Portland Commun

WITHDRAWN

Gender and Genre

Essays on David Mamet

Edited by
Christopher C. Hudgins
and Leslie Kane

palgrave

GENDER AND GENRE

First published 2001 by
PALGRAVE
175 Fifth Avenue, New York, N.Y.10010 and
Houndmills, Basingstoke, Hampshire RG21 6XS.
Companies and representatives throughout the world

PALGRAVE is the new global publishing imprint of St. Martin's Press LLC Scholarly and Reference Division and Palgrave Publishers Ltd (formerly Macmillan Press Ltd).

ISBN 0–312–23869–X

Library of Congress Cataloging-in-Publication Data
Gender and genre : essays on David Mamet / edited by Christopher C. Hudgins and Leslie Kane.
    p.   cm.
Includes bibliographical references and index.
ISBN 0–312–23869-X
    1. Mamet, David—Criticism and interpretation.   2. Sex (Psychology) in literature.   3. Sex role in literature.   4. Literary form. I. Hudgins, Christopher C., 1947-   II. Kane, Leslie, 1945-
PS3563.A4345 Z77   2001
812'.54—dc21
                                                              00–051475

A catalogue record for this book is available from the British Library.

Design by Letra Libre, Inc.

First edition: June, 2001
10 9 8 7 6 5 4 3 2 1

Printed in the United States of America.

Contents

Acknowledgements

We extend our thanks to all of our contributors, a wonderful group of scholars and friends who have worked diligently with us in preparing this book. We are particularly grateful to them for their patience and for their generous and sensitive insights.

Joining a very broad community, we extend our sympathy to the family and close friends of Linda Dorff, who died in the fall of 2000 as we completed preparations for this collection. Linda was a delightful and talented colleague, generous with her students and her colleagues and her fellow scholars of dramatic literature. We will miss her tremendously.

Finally, we thank our editor at Palgrave, Kristi Long, whose good humor, wise suggestions, and general helpfulness we have delighted in over the last several months. Our thanks as well to Sarah Schur, Ms. Long's efficient editorial assistant, and to Palgrave's production staff.

For William J. Hudgins, Jr.
and Cathryn T. Hudgins

For Pamela and David

INTRODUCTION

In "Meritocracy" (1997), David Mamet writes that "advancement, sub-sistence, friendship, regard, in the theatre, is priceless to me and has been, after the love of my family, frankly, the guiding desire of my life: to win and keep a place in our culturally despised profession through merit" (126). At the beginning of the twenty-first century, few know-ledgeable people would deny that Mamet has won his place as one of the most respected, talented, and provocative of American dramatists through merit, though they might argue vehemently about how audi-ences should understand his plays, filmscripts and films, novels, poetry, and essays, especially as that understanding relates to matters of gender and matters of genre.

To put it differently, and more bluntly, critical and popular debate about Mamet's work often centers on whether or not he is a misogynist, or, more broadly, on whether we should read his often misogynist, unlov-able, and unloving characters as reflecting his own misogyny or should recognize some Mametian irony in his depiction of these figures of his fertile imagination. The notion of irony is intimately related to issues of genre and to audience expectations. Those audience preconceptions and those critical debates about gender and genre are often colored by Mamet's celebrity, his fame, and our consequent knowledge about his life, his family, his marriages, his politics, his hobbies. The attention that Mamet has drawn as one of the most important figures in the modern American theater influences our reception of his plays and perhaps skews his aesthetic reputation.

Mamet came to international attention with the premiere of *American Buffalo* at the Goodman Theatre's Stage Two in Chicago on October 23, 1975. That October night, as Richard Christiansen suggests in "The Young Lion of Chicago Theater," was one of the most "significant dates in the history of . . . American . . . theater" (12). Twenty-five years later, Mamet's fulfillment of his early promise has made him successful not only in playhouses around the world but also in movie theaters and in the cutthroat world of literary fiction. But, as he has mused on several occasions upon turning fifty, his life is much different now than when he started as a struggling artist. As Mamet grows older, several new emphases are emerging in his work, including rich meditations on the place of religion in our lives and on the complex relationships between mothers and fathers and children, these more clearly rooted in Mamet's own life than has formerly been the case. In recent years, too, he has created a roster of evocative portraits of complex women—although that strand can certainly be traced back to Margaret Ford in *House of Games* (1987) and Karen in *Speed-the-Plow* (1988). And on occasion, of late, Mamet has produced engaging period pieces, including his adaptation for film of Terrence Rattigan's *The Winslow Boy*, with its specific emphasis on an emancipated "new woman," and his deliciously wicked drawing-room comedy, *Boston Marriage* (both 1999).

Another of Mamet's reverberant triangle plays, *Boston Marriage* is a comedy about two genteel lesbians: the aging Anna fears losing the younger Claire to a still younger woman, which threatens to destroy their "Boston marriage," a euphemism for an intimate, long-term relationship between two women. The earthiness and emotional exuberance of their Irish maid, Catherine, is a delightful counterpoint, "a sort of Greek chorus, interrupting their high-minded chatter with simple yet profound truths" (Hartigan N7). Wonderful complications ensue. As Richard Brucher writes in his review, "Anna's unexpected response to adversity travesties Boston proprieties, collapses class distinctions, and demonstrates the practicality with which sophisticated women, no less than men, will act to secure their interests" (1–2). Similarly, M. S. Mason insightfully recognizes that "Claire's and Anna's barbarity to the maid and to each other, their greedy appetites, and their shallow self concern would be as alarming as Mamet's macho madmen's were it not for the gleaming surface of upper-class propriety, the elegant language (and even more elegant carriage) of the actors, the humor, and the fact that no one seems to feel the barbs too keenly" (20). Although this is "girls night out in Mametville," as Ben Brantley puts it (E1), there is little "psychological distance between Mamet's louts and lesbians" (Siegel D1), especially in the ways Mamet's women reply to fears about aging, the loss of love, and the vicissitudes of life. Indeed, "the wit and thrill" of this comedy, or satire, issues from Anna's and Claire's passions "that, however self-indulgent, rebel against gender restrictions, class roles, and proprieties" (Brucher 1–2).

Still, Mamet has often written about the distinctions between men and women and wishes to protect that vision as it emerges in his work. In 1999, for example, the QuintEssential Theater Company planned to stage seven short plays from *Goldberg Street* (1985) at New York's Limelight Theatre under the title *Mamet Bare*. The playwright rescinded permission for the performance when he learned that the company planned to cast all the characters with women actors. At least one other similar withdrawal of rights to stage a play, in this instance, *Glengarry Glen Ross* (1983), garnered national publicity in recent years, and a production of that play in Las Vegas, not typically a city that attracts national attention for its theater, cast mostly female actors. In his review of the April 1995 production by Los Angeles' Studebaker Studios at the University of Nevada, Las Vegas, Chris Hudgins wrote that the production was horrifically misguided, especially in its changes of lines in Mamet's Pulitzer-winning script to accommodate its casting of women. Critical of these gender shifts, Mamet remarked of the Las Vegas production: "I am reminded of Stanislavski's statement: Any director who does something 'interesting' with the script doesn't understand the text" (letter to Hudgins).

Mamet's decisions to withdraw permissions due to casting women in roles conceived for men have been controversial in some circles, adding to the perception that Mamet is a misogynist. The impetus for this collection of essays was our conversation several years ago about possible topics for a Special Session on Mamet for a Modern Language Association Convention, the venue for the David Mamet Society's annual meeting. We were particularly interested in issues of gender and genre. As Steven Price points out in his chapter in this volume, feminist criticism didn't begin to grapple with Mamet's work to any great extent until Margaret Ford and Karen emerged in *House of Games* and *Speed-the-Plow* as central female figures on his previously largely masculine stage and screen. A controversial 1993 MLA Special Session on Mamet and Pinter, "Playing Misogyny: Pinter *et al.* Stage the Rage," essentially concluded, we think wrongly, that Mamet is a misogynist. Ironically, Mamet's plays, films, and novels began to include compelling portraits of women as his popular reputation as a macho, poker-playing, cigar-smoking gunslinger grew.

Mamet's celebrity and his voluminous output have complicated, perhaps even compromised, his critical and popular reputation. He has written more "occasional essays," often about topics ranging far beyond the theater, than any modern dramatist to our knowledge. Many of those essays have added to his reputation for machismo. That Mamet briefly worked for *Oui* in his youth and, more recently, has written for *Playboy* and been the subject of one of its extensive interviews further contributed to the popular conception of his misogyny in some quarters. His essays often reveal his affections and passionate hobbies to be those that our culture typically regards as quintessentially male—hunting, collecting guns and knives, high-stakes poker, fine scotch, racecar training. His marriages, first to actor Lindsay Crouse and then to Rebecca Pidgeon, an actor and highly respected singer/song writer, added to Mamet's own celebrity. As is so often the case, his success has made his audiences wish to know more about him—which, in turn, allows them to read his work in light of what they believe to know about his life, always a potentially dangerous practice. One might be reminded here of how Arthur Miller's relationship with Marilyn Monroe produced short-sighted reviews of *After the Fall*, or of how Harold Pinter's outspoken and often unpopular political opinions have influenced the reception of his work in recent years.

In a 1997 interview published in the magazine section of *The Boston Globe*, John Koch asked Mamet, "Are you tired of having your work called misogynistic?" Mamet's indignant response is revelatory:

> It's inaccurate and it's a lie, and not only is it that, but it's cowardly. What happened, I believe, was, years ago, I wrote a play called Sexual Perversity in Chicago (*sic*) which was about misogyny, how a nice, healthy relationship between two nice young people was ruined by the incursion of a misogynist. And since then, people have said, "It's been said that you are a misogynist." Well, nothing could be further from the truth, either in my personal life, if it's anyone's business, or in my work. I think if someone wants to make such an unpleasant and demonstrably false assertion, let him or her make it, and I'll respond with whatever small courtesy it deserves. (16)

Mamet's celebrity and the popular conception of his interests and hobbies, then, frequently and unfortunately skew understanding of his work, which can result in unthinking acceptance of a seemingly obvious response. The passionate reactions of audiences and critics to *Oleanna* (1992) is perhaps the best (or worst) example of this phenomenon. As Christine MacLeod suggests, "There is little doubt . . . [t]hat Mamet's own tough-guy persona has been a factor in interpretation. His established reputation . . . and his much publicized fondness for such macho pursuits as hunting, boxing, cigar smoking and poker, correlate all too readily with the essentialist postures of the backlash brigade and hence have tended to overdetermine the critical response to *Oleanna*" (201–02). That response, for MacLeod, has been a nearly universal reading of the play as "a manifestation of backlash sexual politics—that is, as a work characterized by outrage and hostility toward the agenda of contemporary feminism" (199). From her perspective, as a feminist, she emphasizes that what is so very unfortunate about such celebrity-conditioned responses is that "the narrow critical perspective with sexual harassment, political correctness and beleaguered masculinity in *Oleanna* has obscured a far wider and more challenging dramatic engagement with issues of power, hierarchy and the control of language," which she goes on to gloss convincingly (202).

A number of critics of *Oleanna*, of course, go beyond the "backlash sexual politics" readings of this controversial play. Leslie Kane, for example, in *Weasels and Wisemen*, understands *Oleanna* as "an incendiary, unnerving examination of the power dynamic" and concludes that "It is simply too easy to dismiss the play as antifeminist, even misogynist" (141, 184). The central point, here, is that Mamet does not typically comfort his audiences with neatly packaged resolutions. As MacLeod points out, Mamet "confronts his audiences with unresolved conflicts," suggesting that *Oleanna's* intransigent conclusion "points towards the need to conceive of change . . . not as a *reversal* . . . of hierarchical power, but as *transformation*, an actual alternative to the politics of dominance," the idea implied in the folk-song title of the play (212–13).

Still, Mamet's purported misogyny often limits in terribly unfortunate ways the responses of audiences and critics to his work. Certainly, Teach in *American Buffalo* is hostile toward women; even more egregious, the character who utters the line in *Lakeboat* (1970) that "women are soft things with holes in the middle" is no feminist. But responses to such blatantly misogynist lines should be more complex than often is the case. In short, assuming that a character speaks for an author, or that the conclusion of a dramatic plot reflects the author's personal beliefs, is one of the most elementary of interpretive mistakes. At its base, this interpretive problem has to do with the nature of realism and with the broader notion of genre, particularly with regard to Mamet's ideas about "celebration" and dramatic irony and the writer's ideas about the nature of tragedy and comedy.

Mamet's notoriety in certain circles inhibits the recognition of irony or of indirectly implied thematic material. That problem, at its core, is related to issues of genre. As Martin Schaub suggests, Mamet frequently subverts genre conventions, as he does in *The Cryptogram* (1995). Along with several of our contributors, Schaub emphasizes that Mamet celebrates the truth that "we postmoderns long for communion, confession, and forgiveness in an amoral and aleatoric universe." From his perspective, that celebration includes our sad witness to how often that longing goes unfulfilled. Couching his argument as a corrective to much postmodern theory about meaning, Schaub concludes that Mamet reinvents "the rhapsody of a young mind's search for meaning" while staging another negative female in his mother, Donny, who refuses to accept this "truth" about the need for communion. That negative example, though, calls for the audience to "enter a world where joy and suffering, hope and fear, have names, word, meaning" (327–28, 330, 334–35). Belittling Mamet as a sexist who blames Donny for her husband's betrayal, as some critics have, destroys the richness of this complex, ironic response to Mamet's celebration of what is "essential in us all."

Mamet's critical reputation is more complex than those who cry "misogynist" might like. Evolving through several stages, critical attention at first typically centered on Mamet's evocative use of language, especially the patois of his lower-class characters. More insightful critics recognized a disciplined structure beneath that surface, pointing toward Mamet's typical, subtly evoked themes: that human beings are desperate for love; that work, no matter how pedestrian, is central to our lives; that most of us want to do good; that we have difficulty dealing with our mortality in a harsh world.

From the beginning, Mamet's work has been political at some level, typically critical of our economic systems and of the educational structures, formal and informal, that underpin our political economy. Similarly central is the celebration of the struggle men and women endure in their attempts to find the love that in Mamet's view we all wish for, a struggle often marred by hypocrisy and by the wish to control others. Mamet emphasizes that it is hard to live in our modern, decaying world, yet he repeatedly observes that he celebrates human tenacity, even as he presents us with his often negative examples. Complexly, and confusingly for some, in Mamet's work we find a subtly ambiguous admiration even for his most despicable characters as they struggle with the difficult task of living and loving, sometimes to comic effect, sometimes to the nearly tragic.

A partial list of literary influences ranges from Sophocles to Beckett, from Trollope and Thackery to Pinter, from Dreiser to Wilder, and includes the great Russians, Tolstoy, Chekhov, and Eisenstein. Extra-literary figures as diverse as economist Thorstein Veblen and psychologist D. W. Winnicott, in addition to Mamet's knowledge of popular culture and music and an immersion in folk music from Leadbelly to the "neofolk" movement also shape the ideas that emerge in his plays and films.

As he has increasingly balanced his writing between plays and films, Mamet has become a popular icon. Still, most critics regard him as a member of a very small pantheon, the best of American dramatists—in the view of some, the best of this century's dramatists writing in English. The essays in this collection reflect the breadth of critical opinion on matters of gender in Mamet's work and often relate the complicated matter of how audiences respond to Mamet's portrayal of the behavior of women and men together or apart to the equally complex notion of genre. At one end of the spectrum, some feminist critics argue that realism is in and of itself a patriarchal genre, structured by the linear "male Mono-myth" of the quest and prefiguring all women as potential victims of mas-culine aggression. Kellie Bean's chapter, for example, takes this particular feminist notion about genre as its heuristic, as does Linda Dorff's, at least implicitly, in its suggestion that Mamet's work "reinscribes" the "crippling fictions of male mythology."

At the opposite end of the spectrum, several chapters here suggest that Mamet's chilling and/or comic depictions of the flawed relationship be-tween the sexes in our culture implicitly call for a more humane under-standing of our potential for communion. That perspective, in effect, places Mamet's work within the genre of "oblique" or "ironic" comedy, es-sentially both Richard Brucher's and Imtiaz Habib's suggestion. Janet Haedicke argues that a tranformative "feminist ethic" is at work in Mamet's plays, and Steven Price finds elements of what might be called a masculine and a feminine aesthetic in Mamet's work, suggesting that *House of Games* is feminist in that it presents Margaret Ford's journey not as linear but as circular or spiraling, as "creatively productive."

Grappling with the manner of telling a story is central to the analysis of any narrative art form, and chapters such as Ilkka Joki's, focusing on Mamet's novel *The Village* (1994), get at the relationship between genre and meaning in insightful ways. Even in such a specifically genre-based essay, though, the notion of the male narrator's relationship with women characters emerges as central. Representative of the strand of Mamet scholarship that emphasizes the celebratory, Thomas P. Adler cites the playwright's glowing tribute to Thornton Wilder's *Our Town* as suggest-ing that American theater must celebrate the wondrous universality in the banal facts that "people are born, love, hate, are frightened and happy, grow old and die." Robert Corrigan wrote some years ago that "comedy celebrates [man's] capacity to endure," as opposed to tragedy, which "is a celebration of man's capacity to aspire and suffer" (3). Many of the chap-ters here, our own included (Kane's on mothers, Hudgins' on Margaret Ford's journey), evoke that notion of celebration in Mamet's often dark but typically comic work. Several writers use other revealing notions about genre to approach Mamet's work, among them film noir, "Oedipal tragic structure," and cautionary tale or parable, occasionally within reader-response frameworks.

In short, this is a richly varied collection of original essays on David Mamet's canon. Given our topic, it is perhaps not surprising that four of these chapters deal with *House of Games*, all with insightfully different conclusions. Other writers concentrate on Mamet's three children's plays, on *Sexual Perversity in Chicago* (1974), on *American Buffalo, Speed-the-Plow, Edmond* (1982), *Homicide* (1991), *Oleanna, The Cryptogram, Jolly*

(1982/1998), and *The Village*. While we do not agree with all of the opinions expressed herein, we are confident that our contributors' revelatory responses to one of the most important of American dramatists, be he comedic or tragic, feminist or misogynist, Chekhovian satirist or Marxist, will enrich our readers.

൚   ൚   ൚

Taking as his point of departure David Mamet's commentary on Thornton Wilder's *Our Town*, Thomas P. Adler's fine chapter, "Mamet's *Three Children's Plays:* Where the Wilder Things Are," immediately engages our interest in gender, genre, and the metatheatric in Mamet's canon. Adler's study, the first serious consideration of Mamet's largely neglected children's plays—*The Frog Prince* (1984), *The Revenge of the Space Pandas or Binky Rudich and the Two-Speed Clock* (1975), and *The Poet and the Rent* (1974)—richly illustrates both "the inventive ways in which Mamet plays with gender (in *Frog Prince*), with genre (in *Space Pandas*), and with metatheater (in *Poet and the Rent*)," as well as the commonality between Wilderian and Mametian theatrical practice, philosophy, and gendered identity. In Adler's view, Mamet's imaginative retelling of the Brothers Grimm classic fairy tale, "The Frog Prince," which shifts the focus from "the shrewish Princess Patricia" to the Frog Prince and foregrounds motifs of power and patriarchy, is a fable "of helpless submission to something implacable and inexplicable" akin to *Our Town*. He suggests, moreover, that the plethora of metatheatrical tricks, linguistic puns, and the "unlocalized" bare space of *The Poet and the Rent* similarly recall this Wilder classic. And, Adler recognizes striking parallels to *The Skin of Our Teeth* and *The Matchmaker* in *Space Pandas's* portraits of domineering and nurturing maternal figures.

In her provocative chapter, "Plowing the Buffalo, Fucking the Fruits: (M)others in *American Buffalo* and *Speed-the-Plow*," Janet V. Haedicke challenges "the claim of most feminist critics that Mamet and misogyny ring synonymous." Characterizing both plays as Oedipal narratives, Haedicke contends that in these works "Aristotelian form colludes with Freudian content to exalt a quest in which male identity can [ostensibly] be secured by triumph over a female or feminized Other." Yet, she makes a compelling case that a transformative, implicitly "feminist ethic" is at work in Mamet's early and late plays, one that "subverts genre as well as gender, exposing realism and binarism as perceptual and performative." Examining the methods by which Mamet configures gender and attracts attention to "the process of gender-inscription," she asserts that *American Buffalo* and *Speed-the-Plow* parody and condemn the Oedipal quest. Her incisive reading of these plays in each other's light illuminates Mamet's staging of gender-bending as a methodology that "forges a passage from the junkyard landscape of Oedipal Individualism . . . to the dreamscape of American community," one lit by "the fucked, the feminized, the (M)others."

British critic Steven Price's chapter, "Disguise in Love: Gender and Desire in *House of Games* and *Speed-the-Plow*," argues that feminist critics are divided between those who discuss Mamet's women as "misogynist misrepresentation and those who regard them as complex figures," *knowable* in either case through analysis. Price suggests that "such closed readings tend to misrepresent the strategies of the texts," which point toward a fluid conception of identity as performance. Framing his argument with planks from Joseph Campbell, Bruno Bettelheim, and Vladimir Propp, he relies on Janet Brown's definition of feminist structure to demonstrate that Mamet uses the male monomythical form but invests it with a "constant irony of the discrepancy between the desire for structure and progress and the impossibility of their attainment." From his perspective, *House of Games* is feminist in presenting "the structural disruption of female power not as something to be exorcised through closure, but as creatively productive." He concludes that we can no more "know" Karen at the end of *Speed-the-Plow* than Margaret at the end of *House of Games*.

As Richard Brucher succinctly puts it, Mamet's controversial play *Edmond*, in which the title character rejects his life and wife, harasses a woman on a train, beats a pimp, and murders a waitress, is neither "a popular [n]or a well understood play." Eluding audiences and critics alike, who remain baffled and deeply disturbed by its protagonist's hateful views and vicious actions, *Edmond* has elicited little serious critical attention. Taking his cue from Gregory Mosher's observation that Eugene O'Neill could "*see* the culture" and that Mamet, likewise, exhibits clairvoyance in *Edmond*, Brucher's brilliant chapter, "Prophecy and Parody in *Edmond*," contends that Edmond's "racism, misogyny, and homophobia are calculated to offend." Foregrounding the issue of gender, Brucher advances the idea that Edmond, "a middle-class white man, heir to the American Dream and its fallout, is a naive but by no means innocent victim of his race's success," and that Glenna, the waitress Edmond murders, is emblematic of the "incentives," as Thorstein Veblen would have it, "for acquiring women as property." Brucher's enlightening study of Mamet's dark play, which resonates far beyond its closed dramatic world where racism, misogyny, and homophobia have such disastrous consequences, concludes with a perceptive reading of the play's last scene in which Edmond fails to assume responsibility for

Glenna's murder and assumes the role of "wife to his black cellmate." In Brucher's view, this conclusion extends and transcends O'Neill's final scene in *The Hairy Ape*.

In his insightful chapter, "Demotic Male Desire and Female Subjectivity in David Mamet: The Split Space of the Women of *Edmond*," Imtiaz Habib criticizes the notion that Mamet is hostile toward women as misreading the playwright's dramatic discourse. Within a heuristic rooted in essays by feminist critics Ann Hall and Dorothy Jacobs, Habib argues in Foucauldian terms that Mamet's women characters "interrogate demotic male desire and . . . function as agents of recovery." Positing that these women are "at once figures of an oppressed female selfhood and elements of a male critique," Habib suggests that in *Edmond* women's oppression springs from the male need for "validation," which frequently women refuse to provide, a "simultaneous acknowledgment and contravention of contemporary fantasies of masculine power." He concludes that Edmond's nostalgic regret for his failed marriage and his need for love are what "the experience with Glenna has brought about in him," which "lives most strongly" in his scenes with his cellmate. Thus, the "abuse of women by men, and the sexual and racial prejudice that are its accompaniments . . . are the demotic desires that Mamet cathartically ferrets out and purges in plays like *Edmond*."

"When *Oleanna* premiered in 1992 in Boston and New York under the direction of its author," observes Robert Skloot, "critics were quick to point out that the two-character play presented a devastating vision of the tense relationships between men and women in contemporary society." However, in "*Oleanna*, or, The Play of Pedagogy," Skloot posits that when looked at through the ideology of Paulo Friere, the theater of Augusto Boal, and the educational demands of bell hooks, *Oleanna* becomes "a metaeducational text" in which "the shifting dynamic of power between the [male] teacher and [female] student reveals their antagonistic identities and the gestural essence of their struggle." In this fresh approach to Mamet's polemical play, using its epigraph from Samuel Butler's *The Way of All Flesh* as a catalyst, Skloot aligns *Oleanna* with Mamet's "preoccupation with the issue of *teaching*" as it "'performs it.'" Noting that our attention is drawn to evaluating the validity and impact of Carol's accusation "that John has 'raped' (forcibly disabused) Carol of her academic expectations," Skloot avers that Mamet opens a space for gendered readings of Carol as "the *type* of women who 'cry rape' when they feel aggrieved by men and/or powerless in their presence." Despite the implied shift of power in this play, he contends that neither the male professor nor the woman student wins in the educational arena.

Kellie Bean's chapter is representative of feminist criticism that regards Mamet's work as misogynistic and regards American realism, in general, as "a conservative generic paradigm" that, by definition, circumscribes "troublesome female characters . . . within . . . patriarchal borders." In "A Few Good Men: Collusion and Violence in *Oleanna*," Bean understands Mamet's theater to rely on outmoded, "static, oppositional notions of gender" and suggests that Mamet "creates John's image . . . at the expense of the [stereotypical] female characters"—the "emotionally needy wife," the "hysterical student," the "castrating feminist." She convincingly suggests that John's efforts to appease Carol are "efforts to reconcile himself with the Tenure Committee"; when John fails in his attempts to retreat into a "non-ideological rhetoric" of the human, his resorting to physical violence celebrates "John's power over Carol." Bean's reading depends on perhaps her most controversial assertion, that Carol does not realize that "the vast misogynist tradition of patriarchy stands behind her masculine professor" and her suggestion that the tenure committee will grant John's tenure.

Karen Blansfield's "Women on the Verge, Unite!" argues that many critics misread Mamet's attitudes toward women, particularly the absent or "marginalized women" in his early "macho" plays. In works where women exist on the periphery of male worlds, Blansfield trenchantly observes, "women wield a strange and startling power . . . for they are central to the men's image of themselves, to their sense of power—or lack of it." Blansfield observes that when women do appear in early Mamet, they easily manage "to undercut the male's shaky or self-inflated ego." In later works such as *Speed-the-Plow* and *House of Games*, she concludes, even if they lose in the end, Mamet's central women characters "disrupt the balance of the men's world." Agreeing with Christopher Bigsby that the absence of women in Mamet's early plays "underscores the emptiness" of the frontier myth of masculine self-sufficiency, Blansfield suggests that "Mamet's women are more potent than initially seems apparent," their power generated by the male fear of women, by men's insecurity, and by their "pathetic dependence on women" for identity.

In her insightful "'It's the way that you are with your children': The Matriarchal Figure in Mamet's Late Work," Leslie Kane suggests that several of Mamet's recent plays demand a reconsideration "of the matriarch and the place of home in [Mamet's] work." Convincingly arguing that Mamet renders "ambivalent, unsentimental portraits" of women who are profoundly human, at once "tender, fallible, destructive," Kane finds that in *The Cryptogram* Donny's impatience with John shatters our presumptions about maternal love. She suggests that Donny's attempt to shield her son from the truth about his father's abandonment is a generous deception that miscarries. In act 3, after Donny's more straightforward, adult talk devastates John, Kane carefully argues, John's continuing his search for the blanket, knife in hand, is an image of his seeking love and "right behavior," not an image of suicide. And, in *Jolly,* she finds "an incisive work whose poignant look at sibling ties . . . is an integral complementary component of the playwright's exploration of maternal love and abuse." Here, she engagingly suggests that parenting has allowed Jolly to exhibit the love that she and her brother were not allowed to show as children and that such possibility depends on Jolly's struggle as an adult with her early relationship with her own mother. Aptly expanding our understanding of both gender and genre in Mamet's work, Kane movingly concludes that Mamet shows his most courageous characters possessing "the potential to relinquish pain, to conserve heritage, and to choose life" by painfully giving birth to themselves.

In "Reinscribing the 'Fairy': The Knife and Male Mythology in *The Cryptogram,*" Linda Dorff casts light on a seeming universe of the Other, which, like much of "Mamet's con-game drama and cinema," is full of tricks, not the least of which is that "the characters negotiate their relationship to each other through a system of mythical objects that represent the absent father, positioning him as the (present) subject of the play." "Disguised as the inverse of *American Buffalo,*" *The Cryptogram,* suggests Dorff in her fine analysis of male mythology and iconography, "pretends to be a family play . . . a drama of Others, a woman, a gay man, and a child." Although Dorff posits that the setting of an American family home and the absence of a white heterosexual male character might appear at first glance as Mamet's response to charges of misogyny and homophobia, in her view *The Cryptogram* presents a fascinating departure from Mamet's earlier depictions of "world[s] of men." Approaching "male mythology in Mamet's plays as deeply conflicted," given that his characters both desire intimacy and "avoid intimacy—coded as femininity/castration," Dorff maintains that *The Cryptogram*'s "hyper-coded stage props"—a photograph, a blanket, and a knife—impede, rather than enable, their meaning to be decoded by the characters and audience alike.

An intriguing chapter on genre, Ilkka Joki's "Mamet's Novelistic Voice" argues that *The Village* is "a novel whose form and structure reflect the genres of theatre and the cinema," especially in its "segmented format." Noting the novel's similarity to Wilder's *Our Town,* Joki discusses the generic distinctiveness of drama and novel in Bakhtinian terms. For him, the most difficult interpretive task in *The Village* is to understand the narrator, who is ironically distant from some characters but shares a worldview with others and who is reserved or inconsistent about taking "the reader into his confidence." Joki argues that "sex and gender . . . play a role in Mamet's idealization [of audience]," for the narrator and the audience identify with Henry, who cannot effectively tell his wife his stories with any interest or attention. Carefully reading Mamet's narrator's use of the "representational option," telling the story in almost cinematic pictures with "contrasting narrative comment," Joki describes several gender inflected narrative techniques. A fascinating analysis of the narrator's depiction of the Minister's "out-loud speech" and Dickie's "inner speech" allows Joki to conclude that "in its ability to accomplish all this with such ease, as a unified artistic utterance, the novel would indeed seem to be superior to the dramatic genres, at the same time as it shamelessly borrows its scenic, dramatic structure from them."

In his engaging chapter, "'A small price to pay': Superman, Metafamily, and Hero in David Mamet's Oedipal *House of Games*," Christopher C. Hudgins turns his keen eye to Mamet's first film. Taking his cue from the centrality of "the Oedipal plot of revelation and recognition" in Mamet's works, which encourages an "intended retrospective" reading of *House of Games*, Hudgins reveals that which has remained uncovered in the shadowy world of this film noir. Reading the film as "a courageous search for knowledge," he finds that "beneath its film noir trappings, *House of Games* is about the nature of love in the time of midlife crisis." Framing his analysis in audience response theory and in Mamet's expository essays, Hudgins makes a compelling argument that we have not heretofore understood Maggie's role nor perceived the full extent of her transformation. In fact, he cogently convinces us that the film's "implicit call for us to 'reconsider' . . . its ambiguity" informs the film's presentation of psychiatry, Mike's desire for intimacy and his concomitant "fear of women's control," and Maggie's longing for communion. Conversely, Hudgins sees Mike, who playfully reveals a "sincere affection for Maggie" but rejects both the specter of communion and the acknowledgment of vulnerability, as emblematic of the response of males who reject "emotional involvement with women altogether," seeking "refuge in work, in the club, in the locker room—or in the metafamily that frequents the House of Games."

In "Man Without a Gun: Mamet, Masculinity, and Mystification," Diane M. Borden suggests that Mamet's plays and films do not attempt to answer the question "What does it mean?" but rather to "remystify the moral, psychological, and philosophical closures" that many critics attempt to impose on his work. She equates such mystification in *House of Games* and *Homicide* with the sublime, suggesting that in both films "an initiate is seduced, gives himself or herself over to the Other in a state of eroticized desire, only to be conned . . . just when he or she thinks that they are about to become a member of the family." Intriguingly, Borden associates the sublime with psychological defense mechanisms that are independent of gender but based in "transference love," desires centered around parental or sibling figures. Arguing that the world of both films is

seen through the "subjectivity" of the protagonist, she understands the audience to be "Enraptured by narrative disclosure," experiencing "unconcealments that bring a simultaneous mixture of horror and delight."
Relating the sublime to Mamet's use of the gun and other phallic signifiers that "remystif[y] issues of gender and genre," Borden concludes that
Mamet manipulates both gender and genre expectations through a
process of deliberate obfuscation which suggests that "the promise of
meaning is nothing but a con."

Most of the chapters that follow seek to understand Mamet's complex,
evocative stories of his men and women, some centering their attention
on the notion of ambiguity that Borden concludes results from obfuscation. These chapters provide what we think are provocative critical perspectives in our ongoing attempts to read a controversial artist who has
stretched the boundaries of the American theater and cinema.

WORKS CITED

Brucher, Richard. "*Boston Marriage.*" *The David Mamet Review* 6 (1999): 1–2.
Christiansen, Richard. "The Young Lion of Chicago Theater." *Chicago Tribune Magazine* July 11, 1982: 9+.
Corrigan, Robert W. "Comedy and the Comic Spirit." Introduction to *Comedy: Meaning and Form.* Ed. Robert W. Corrigan. San Francisco: Chandler, 1965.
Hartigan, Patti. "Three Women, One Mamet: The Thing About 'Boston Marriage.'" *The Boston Globe* May 20, 1999: Arts and Film N7.
Hudgins, Christopher C. "*Glengarry Glen Ross.*" *The David Mamet Review* 2 (1995): 2–3.
Kane, Leslie. *Weasels and Wisemen: Ethics and Ethnicity in the Work of David Mamet.* New York: St. Martin's, 1999.
Koch, John. "Interview with David Mamet." *Boston Globe Sunday Magazine* November 9 1997: 16.
Mamet, David. "Meritocracy." *True and False: Heresy and Common Sense for the Actor.* New York: Pantheon, 1997.
———. Letter to Chris Hudgins, July 21, 1995.
Mason, M. S. "'Boston Marriage': Barbs Beneath Victorian Propriety." *The Christian Science Monitor* June 18 1999: Theater 20.
MacLeod, Christine. "The Politics of Gender, Language and Hierarchy in Mamet's 'Oleanna.'" *Journal of American Studies* 29 (1995): 199–213.
Schaub, Martin. "Magic Meanings in Mamet's Cryptogram." *Modern Drama* 42 (1999): 326–37.
Siegel, Ed. "At ART, A 'Marriage' Made by Mamet." *The Boston Globe* June 11, 1999: Arts and Film D1.

MAMET'S
THREE CHILDREN'S PLAYS

WHERE THE WILDER THINGS ARE

THOMAS P. ADLER

In his essays and interviews, David Mamet rarely has much to say about a specific play other than one of his own. "Notes on *The Cherry Orchard*" from *Writing in Restaurants* (1987) might at first appear to be an exception, but he had recently completed an adaptation of the Chekhov classic when he wrote it. So it comes as something of a surprise—especially given what would seem to be stark differences between their philosophies—to find him singling out enthusiastically (in his commentary on "Stanislavsky and the American Bicentennial") a production of Thornton Wilder's *Our Town* (1938) that he had seen at Chicago's Goodman Theatre. "I left," Mamet says, "feeling much better than when I went in. I thought: isn't it the truth: people are born, love, hate, are frightened and happy, grow old and die. We as audience and we as artists must work to bring about a theater, an American Theater, which will be a celebration of these things" (*Restaurants* 30). To rescue the commonplace from apparent banality and "ratify [its] universality" has, indeed, long been recognized as a defining characteristic of Wilder's drama.

Mamet uses these same key notions—"truth" and "celebration"—again when he talks about the interaction between the narrator of a tale and the audience that responds to what it hears: "'The only profit ... to those who participate as storytellers or as listeners ... is the shared experience itself, the celebration of the tale, and its truth'" (Geis 64). A number of critics have emphasized recently the centrality, even ubiquity, in Mamet's works of storytelling as a performative act that potentially brings order out of chaos and community out of aloneness and alienation; C. W. E.

Bigsby, for example, concludes that "At the heart of all Mamet's plays are story-tellers whose stories shape their world into something more than random experience, decay and inconsequence. . . . They create drama and by doing so give themselves a role" (206). Mamet himself would succinctly put it this way: "The simple magic of the theater rests in the nature of human perception—that we all want to hear stories. And the stories we like the best are those told most truly" (*Freaks* 62).

As Bigsby also notes, among "the writers most frequently quoted by Mamet" (along with such others as Veblen, Tolstoy, Freud, and Kafka) is the psychologist and author of *The Uses of Enchantment: The Meaning and Importance of Fairy Tales*, Bruno Bettelheim. In his reading of Bettelheim's "theory" of the fairy tale, Mamet likens the appeal of those stories, like that of drama itself, to the dreams and wish-fulfillment fantasies of adult listeners and emphasizes the tales' ability "finally, to *affect*, because we listen to [them] nonjudgmentally—we identify *sub*consciously (noncritically) with the protagonist. We are allowed to do this, [Bettelheim] tells us, because the protagonist and, indeed, the *situations* are uncharacterized aside from their most essential elements" (*Restaurants* 13). Such a presentation of character and action stripped down to their barest essentials—and thus rendered less individual and more universal and, consequently, better able to embody and convey the commonalties of human experience—is a dramatic strategy Mamet undoubtedly noticed, as others have, in Wilder's play as well.

I

Mamet relates that as a high school student he "occasionally . . . played piano for the kids' shows [at Second City in Chicago] on the weekend" (*Cabin* 97); he also worked for a children's theater company in his hometown during the early 1970s (Carroll 8). When he composes his own stage version of the classic fairy tale, *The Frog Prince* (first performed in 1984 by the Milwaukee Rep, and then a year later at New York's Ensemble Studio Theatre), he uses virtually nothing of the material from the 1815 edition of the Brothers Grimm on which Bettelheim focuses his analysis. In that telling, entitled *The Frog King, or Iron Henry*, the frog (formerly a prince who fell victim to the "spell" of a "wicked witch" for an undisclosed reason) rescues the precious golden ball of the pampered and beautiful-beyond-belief, if egotistic, princess from a deep well in a "dark forest," with the promise that he will now become her dearest friend and share her life and bed. But she has no intention of keeping her bargain with this "ugly" and "nasty" creature, and so only under pressure from her father, the king, does she appear on the surface to fulfill her word. Underneath, however, she remains so rebellious that she throws the frog from her bed against the wall, whereupon he is transformed back into a prince who is then given her hand in marriage by the king—though the discordant question of just why the prince would ever want to marry so selfish and self-centered a golden girl is never even broached. In the tale's coda, they go off in a coach drawn by white horses and driven by "faithful" Henry, who experiences the loosening of the iron bars around his heart now that his master again lives "free and happy." Although various renditions differ in their explicitness about just how many nights, if any, the frog actually spends in the princess's bed, Bettelheim (in what Alison Lurie among others would generally regard as readings "overdetermined by orthodox Freudianism" yet "thoughtful, humane, and sensitive" [23]) interprets the ball as her "underdeveloped narcissistic psyche" suddenly made aware of a more "complicated" and "darker" sexual reality than she previously knew existed: her erotic anxiety expresses itself first in anger and disgust, but then gradually alters into "responsible" love through continued intimacy under the guidance of the wise parent, as she comprehends that beauty can emerge even from a once repulsive animal-like nature. On his part, the initially "repugnant" frog, himself beginning like a dependent, mother-fixated child, undergoes a painful metamorphosis into a mature individual (Bettelheim 286–91).

Mamet's *The Frog Prince* takes its viewers into the woods and remains firmly there through the cyclic passing of a year from summer in scene 1 to spring in scene 4, never venturing back out into kingdom and castle. Indeed, rather than focus on the princess's initiation into maturity that Bettelheim regards as central to the original, Mamet keeps her offstage, a peripheral figure, while the prince, reduced by the Peasant Woman's spell from his human form and thus made Other, is foregrounded. Mamet fills in the earlier part of the story, left untold in Grimm, of how the prince becomes a frog in the first place, thus writing what is, up to a point, almost a "prequel" of the more widely known narrative. At the opening, the engaged-to-be-wed prince, accompanied by his servingman—here renamed Bill—is out admiring the flowers in land that has summarily been laid claim to for a royal park or enclosure. When the old woman asks him to give her the flowers he has picked for his betrothed, he refuses and offers her money instead, which points to a kind of class arrogance in him. She, in turn, puts her curse of "dwell[ing] in misery" upon him, metamorphosing him until some "pure woman"—to whom he must not reveal his former state—plants a "selfless kiss upon his lips" (63). On the eve of the princess's wedding to another suitor, Frog and Bill encounter the Milkmaid, whose cow has been carted off by the bailiffs and whose fiancé has been dispossessed and sent into exile; rule by the shrewish Princess Patricia is hardly of the kinder and gentler variety that might be predicted of a woman—the patriarchy in the original tale acted, in fact, much more humanely and responsibly. The simple regendering of power does not in itself necessarily effect change. In the princess's repressive kingdom where borders are closed down before dark, civilized law has disappeared and been replaced by a system in which might equals right. When Bill goes off to have the prince's gold sword melted down to buy food for the Milkmaid, he is killed in the process.

Through the example of Bill's self-sacrifice and the Milkmaid's kindness in giving the Frog her shawl to warm himself, the Frog Prince comes to admit that his first inclination had, indeed, been to take advantage of her, but that he has changed. For her part, the Milkmaid (who here never conveniently turns out to be a princess by birth) would have kissed him had she felt free to do so, but was constrained by her commitment to her fiancé. Now when she does kiss him, he is transformed back into the prince—only, however, to be tested yet again. On his way to place flowers on Bill's grave, he once more encounters the Peasant Woman, who demands that if the flowers are not given to her, she will cast the curse another time. Fidelity to one's word is privileged. Only very reluctantly does the prince agree, finally understanding that perhaps the initial curse was somehow a punishment for his arrogance: in Mamet's retelling, the clear implication is that all property is suspect, because it entails an usurpation of what perhaps should be shared, if not communally, at least with those who have less. When the prince exits the stage, over his uniform he wears the shawl the Milkmaid so generously shared with him, indicating visually the need for a fusion, for power to be clothed in kindness and generosity. In a sense, he has discovered his "princess" in the nurturing Milkmaid, but she is the forbidden mother as well. So he sets out alone, without either servant or wife, let alone a kingdom, with only his individual ingenuity and self-reliance to depend upon. As Dennis Carroll asserts, in Mamet's hands this has become a dark tale, yet Carroll does not specify precisely why (142). If the old woman functions as the Frog Prince's teacher on his journey of initiation, she appears to serve as a portent that there exists a capricious force that sometimes prevents us, without apparent reason, from acting on our best instincts: however good and noble the desire to honor the faithful servant in death, that inclination must be curbed, must be subservient to the workings of a mysteriously ambiguous fairy godmother/wicked witch who controls the prince's actions. That a heartfelt instinct should be deemed somehow malignant seems perverse. The overall effect, therefore, is less one of a fable of subversive resistance to unjust domination than of helpless submission to something implacable and inexplicable.

This may seem a dark "moral" for a children's play, but then there are several elements in Mamet's revisioning of *The Frog Prince* that would not be immediately accessible to many young people. While precocious children might enjoy the slangy language ("what's it to you?" [61]; "blow this joint" [74]), even they should not be expected to understand words like "portentous," "equilibrium," "mercantile," "perverted," "promiscuous," and "atavistic." Furthermore, the discussion of the necessity for "contrast and balance" in both art and life (57) that begins the play would also be over their heads, as would the multiple meanings of lust, blood, pride, and a good heart associated with the word "red" in the Prince's ballad. Finally, the very Wilderian question, "Do you think we never know good things 'til they've passed?" (84)—echoing Emily's "Do any human beings ever realize life while they live it?—every, every minute?" from *Our Town*, followed by the Stage Manager's reply, "The saints and poets, maybe—they do some" (100)—requires a degree of reflection about apprehending goodness only after it has been lost that would be beyond most youths.

II

Of Mamet's three plays for children, the one that is most readily accessible, if also the least consequential and resonant, is *The Revenge of the Space Pandas or Binky Rudich and the Two-Speed Clock*, written in 1975 for St. Clement's Theatre with a grant from the New York State Council on the Arts. The play's talking animals—Bob, a sheep from Earth, and Boots and Buffy, pandas from up on Crestview—could, of course, be indebted to numerous sources other than the dinosaur and mammoth in Wilder's *The Skin of Our Teeth* (1942). But the manner in which Mamet describes the play's setting, "Waukegan, Earth and Fourth World in the Goolagong System" (90) sounds at least slightly reminiscent of the way a minister in Wilder addresses a letter to a sick parishioner so that it conveys a spatially unrestricted, ahistorical perspective: "United States of America; Continent of North America; Western Hemisphere; the Earth; the Solar System; the Universe; the Mind of God" (*Town* 45). What is more, the emphasis on the perennial need for "wonder" and "adventure" in life, for turning oneself loose to experience the unexpected and the unknown, echoes several passages from Wilder's *The Matchmaker* (1955), culminating in Barnaby's statement of the play's moral to the audience: "I think it's about adventure. . . . So that now we all want to thank you for coming tonight, and we all hope that in your lives you have just the right amount of—adventure!" (401).

Space Pandas also owes much to Saturday morning science fiction serials on TV. Binky (Leonard) Rudich, a twelve-year-old cub scientist, successfully experiments with time and space travel, so that he, Bob the sheep, and a neighbor girl with the humorous name of Vivian Mooster—much is made of its being easily mistaken for Rooster—wind up on the suburban-sounding Crestview (named, like Glengarry Glen Ross, to attract investors), 50 light years away, and where the inhabitants have not seen a sheep in several thousand years. Mainly, the three travelers wanted to escape from the domestic domain of Binky's mother, who insists they suspend their fun and observe a proper lunchtime, eating her much-hated casserole. But the food on Crestview, ruled by George Topax, a supremely godlike figure alternately adulated as "Magnificence," "Persuasive Powers," "Scourge," and "The Greatest Thing since Sliced Bread" (*Pandas* 110), is hardly more appetizing, featuring something called Lunafish. Besides, George wants Bob's wool for making the school letter sweater he never had and so, like Mamet's Peasant Woman, casts his executive order in the form of an incantatory rhyme to keep them there. But in a metatheatrical moment, the Derelict, really the out-of-work-because-too-old-to be-a-star Edward Farpis, who once played Colonel Drurik in the movie *The Revenge of the Space Pandas*, rescues the three Earthlings from being pelted by a giant pumpkin. Through the device of spatial relocation, the time travelers are suddenly back home in Waukegan again, all too happy to eat the casserole still waiting for them.

Although, given its preadolescent characters, there naturally can be no romantic interest here, Mamet is still working—as the designation he gives the printed text attests—within the traditional generic pattern of the romantic comedy, for which critics such as Northrop Frye delineate a tripartite structure: rejection by a restrictive, "anticomic society"; a "period of confusion" or "temporarily lost identity" away from that society; and a "discovery of identity" and return and reintegration into "a new society" (72–79). Binky's mother with her rules and orders serves as the "blocking" force; but if the child cannot survive on his own, free of dependency on the parent, he also needs gradually to escape from it. So the child uses his creativity (here in the form of scientific experimentation) to help author or write the text of a more independent self. If Crestview is not exactly a Shakespearean green world in that it is even more fraught with danger than home, what occurs there from the point of view of learning about one's vulnerability as well as one's capacity for moral growth through recognizing good and evil—the encounter with the Derelict who becomes their savior—is similar. Upon their return, they are better prepared to accept the necessity for a balance between freedom and increased responsibility. And yet the family community they reenter, though it has stood still in time, has also, if somewhat inexplicably, grown in wisdom, for now Mrs. Rudich sees the rejuvenating and maturing value of adventure, of exploring, if you will; the once repressive society has become less so. The line between allowing children the necessary room to grow, even if it entails permitting the out-of-ordinary or rebellious, and exercising a sensible control is a fine one. The play's seize-the-day verse *L'envoi*, which like the epilogue in plays of old reaches out across the footlights to directly involve and embrace everyone in the audience, generalizes this insight or epiphany that as life moves toward death, we will treasure those moments when we were most fully alive: "As decrepit we grow / It's a comfort to know / We have been to the Goolagong" (155). And so the characters' journey to Crestview becomes analogous to the audience's own sojourn in the theater, or a listener's enraptured attention to a fairy tale: entry into a temporary world of the imagination where something is learned before one returns, enlightened, to the world of everyday reality.

But the lesson learned may be less obvious and psychologically more engaging than simply the Wilderian need to embrace a considerable amount of adventure in one's life; it may, instead, have more to do with being wrenched traumatically from and then returning to mother and home. Among Mamet's collected essays, "Kryptonite: A Psychological Appreciation" from *Some Freaks* (1991) can perhaps throw light on this deeper motif. Tellingly enough, the essay begins with Mamet's return to Chicago and remembrance of an event from his own childhood when his mother reined in his freedom: during the polio epidemic, she only "grudgingly" let him out of the house to play, and absolutely forbade his drinking from the public water fountains in the park. Now revisiting that same park, he notices a bicycle with the "trademark Kryptonite" on its lock and recalls the Superman comics, with their hero who was impervious to all dangers except the threat posed by a piece of rock from the destroyed planet of his birth. Mamet tries to puzzle out the "deeper meaning of the Superman story," whose "power" not only is "obtained at the expense of any possibility of personal pleasure," but also whose seeming "strength reiterate[s] a very deep cry for help," since "ultimately he must fear [the] childhood home" of which the talismanic rock is a relic. Superman "can never reintegrate himself by returning to that home," and this lack of integration will forever prevent "any happy sexual manhood, of intimacy, of peace" (177–79). Interpreting the Superman narrative in this way might be seen as a kind of negative object lesson or inverse gloss on *Space Pandas*, since the characters in Mamet's play not only can but *do* go home again to reconnect with a more sympathetically understanding, nurturing mother and continue their process of individuation. Thus, while flights of imagination are validated as an essential part of the maturation process, so, too, is the security of home until the proper time comes to exercise full independence and break completely free.

III

The mark of Wilder on Mamet's children's plays is most visible in the metatheatrical techniques employed in the earliest of the three, *The Poet and the Rent* (performed in 1974 by Chicago's St. Nicholas Theater Co., and then in 1979 in New York at Circle-in-the-Square). The drama's subtitle, "A Play for Kids from Seven to 8:15," contains a very Wilderian pun, literally specifying the hour and a quarter audiences can expect to be in the theater but also, before making its unexpected turn to clock time, suggesting a suitable chronological age for the youngest viewers; the cast of characters includes a similar linguistic pun, describing Spuds O'Malley as "a cop who keeps his eyes peeled" (10). The play's setting, on a mostly bare stage "in a theater," recalls the locale of works like Luigi Pirandello's *Six Characters in Search of an Author,* but may be seen as alluding directly to Wilder's minimalist *Our Town* as well, for which there is "No curtain. No scenery" (5); the unlocalized space is thus a universalized anywhere and everywhere, just as the address of the factory in *Poet and Rent* is "1234 Yourstreet, Anytown, U.S.A." (35). With the ambiguous comment that most of his characters "in their time play many parts" (11), which refers to doubling of roles but might equally well hint at role-playing, Mamet draws upon the Shakespearean notion of "all the world's a stage" and "all the men and women merely players." This decided emphasis upon the human tendency to theatricalize life contributes to the audience's self-reflexivity about being in a theater watching a play. Mamet goes on, as Wilder before him had, to let out all the stops in his dramatist's bag of tricks, making this the richest of these plays for children in sheer theatricality, if not necessarily in insight.

In his important essay, "Some Thoughts on Playwriting," (1941), Wilder—who like Mamet valorizes the "storyteller" function of the dramatist—argues that the theater in its greatest ages (Periclean Athens and Elizabethan England, for example) has always depended heavily upon conventions by building upon what he calls an "agreed-upon falsehood, a permitted lie" as a means of more closely approaching the truth (3, 8). Such accepted conventions, understood to be "pretense" by all involved, help to break down the artificial boundary between play and audience by inviting a fuller imaginative collaboration in the action; by increasing the audience's self-consciousness as an audience; and by emphasizing the communal and ritualistic nature of the theatrical experience. In Wilder's view, the traditional box set, because it localizes the action to a particular place and restricts it to a definite time, renders the action less universal and hinders its ascent into the desirable realms of parable, allegory, and myth. In contrast, Wilder sought a theater wherein the large, recurrent outlines of the human story could be told through particular examples less important in themselves than the universal patterns they stand for and embody forth. Following Wilder's lead in his reliance upon recognizable stylistic conventions of the nonrealistic theater, Mamet in *Poet and the Rent* gives us a narrator, Aunt Georgie, who sets the time and place and underlines the moral (often rewarded with a pie in the face for her sententiousness); a storyteller, Sergeant Albert Pressman; a Mountie, with his sidekick wonderdog, Kodiak Prince (who sometimes recites absurd doggerel verse, such as "Life is a dream of Geometry / Life is a dream of Space / Life is a dream of some Orient Queen / Who got whacked in the head with a mace" [21]); characters who address the audience directly, who double as stagehands changing the modest sets and props from apartment to park to factory to jail, and who even become a chorus—and a singing one at that in the grand production number and finale; an actor who temporarily steps out of character to take a phone call from his domineering mother; allusions to several other literary texts (including ones by Dostoyevsky and Dreiser and Mamet's own *Duck Variations*) and lines of dialogue that revise lyrics from well-known songs (such as "This must be love, because I feel so bad" [14]); and, finally, characters reminiscent of Lily Sabina Fairweather from *Skin of Our Teeth*, who make caustic comments about the goings-on and otherwise criticize "faults" in the action, such as coincidences or digressions from the central plotline.

The plotline itself, which traces the young Poet's journey to a truer awareness of the nature of his vocation, is frenetic if fairly straightforward. The Poet lacks the 60 dollars he needs to pay the rent owed to his landlord, portrayed as a "capitalistic parasite," exploiter of the artist and the working man. When selling poems brings in only a quarter, he decides he had better take a job as a night watchman, where the boss specifically forbids him to engage in any writing. So he gets mixed up with two thieves, but they bilk him out of his part of the take. While in jail, he manages to win the needed 60 dollars at cards to pay the rent, but now still lacks the money for bail. After a rich girl he knows fails to come to his immediate rescue—though she later does offer two year's rent on his apartment—salvation finally seems to be at hand when an advertising agency offers him enormous sums to write copy for Wacko Products. Ultimately, however, the Poet resists the temptation to prostitute his art. The anti-business bias of the play, with its criticism of a society that deems the artist superfluous and expendable because he "ain't got no marketable skills" and therefore is of "no use" (31), brings *Poet and the Rent* closest of any of Mamet's children's plays to a pervasive thematic current that typifies such well-known dramas as *American Buffalo* and *Glengarry Glen Ross*. Speaking of those plays as exempla of the American Dream and its "divisive" myth of success, Mamet feels they demonstrate how "one can only succeed at the cost of, the failure of another"—even to the point of promoting dishonesty: "The effect on the little guy is that he turns to crime. And petty crime gets punished; major crimes go unpunished" (qtd. in Roudané 74).

But just as Sabina in a Brechtian moment at the close of *Skin of Our Teeth* reminds the audience that "We have to go on for ages and ages yet" and do our part in completing "The end of this play [that] isn't written yet" (250), so, too, the Poet in recommitting himself to his vocation as artist knows that he must "go home and go to work," since "There's a whole society to be explained out there" (52). Earlier, he had defined more explicitly than anyone else in all of Mamet's dramatic canon the social function and high moral calling of the poet/artist: "he's the man that lays it on the line and sums *up* this whole cockamamie flea market that we call 'life,' for each and every one of us—to help us live our humdrum, day-to-day and oftentimes fraught-with-pain excursions from womb to tomb with dignity and strength" (17). Muting the happily-ever-after ending of traditional children's tales—already severely undercut by the production number's warning of farcical pies-in-the-face and pants-catching-on-fire before "Misfortune will Retire"—Aunt Georgie's curtain line, "And they all lived as contentedly as possible, under the circumstances, for a reasonable length of time" (53), insists on the realities of disappointment, unpredictability, uncontrollability, and transitoriness that form not only an ineradicable part of daily existence but also contribute to its infinite variety and challenge.

Even more than the "refreshing [freedom from] the innocuous, patronizing fustian often associated with such plays" and the "quite complicated narratives" that Dennis Carroll argues mark Mamet's children's scripts "as suitable for parents as for children" (141), the inventive ways in which Mamet plays with gender (in *Frog Prince*), with genre (in *Space Pandas*) and with metatheater (in *Poet and the Rent*)—and even occasionally overturns audience expectations in the case of the first two—help make these dramas not just for children, who would, in fact, be at a loss to explain much of their richness. And if tonally, though admittedly not always thematically, they seem atypical of Mamet's canon, they do, perhaps even more obviously than his works exclusively for adults, fulfill the purpose that he designated for all "work[ers] in the true theater" during the Theodore Spencer Memorial Lecture he delivered at Harvard the same year (1986) that *Three Children's Plays* reached print: "to bring to your fellows, through the medium of your understanding and skill, the possibility of communion with what is essential in us all: that we are born to die, that we strive and fail, that we live in ignorance of why we are placed here, and, that, in the midst of this we need to love and be loved, but we are afraid" (*Restaurants* 116–7). Wilderian notions all!

This essay is dedicated to the memory of Brian Mexicott, himself a playwright as well as a student and scholar of Mamet. Brian was at work on a doctoral dissertation on Mamet and Masculinity when he died of AIDS on January 5, 1996.

WORKS CITED

Bettelheim, Bruno. *The Uses of Enchantment: The Meaning and Importance of Fairy Tales.* New York: Knopf, 1977.

Bigsby, C. W. E. *Modern American Drama, 1945–1990.* Cambridge: Cambridge UP, 1992.

Carroll, Dennis. *David Mamet.* New York: St. Martin's, 1987.

Frye, Northrop. *A Natural Perspective: The Development of Shakespearean Comedy and Romance.* New York: Harcourt, Brace, 1965.

Geis, Deborah R. "David Mamet and the Metadramatic Tradition: Seeing '"the Trick from the Back.'" In *David Mamet: A Casebook.* Ed. Leslie Kane. New York: Garland, 1992, 49–68.

Lurie, Alison. *Don't Tell the Grown-Ups: Subversive Children's Literature.* Boston: Little, Brown, 1990.

Mamet, David. *The Cabin: Reminiscences and Diversions.* New York: Random House, 1992.

———. *The Frog Prince.* In *Three Children's Plays.* New York: Grove, 1986, 55–87.

———. *The Poet and the Rent.* In *Three Children's Plays.* New York: Grove, 1986, 9–53.

———. *The Revenge of the Space Pandas or Binky Rudich and the Two-Speed Clock.* In *Three Children's Plays.* New York: Grove, 1986, 89–155.

———. *Some Freaks.* New York: Penguin, 1991.

———. *Writing in Restaurants.* New York: Penguin, 1987.

Roudané, Matthew C. "An Interview with David Mamet." *Studies in American Drama, 1945 to the Present* 1 (1986): 9–53.

Segal, Lore and Maurice Sendak. "The Frog Prince, or Iron Henry." In *The Juniper Tree and Other Tales from Grimm*, vol. 2. New York: Farrar, Straus, 1973, 169–77.

Wilder, Thornton. *The Matchmaker.* In *Three Plays.* New York: Harper Perennial, 1985, 251–401.

———. *Our Town.* In *Three Plays.* New York: Harper Perennial, 1985, 1–103.

———. *The Skin of Our Teeth.* In *Three Plays.* New York: Harper Perennial, 1985, 105–250.

———. "Some Thoughts on Playwriting." In *Aspects of the Drama: A Handbook.* Ed. Sylvan Barnet et al. Boston: Little, Brown, 1962, 1–11.

Plowing the Buffalo, Fucking the Fruits

(M)others in *American Buffalo* and *Speed-the-Plow*

Janet V. Haedicke

Since a line from Mamet's earliest play, *Lakeboat*, defines women as "soft things with a hole in the middle" (59), I risk heresy in challenging the claim of most feminist critics that Mamet and misogyny ring synonymous. The aggressively male dramaturgy charted by this first effort has served to cement this damning equation, as most Mamet plays feature men in traditionally male environments and include women only as minor characters when they are included at all; as Hersh Zeifman so vividly puts it, Mamet stages the "Phallus in Wonderland." A shift, moreover, from a form that the playwright now dismisses as immature, "episodic glimpses" ("Interview," Harriott 78) to a more traditional, linear theater has further validated the Mamet-misogynist label since feminist drama theory condemns realism as an endorsement of dominant ideology in its illusion of an objective reality, fixed truths, and stable identities.[1] In such Oedipal narratives, Aristotelian form colludes with Freudian content to exalt a quest in which male identity can be secured by triumph over a female or a feminized Other.[2]

Mamet's first such linear narrative, *American Buffalo* in 1975, certainly reeks of this collusion as the junkshop setting frames a quest by the three male characters to "take off this fucking fruit's coins" (54); similarly, the first such linear narrative to include a female character, *Speed-the-Plow* in 1987, exudes Oedipal desire as the Hollywood setting frames a quest by two male characters to secure profit and vanquish the "Pussy" (78). Yet I

am convinced that there emerges in Mamet a feminist ethic; these plays
ultimately subvert gender as well as genre, exposing realism and binarism
as perceptual and performative. In undermining the Newtonian/Carte-
sian foundation of both classical realism with its illusion of objective truth
and of the "sex-gender system"[3] with its illusion of fixed identity, Mamet
opens the possibility of transformation beyond an epistemology of linearity and stability. Subsequent plays have further testified to his subversion
of the gendered assumptions of realism through realism itself and thus inevitably have included increasingly more significant female characters; in
fact, two recent plays, *The Cryptogram* (1995) and *The Old Neighborhood*
(1997), shift to a domestic setting, affirming Mamet's focus on the *process*
of gender and on the exigency of transformation.[4]

What emerges on Mamet's stage in critical need of transformation is
America itself. In defining the American Dream as a dead end of "raping and pillage" ("David Mamet" 133), the playwright confirms the gendered nature of the quest; seeking power through the feminization and
defeat of an Other, Mamet's males bear witness to the polarization inherent in the ideal of American Individualism. This taint being excruci-
atingly vivid in the sanctified realm of Business, Mamet is convinced
that its corrosive, hierarchical system is "what America is about" ("David
Mamet" 137) and that the separation of the professional from the personal (feminism's fundamental target) exonerates unethical, even violent,
behavior ("An Interview," Roudané 74). Thus do many of his plays concern business, where success manifestly comes at the expense of another,
cast as female in subjugation: "buggering" a customer assumes the "intensity of coition" (Almansi 207) since, as Mamet notes, "American capitalism comes down to one thing. . . . The operative axiom is 'Hurrah for
me and fuck you.' Anything else is a lie" (qtd. in Dean 190). Even in this
homosocial world, the violence is gendered—a rape whose corrosion
constitutes Mamet's overriding subject: "All plays are about decay. They
are about the ends of a situation which has achieved itself fully, and the
inevitable disorder which ensues until equilibrium is again established. . . . That is why theatre has always been essential to human psychic equilibrium" (*Writing* 111). In the entropic environment of Mamet's
plays and of Mamet's America, this possibility of regeneration is signaled
by those at the borders of the stage and of society, who transgress those
borders and thus destabilize the binary territory that they have been re-
cruited to frame.

The "fucked," on or off Mamet's stage, bear notice, then, as they fore-
ground the very process by which they are so feminized. This engendering
of gender lurks in that "Mamet-speak" (Kroll 72) about which much critical controversy has erupted since "our foremost warrior-philologist"

(Savran 132) loosed his linguistic frontal assaults. Mamet's males deploy words—often obscenities along the order of "Fuck you"—to dominate, but their elliptical, fragmented "'grammatical chaos'" (Cohn 111) only displaces the communication, identity, and stability that they seek, revealing consciousness as ever mediated by language. As Mamet insists, "our rhythms *prescribe* our actions" (qtd. in Wetzsteon 39); his characters are therefore exposed as performers, their litanies through artifice and excess flouting rather than flaunting social realism: "All realism means is that the language strikes a responsive chord. The language in my plays is not realistic but poetic" ("An Interview" 76).[5] As the language cracks under its excess, so, too, does the realism as Mamet's characters frantically strive to perform into existence a stable, objective reality in which identity is fixated or gendered and such binaries as male/female, professional/personal, and rich/poor remain reassuringly hierarchical.[6] These performances emerging as parodies of the Oedipal quest, Mamet answers the call of feminist theorist Teresa de Lauretis for work that is "narrative and Oedipal with a vengeance, for it seeks to stress the duplicity of that scenario and the specific contradiction of the female subject within it" (*Alice* 157). Mamet stages just this contradictory space, exposing genre and gender as performative.[7] His determined choice of linear narrative reflects, not the enthroning of an objective truth, which he adamantly disclaims ("Interview," Harriott 79), but the foregrounding of perception, which "connects random events" and "equals truth" ("Two Gentlemen" 12).

Thus, Mamet's focus emerges as ultimately more epistemological than social, his call resounding for a consciousness that abdicates the throne of Oedipally forged Truth and Identity since "the purpose of the theatre is to transcend the individual conscious mind, to put the spectator in a communion with his or her fellows on the stage and also in the audience, so as to address problems which cannot be addressed by reason" ("Celebrating" 90). Regeneration, in our state of "rational uncertainty" (*Writing* 9), will spring from the dream or the drama, where borders blur between logic and illogic, order and chaos, public and private—oppositions coded as male and female within the hierarchical binarism of Western thought. In this liminal, transformative realm, "feminine" chaos inhabits rather than opposes "male" order, perturbing it, in the terminology of chaos theory, to a point of bifurcation at which entropy becomes a positive state from which a new order can evolve.[8] It is this realm beyond America's dead end, where essentialist masculine and feminine principles are not merely inverted but displaced and where Oedipus in exile recognizes his narrative as perception, that Mamet's drama envisions, even those plays so male-in-extremis as the first and last of what Ruby Cohn terms the "Business Trilogy" (109)—*American Buffalo* and *Speed-the-Plow*.

The short scenes of previous plays giving way to two linear acts, *American Buffalo* shifted Mamet's course not only in form but also in setting and subject. Portraying three petty thieves in "Don's Resale Shop," the play is too often regarded as a prequel to the 1983 Pulitzer Prize-winning portrayal of conniving salesmen in a real estate office. Yet Mamet regards *Glengarry Glen Ross* as "not as good a play as *American Buffalo*" ("Celebrating" 92), its "gang comedy" form pitting a multicharacter protagonist against the environment. Conversely, *American Buffalo*, in evoking "vehemently opposed aspects of one individual" (93) through intercharacter conflict, constitutes a tragedy and the more fitting analogy to *Death of a Salesman*; moreover, seeing Miller's play as a tragedy of family rather than business, Mamet extends the comparison beyond form to subject: "*American Buffalo*, sneakily enough, is really a tragedy about life in the family— so that is really the play which is closest to *Death of a Salesman*, though it's something I only realized afterwards" ("Celebrating" 93). It is something that critics have yet to realize, most concurring with Matthew Roudané in praising Mamet's resistance to American drama's "(over)reliance on the primal family unit" (6).

The playwright's labeling as domestic drama a play in which the characters are not related and in which not even a subjugated woman like Linda Loman appears validates a reading of *American Buffalo* beyond the sociological focus on America's business ethos. To be sure, the junkshop, whose owner wants to steal back a buffalo nickel that he has sold for 90 dollars, does emblemize an America that has sold out its frontier to become a cluttered, yet barren, landscape. But the play traces this dead end to its source, not in business competition, which is symptom, but in familial hierarchy, which is disease. As sanctioned site of values (and of fucking), the Family as icon provides prototype and paradigm for the engendering of gender—a process of power through subjection or "raping," which defines the entropic, violent American Dream.[9] Inscribing sex as gender, the Family has bequeathed to America an Oedipally prescribed trajectory of fixating identity through the conquest of a (M)other, a trajectory ascendant in the frontiersmen's conquest of Nature trophied by the eradicated buffalo.

In *American Buffalo*, the Lord, as the epigraph suggests, may have come in glory to the Republic, but now "He is peeling down the alley in a black and yellow Ford" (n.p.). This is an America of speed and of things, in which not buffalo but buffalo nickels are valued. The play opens on (the) Don schooling Bob, his "gopher," on the "Skill and talent and the balls to arrive at your own *conclusions*" (4) and on the principle that "there's business and there's friendship" (7). Exemplification of this "balls" sensibility arises in Don's vindictiveness toward the coin purchaser and justification of their friend Fletcher's screwing Bob's protector, Ruthie, out of her pig iron. Yet, even though Bobby has blown his stake-out of their "mark," Don's tone remains tender, if misguided, until the entrance of Walter Cole, whose nickname, Teach, presages his supremacy in what Pascale Hubert-Leibler describes as Mamet's Foucaultian "teacher-student paradigm" (73). The three become a parodic Oedipal triangle with Bobby as object-child of conflicting dynamics, which reflect Don's internal struggle.

It is fitting, then, that Teach's first words, other than a perfunctory "Good morning," assault one of the play's two absent females: "Fuckin' Ruthie, fuckin' Ruthie, fuckin' Ruthie, fuckin' Ruthie, fuckin' Ruthie" (9).[10] With Don's comic "What?" prompting an emphasized "Fuckin' *Ruthie,*" Teach's tirade, like many Mamet litanies, underscores a divide that is both gendered and linguistic. Here is a language where words fall in the cracks ("I sit down at the table Grace and Ruthie" [10]), exposing a void of that meaning which gendered representation struggles violently to deliver. Humiliated by Ruthie's sarcasm about his eating of Grace's toast, Teach relegates the woman to Other regionally and sexually, declaring Ruthie a "Southern bulldyke asshole ingrate of a vicious nowhere cunt" and concluding that "The only way to teach these people is to kill them" (11).

Teach thus immediately captures the apex position of the triangle,[11] "out-maling" Don in his ironic insistence on the money/friendship separation so "maybe we can deal with each other like some human beings" (15). Blaming his unmanly poker losses on the women's cheating, Teach eventually persuades Don that, "simply as a *business* proposition" (35), loyalty to Bob cannot be allowed to interfere with judgment in planning the coin heist. In agreeing to cut out the "kid" (34) as unfit for the "thing" (44) and let Teach "go in there and gut this motherfucker" (35), Don capitulates to his masculinist ethos of reducing to Other any threat to dominance: to a cuckold, their fence ("Guys like that, I like to fuck their wives" [28]); to a "fucking fruit" (54), their victim; to an oxymoronic "dyke cocksucker" (54), Ruthie; and to a "Cocksucker" (72), Fletcher, a Godot figure whom Don does insist be a third party in the theft.

This technique of power through negative mimesis undergirds Teach's definition of America's founding principle:

You know what is free enterprise?. . . .
The freedom . . .
Of the *Individual* . . .
To Embark on Any Fucking Course that he sees fit. . . .
In order to secure his honest chance to make a profit. . . .

The country's *founded* on this, Don. . . .
Without this we're just savage shitheads in the wilderness. . . .
Sitting around some vicious campfire. That's why *Ruthie* burns me
up. (72–73, some ellipses added)

The illogic of an "honest chance" being referred to larceny escalates in
the non-sequitur implication that Ruthie has somehow attacked free enterprise in criticizing Teach. His ethos an illusory Newtonian order of hierarchy and logicality, Teach ultimately subverts his own insistence on
objective truth; having instructed Bob that "Things are what they are"
(39), he insists to Don that "A fact stands by itself. And we must face the
facts and act on them" (75), a stance only he has the "balls" to take. When
Don resists the comically specious scenario of there existing a written
combination to the "fruit's" safe, Teach erupts: "Fuck you. (All day long.
Grace and Ruthie Christ). . . . I am not Fletch" (79). This feminization
of Don for his refusal of "fact" aligns him with the other "cocksuckers"
whom Teach must scapegoat to defend his male identity, a bulwark
strengthened further by his gun—"A silly personal thing" (85) that "helps
[him] to relax" (84). He thus needs this "thing" to accomplish "the thing,"
"The light of things as they are" (85). Mamet's repetition of the word
"thing" over sixty times in the play as well as the junk "things" in Don's
shop not only render ironic the clawing search for an objective reality and
fixed identity but also indict the inevitable violence in this "thing" of
Oedipal Individualism, where it is "either him or us" (84).

The "him" must be scripted as a (M)other, who is "buffaloed" or
"fucked" to maintain the illusion of a stable hierarchy. Frustrated by Bob's
confused account from the women of Fletcher's mugging by "Some spics"
(92), Teach teaches the "young fuck" (93) a lesson by striking him with "*a
nearby object,*" a "thing" to confirm referentiality: "Grace and Ruthie up
your ass, you shithead" (94). Bob's tears only cement his female positioning: "That don't mean shit to me, you fruit" (94). Though Don, who
shared Teach's stance that the "thing" in business is logic and "Action" (4),
initially condones the violence against Bob, he finally acknowledges the
perceptual and mediated, even contradictory, nature of truth and consciousness; this Saussurian epistemology, as Thomas King points out
(541), was ever implicit in Don's edict that "Action talks and bullshit
walks" (4). A phone call from Ruthie confirming the partial truth of Bob's
narrative thus revives Don's loyalty to Bob, who confesses that he has purchased the buffalo-head nickel that he brought to sell to Don. Attracted
to "the art on it" (64), Bob again defies the logic of business in replying
to Teach's "Why would you do a thing like that?" with a simple "For
Donny" (99).

Teach's disgust and disbelief that Bob has not beaten them to the "fruit's" coins erupt in an assertion of his racial and sexual dominance in the face of Don's command to get his car to take Bob to the hospital: "I am not your nigger. I am not your wife" (100). Finally recognizing that, as Mamet claims, he has been "tempted by the devil into betraying all his principles" ("Celebrating" 94), Don consciously chooses personal connection over professional action, despite a confusion of facts and sacrifice of profit, and exorcises Teach's predatory sensibility: "You stiff this one, you stiff that one . . . you come in here, you stick this poison in me . . . (*hitting him*). . . . You make life of garbage" (101, some ellipses added). Part of Teach's poison, Don's violence dissipates with Bob's confession that he lied about seeing their mark leave home. Their Business "thing," their quest thus revealed as an a priori dead end, Teach trashes the junkshop "things" that he had so esteemed as truth-tokens, lamenting that "The World is Lies. . . . Every Fucking Thing. . . . I fuck myself" (103–04). His tool (irresistible!) of destruction is yet another pig iron, a "thing that they stick in dead pigs keep their legs apart all the blood runs out" (35). Male violence ultimately turning on itself, Teach's fear reduces all to such a splayed position; thus does he see himself as "a sissy" in the self-fashioned paper rain hat donned to get the car.

Don, however, bemoans no such male/female inversion since he has spurned the hierarchical binarism of hetero/homo, professional/personal, Self/Other, fact/fiction. Straddling the boundaries of a mediated consciousness, he does not "*care* anymore" (100) about the truth of Bob's story or feel anger at Teach that his "shop's fucked up" (104). Into this "ruthless and graceless" (Zeifman 129) world where junk becomes a valued "thing," into this America where the buffalo adorn not a fruited plain but the barren coin of the realm, into this junked shop enters the shadow of Grace.[12] Bob and Don in the final scene evoke the possibility of resurrection through a communal rather than individualistic ethic; in a realm where Ruthie and Grace are no longer "'ghosts'" (Zeifman 126) but transgressors of presence/absence borders,[13] we can embrace the communality resonating in Don's exit-line: "That's all right" (106).

America will not be all right, however, so long as violent performances of gender "make life of garbage"—an alchemy at its extreme in the Hollywood setting of *Speed-the-Plow*. An image-factory "flooding the market with trash" (Mamet, "An Interview" 78), Hollywood not only reproduces but produces culture and hence is complicit in the making of America as a junkshop. Thus, this play's protagonist, a newly promoted Production Head, concedes of the movie business "with its own unchanging rules" that "It's not all garbage, but most of it is" (29). The only voice raised against the inevitability of junk values is female. Karen, the first of a series of women characters in all of Mamet's subsequent plays, questions, "But why should it all be garbage?" (29) and raises the central issue of the play. Another Faustian conflict, *Speed-the-Plow* depicts the battle for the soul of Bobby Gould as Karen, his temporary secretary, takes on the Mephistophelian Charlie Fox.

This quest for Gould is, to the sly Fox, a quest for gold in the form of Hollywood's favored commodity, "A *Buddy* Picture" (11) for which he has secured a star and that he wants Gould's studio to produce. A prison film is "the *thing*" (10) since it contains "Action, blood, a social theme . . ."(13), a standard that authorizes not only sexism but racism and homophobia ("And the black guys going to rape his ass" [11]). Though Gould at play's opening has decried his job as a "monster," a wilderness territory between "'Art'" and "'Entertainment'" (3), he succumbs to Fox's proposal to co-produce this shameless paean to a male gaze as tribute to their friendship. Gould's assertion that "Money is not Gold" (21) because theirs is a "People Business" (22) facilely yields to Fox's that "We're gonna kick the ass of a lot of them fucken' people" (22). As in *American Buffalo*, the imperative of Business, "the thing," is to fuck or feminize any threat to coherent identity; no longer suffering the "monster" of ambivalence, Gould heralds their future: " . . . it's Boy's Choice: Skate in One Direction Only" (23).

Karen, on the other hand, as "just a temporary" (27), embodies the intrinsic nature of ambivalence. Her entrance with a tray of coffee confirming her gendered inscription, she nonetheless transgresses boundaries in resisting the Hollywood-sanctified coding of women as Mother or Monster, Madonna or Whore. This transgression, foregrounded in the casting of the singer/actress Madonna for the New York production, is signaled by Fox's assertion that "she falls between two stools. . . . That she is not, just some, you know, a 'floozy' . . . on the other hand, I think I'd have to say, I don't think she is so *ambitious* she would schtup you just to get ahead" (35, some ellipses added). To counter their self-described positioning as "Two Whores" (26), the men script Karen as a commodity in the sex-gender system by wagering $500 that Gould "can screw her" (38). To Karen's inquiry about the Buddy Picture being a "good film," Gould equivocates that it is a "commodity" (41) and that his job is to turn a profit rather than to change the world. Through talk of purity and a proposal that she report that evening on the filmic potential of the "artsy" book on his desk, Gould gains assurance that this commodity, too, will turn a profit.

Though Gould does "schtup" Karen when she comes to his apartment, it is she who prevails in this private sphere. Feeling "Empowered" (48) after reading the book, entitled *The Bridge or, Radiation and the Half-Life of Society* (42), Karen embraces its call for transformation from "a life lived in fear" (49) and asks to work on the film version; here, her desire echoes Mamet's for theater: "In a morally bankrupt time we can help to change the habit of coercive and frightened action and substitute for it the habit of trust, self-reliance, and cooperation" (*Writing* 26–27). Although enchanted by her "*freshness*" in sharing "this thing" (50), Gould scorns the book as one about "the End of the World" that "won't Get the Asses in The Seats" (53) since people "require" just "*the thing everyone made last year*" (56). His upholding of what Karen terms the "*degradation*" (55) of dominant ideology falters, however, with her confession that she came in full knowledge of his sexual ploy and that she, too, sought connection. Reading to him from the book, Karen urges Gould to transform himself and his images: "'What was coming was a return to the self, which is to say, a return to God. It was round'"(58). In countering the linearity of Western thought, the "Eastern Sissy Writer" (23), albeit excessively and obtusely, provides for Karen a paradigm of liminality, one in which the borders between male and female, professional and personal, dissolve. Her presence as a desiring subject, a sexual (M)other, suggests, not essentialist Womanhood, but a permeation through "disruptive excess" (Hall 139) of Madonna/Whore, Mother/Monster boundaries; by "greenlighting" the not-Art, not-Entertainment film, Gould affirms as not-"monster" both his job and that no man's land (literally) of differences beyond boundaries.

It is, however, Karen's transgressive sexuality that Fox publicly attacks to stifle this transformation. Back at the studio the following morning, Fox mocks Gould's recognition that his "life is a sham" (69) and his decision "To do something which is right" (68) by making the Radiation film instead of the Buddy Picture: "you're gonna spend ten million dollars for a piece of *pussy*, you were 'up all night . . .' You were up all night boffing the *broad*. Are you getting *old?* What is this? *Menopause?*" (69). Having scripted Gould as an old woman or "some Eastern Fruit" (66) in abandoning the quest for gold, Fox takes a stand on the masculine pole of heterosexual versus homosexual, young versus old, public versus private, Western versus Eastern, logic versus liminality. His own gendered stability threatened by the book's notion "That silver is more powerful than gold; and the circle than the square or triangle" (73), Fox seeks an Oedipal victory over the feminized; like Teach, he resorts to the violence intrinsic in binary scripts:

> *Fuck* you . . . *Fuck* you . . . (*He hits* GOULD.) *Fuck* you. Get up. (*He hits him again.*) I'll fucken' kill you right here in this office. All this bullshit; you *wimp*, you *coward* . . . now you got the job, and now you're going to *run* all

over everything, like something broke in the *shopping* bag, you *fool*—your
fucken' sissy film—you squat to pee. You old *woman.* . . . (70)

Yet it is not gendered violence that delivers Gould and gold but the
revelation of Truth—Oedipus's deepest desire. To defend masculine territory, Fox must refute ambivalence, including his own "two stools" perception of Karen; reestablishing the absolute border between Madonna
and Whore, he sets out to prove her "A Tight Pussy wrapped around Am-
bition" (78) through a forced admission that sex was contingent upon
Gould's endorsement of the Radiation film. In informing Karen that
"You're living in a World of Truth" (77) and demanding an unequivocal
answer, Gould yields to Fox's negation of provisional truths that belie
Truth, differences that belie difference, and chaos that belies linearity.
Thus is he indeed "lost" (78), not, ironically, in blurring the borders but
in retracing them by choosing Fox's narrative over Karen's. Fox's erection
(again irresistible!) of a masculine tower from which the gaze reigns
supreme is founded on the expulsion of Karen as a trespasser, a violator of
bounds whose "moment of suspension" (Nelson 74) or "mistress plot" (77)
disrupts the master narrative of causality and coherence. Reminding
Gould that they have a meeting about their film, Karen sounds the death
knell for transformation as she ingenuously validates Fox's image of a
monster of unfeminine femaleness connected with neither romantic love
nor "Hearth and Home" (72). Her concern that Gould be "a good man"
(81) by countering Hollywood's production of America is cast as perverse
in Fox's one-dimensional image of manhood through triumph over the
frontier, the homosexual, the woman.

Reinstating gendered identity in banishing Karen ("See you at the A
and P" [80]), Fox aborts Gould's salvation (as evidenced by *Bobby Gould
in Hell* in 1989). Once again, Grace is absent from the stage, from the
screen, from the world as the illusion of male presence is fostered by female absence. The Buddy film having vanquished *The Bridge* project,
Fox's ethos of Individual over Other has blown up the bridge, which
"'brought grace'" (4). Warning Gould that they are not destined "To
Share Our Burdens," Fox sentences his "buddy" to the "buddyless," unre-
deemed life of the Individual: "And what *if* this fucken' grace' exists? It's
not for you. . . . You have a different thing" (81). This "thing"—the objective, linear "reality"—for the Production Head is reproducing and producing culture through mythologized image; to Fox's query, "What are
we put on earth to do?," Gould concedes, "We're here to make a movie"
(82). His soul damned to a Dantesque repetition of Hollywood's homage
to the male gaze, Gould will speed his plow and spread his seed on
ground overplowed and overcultivated, demeaning Thackery's evocation

of "duty" in the play's epigraph: "'to each some work upon the ground he stands on, until he is laid beneath it'" (n.p.).[14] Karen, however, who, "'descends to the ground, and takes [her] part in the contest'" (n.p.), evokes another consciousness, another field to be plowed and sown. Her recognition of gender, sexuality, and identity as performance evinces a gaze beyond the binary,[15] one that envisions a fruited plain and an America on which God's grace is shed.

To reap a harvest from this plain, the work of each of us upon the earth is that which, according to Mamet, Christ taught: "It's not our job to change the world. It's our job to act according to precepts we perceive to be right" ("Two Gentlemen" 12). Mamet here again affirms an observer-influenced reality but emphasizes our ethical imperative within it. In staging a realism whose fissures subvert the Newtonian/Cartesian epistemology of classical realism, Mamet opens the genre to the possibility of alternative worlds at the borders of its proscenium. In staging a binarism whose fissures subvert the Oedipal epistemology of naturalized gender, Mamet opens subjectivity to the possibility of alternative futures at the border of masculine and feminine. With his performing males mimicking that "certain amount [of American men]. . . . For example, all" ("Interview," Harriott 84) who are misogynists, Mamet's theatrical purpose is explicitly transformative, hence implicitly feminist: "I have always thought that mixed media and performance art was [sic] basically garbage, very decadent, and the sign of a deep unrest, the sign really of a cultural disease—a turning of one's back on a regenerative cultural institution" ("Celebrating" 90).

Even if theatrical communion signifies only, as Herbert Blau suggests, "*a community of the question*" (12), it nonetheless forges a passage from the junkyard landscape of Oedipal Individualism, American style, to the dreamscape of American community. And if, indeed, "the oppressed must free the oppressor" (*Writing* 33) in any hierarchical system, then the fucked, the feminized, the (M)others light the passage so that we may emerge from the American Dream's dead end of raping to an open, unstable, liminal realm where the females, the fruits, and the buffalo roam across borders no longer perceived even by Oedipus as real.

NOTES

1. Following Artaud and Brecht in indicting the conservatism of realistic representation, Jill Dolan, for example, warns that "American realism's 'craving for a referent'—that is, its mimetic representations of 'the real'—situates the spectator as a subject of coherent identity who can be

appealed to through the text's construction to authorize its illusion" (96). And since representation fails to construct women as subjects, Sue-Ellen Case's warning has been heeded: "Cast the realism aside—its consequences for women are deadly" (297).

2. As Teresa de Lauretis insists, "if the crime of Oedipus is the destruction of differences, the combined work of myth and narrative is the production of Oedipus. . . . Therefore, to say that narrative is the production of Oedipus is to say that each reader—male or female—is constrained and defined within the two positions of a sexual difference thus conceived: male-hero-human, on the side of the subject; and female-obstacle-boundary-space, on the other" (*Alice* 120–21).

3. Naming a founding principle of feminism, Gayle Rubin first used this term in 1975 to emphasize that sex is not gender.

4. See de Lauretis for a cogent argument that "*the construction of gender is the product and process of both representation and self-representation*" (*Technologies* 9).

5. Though most critics regard Mamet's language as that of the street, some do perceive its attenuation beyond realism: Bigsby insists that this is not "transcribed speech" (350); Cohn, that "accurate ear" claims are "nonsense" (109); Schvey, that the "obliquities" reflect a power game (106); and Dean, that Mamet writes "free verse" (22).

6. Jacques Derrida points out that "*the* metaphysical exigency" is a "hierarchical axiology" (93) that, in prioritizing oppositions, posits the possibility of a return to an original, ideal, and unified state.

7. Judith Butler convincingly argues that gender is an "identity instituted through a *stylized repetition of acts*" (270).

8. See, for example, Ilya Prigogine and Isabelle Stengers' postulation of positive entropy and order arising out of chaos in the form of dissipative structures, a concept that won Prigogine the Nobel Prize.

9. De Lauretis insists that "the story of Oedipus weaves the inscription of violence (and family violence at that) into the representation of gender" (*Technologies* 44).

10. According to Almansi, Mamet's "fucked up" males often complain of an individual woman; or that "prickteaser" woman, America; or that malevolent "female God, Mother Nature" (193).

11. A Lacanian reading would view Teach as representing the symbolic Law-of-the-Father in a phallogocentric culture.

12. In the essay "In The Company of Men," Mamet describes male community as sometimes "an experience of *true* grace" (90).

13. Though Zeifman exonerates Mamet from equation with his misogynist characters, he finds problematical the "essentialist reduction of women to a gender stereotype" (133) embodying spiritual values. This concern, while valid, can be alleviated by recognition of Mamet's epistemological subversions rather than inversions of oppositions.

14. Tony Stafford considers the themes of contest and work in the play through comparison with Thomas Morton's 1800 play *Speed the Plough*.

15. Although Laura Mulvey initially conceptualized the male gaze, which was to undergird feminist film and drama criticism, she has since urged evolution beyond this ironically binary perspective, an evolution that most drama critics ignore but that Mamet seems to suggest.

WORKS CITED

Almansi, Guido. "David Mamet, A Virtuoso of Invective." *Critical Angles: European Views of Contemporary American Literature.* Ed. Marc Chénétier. Carbondale: Southern Illinois UP, 1986, 191–207.

Bigsby, C. W. E. *Beyond Broadway.* Cambridge: Cambridge UP, 1985. Vol. 3 of *A Critical Introduction to Twentieth-Century American Drama.* 3 vols.

Blau, Herbert. "Hysteria, Crabs, Gospel, and Random Access: Ring Around the Audience." *Studies in the Literary Imagination* 21 (1988): 7–21.

Butler, Judith. "Performative Acts and Gender Constitution: An Essay in Phenomenology and Feminist Theory." *Performing Feminisms: Feminist Critical Theory and Theatre.* Ed. Sue-Ellen Case. Baltimore: Johns Hopkins UP, 1990, 270–82.

Case, Sue-Ellen. *Feminism and Theatre.* New York: Methuen, 1988.

Cohn, Ruby. "How Are Things Made Round?" Kane, 109–21.

Dean, Ann. *David Mamet: Language as Dramatic Action.* Rutherford: Associated UP, 1990.

De Lauretis, Teresa. *Alice Doesn't: Feminism, Semiotics, Cinema.* Bloomington: Indiana UP, 1984.

———. *Technologies of Gender: Essays on Theory, Film, and Fiction.* Bloomington: Indiana UP, 1987.

Derrida, Jacques. *Limited Inc.* Evanston, IL: Northwestern UP, 1988.

Dolan, Jill. *The Feminist Spectator as Critic.* Ann Arbor: U of Michigan P, 1991.

Hall, Ann C. "Playing to Win: Sexual Politics in David Mamet's *House of Games* and *Speed-the-Plow.*" Kane, 137–60.

Hubert-Leibler, Pascale. "Dominance and Anguish: The Teacher-Student Relationship in the Plays of David Mamet." Kane, 69–85.

Kane, Leslie, ed. *David Mamet: A Casebook.* New York: Garland, 1992.

King, Thomas L. "Talk and Dramatic Action in *American Buffalo.*" *Modern Drama* 34 (1991): 538–48.

Kroll, Jack. "Phantoms in the Dark." *Newsweek.* February 20, 1995: 72.

Mamet, David. *American Buffalo.* New York: Grove, 1976.

———. "Celebrating the Capacity for Self-Knowledge." With Henry I. Schvey. *New Theatre Quarterly* 4 (1988): 89–96.

———. "David Mamet." *In Their Own Words: Contemporary American Playwrights.* David Savran. New York: Theatre Communications Group, 1988. 132–44.

———. "An Interview with David Mamet." With Matthew C. Roudané. *Studies in American Drama, 1945-Present* 1 (1986): 73–81.

———. "Interview with David Mamet." *American Voices: Five Contemporary Play-wrights in Essays and Interviews*. Esther Harriott. Jefferson, NC: McFarland, 1988. 77–97.

———. "In the Company of Men." *Some Freaks*. New York: Viking, 1989. 85–91.

———. *Lakeboat*. New York: Grove, 1981.

———. *Speed-the-Plow*. New York: Grove, 1985.

———. "Two Gentlemen of Chicago: David Mamet and Stuart Gordon." With Hank Nuwer. *South Carolina Review* 17 (Spr. 1985): 9–20.

———. *Writing in Restaurants*. New York: Viking, 1986.

Mulvey, Laura. *Visual and Other Pleasures*. Bloomington: Indiana UP, 1989.

Nelson, Jeanne-Andrée. "*Speed-the-Plow* or Seed the Plot?: Mamet and the Female Reader." *Essays in Theatre* 10 (1991): 71–82.

Prigogine, Ilya, and Isabelle Stengers. *Order out of Chaos: Man's New Dialogue with Nature*. New York: Bantam, 1984.

Roudané, Matthew C. "Mamet's Mimetics." Kane, 3–32.

Rubin, Gayle. "The Traffic in Women: Notes toward a Political Economy of Sex." *Toward an Anthropology of Women*. Ed. Rayna Reiter. New York: Monthly Review, 1975, 157–210.

Savran, David. "David Mamet." *In Their Own Words: Contemporary American Playwrights*. New York: Theatre Communications Group, 1988, 132–44.

Schvey, Henry I. "Power Plays: David Mamet's Theatre of Manipulation." Kane, 87–108.

Stafford, Tony J. "*Speed-the-Plow* and *Speed the Plough:* The Work of the Earth." *Modern Drama* 36 (1993): 38–47.

Wetzsteon, Ross. "New York Letter." *Plays and Players*. Sept. 1976: 37+.

Zeifman, Hersh. "Phallus in Wonderland: Machismo and Business in David Mamet's *American Buffalo* and *Glengarry Glen Ross*." Kane, 123–35.

DISGUISE IN LOVE

GENDER AND DESIRE IN *HOUSE OF*
GAMES AND *SPEED-THE-PLOW*

STEVEN PRICE

They'd had this date from the beginning. David Mamet had been on a collision course with feminist criticism since 1970, when he wrote the all-male *Lakeboat* and began to develop the scatalogically colloquial dialogue for which he would become known. This, after all, was the piece in which a man describes women as "soft things with a hole in the middle," a line that one critic thought sufficiently representative to use in the epigraph to a scathing essay on the playwright published in 1991 (Nelson 71). Nevertheless, it took a long time for such criticism to appear. As recently as 1989, a collection, *Feminist Rereadings of Modern American Drama*, was published for which no articles on Mamet were even submitted (Schlueter 11–12). The situation changed only after the appearance of two works that presented a woman character as enigma within a predominantly masculine world: Margaret Ford, the psychoanalyst who alters her appearance and behavior at the end of *House of Games* (1987); and Karen, the Hollywood secretary whose motives remain uncertain in *Speed-the-Plow* (1988).

In an interview following the release of *House of Games*, Mamet stated: "I think it's absurd to accuse me of misogyny, simply because I have been unable or unwilling to describe female characters as readily as men. It's just that I know men better and it's the duty of a writer to describe what he knows best" (qtd. in Ranvaud 232). This was essentially the same response he had given to interviewers in 1976 (Fraser 7) and 1984 (Harriott 84). Interviewers sometimes suspect that Mamet is "kidding" them (for example, Cinch 50), and one may often feel that his essays and interviews form part of an elaborate confidence game; but there is good reason to suggest that at the time of writing *House of Games* and *Speed-the-Plow* he was still uncertain of his ability to create convincing female characters, and perhaps saw these works as being more about men than women.

Given this self-appraisal, "[i]t is no surprise . . . that feminist viewers may be a bit skeptical when Mamet begins to create female characters" (Hall 138). Such skepticism is exemplified in Carla J. McDonough's assertion that "[w]omen and the female in Mamet's plays are always allotted a negative position. They are what is most feared and most confusing for his men, and they appear, when they appear, only in caricature or as stereotype of both male fear and fantasy. They are basically men without power, castrated men, failed men, failed salesmen" (200). A contrary position is taken by those critics, including some hostile ones, who argue that, perhaps unknowingly, Mamet's plays reveal a resistant femininity that exposes the blindnesses in masculine perceptions of women. Jeanne-Andrée Nelson, for example, asserts that Mamet glorifies "the supremacy of male modes of being and thinking," and that "very little hope is left to rescue any of his work outside of the phallocentric system of representation" (73–74). Nevertheless, her reading of *Speed-the-Plow* allows her to "rescue" this play, which is "unique in the *oeuvre* of Mamet" because in Karen it contains an active female "reader" who "mirrors the interpretative effort of her female counterpart in the audience who refuses to participate in the misogynistic discourse of the patriarchal authority" (74). Ann C. Hall, in a more sympathetic essay, similarly emphasizes the disruptive effects of a feminine excess or *jouissance* that escapes masculine representation: "[b]y challenging the power structures established in the plays, and, more importantly, by challenging the expectations of other characters and their audiences, Dr. Ford in *House of Games* and Karen in *Speed-the-Plow* embody this revolutionary femininity" (139). Consequently, "[w]hile the scripts appear to grant power to the male characters, the women in these plays are the blind spots which violate our sense of closure" (157).

The paradox is that in tracing such "blind spots," both Hall and Nelson are led at times into affirming a feminine essence, or at least a knowable subjectivity, the denial of which they elsewhere see as a prerequisite of resistance. Although feminist critics of Mamet's female characters are broadly divided between those who dismiss them as misogynist misrepresentations and those who regard them as complex figures possessing a deep psychology, in either case the characters become knowable under analysis. Consequently, these studies usually have a considerable investment in the power of psychoanalytical reading. The problem is that these closed readings tend to misrepresent the strategies of the texts, which frequently jam the mechanisms of psychoanalysis and unsettle attempts to maintain a secure awareness of both character and interpretive strategy.

Both Hall and Nelson see Mamet's women as figures possessing the qualities of the analysand in a case study. In particular, both are finally drawn to vouch for Karen's sincerity and to tell us what she is really thinking: "Karen is sincerely straightforward" (Hall 157), and quite simply "is not . . . guilty of manipulation" (Nelson 80). Nelson even provides information about what went on in Karen's mind *off*stage: when Karen reads the words of *The Bridge* she "is sure about the incorruptibility of their truth," and "her voice duplicates the emotion she felt when she read alone" (77). As Andrew K. Kennedy once noted, however, "'[s]incerity' can seldom be taken for granted in dramatic dialogue" (23), since the very nature of performance compels the recognition that sincerity can be simulated; and this is a problem foregrounded in Mamet's con-dramas. Karen's admission that she would not have gone to bed with Gould if he hadn't greenlighted *The Bridge* does not settle the question of her true motivation one way or the other: it leaves it, precisely, indeterminable.

The slippage between materialist and essentialist views of the self in these essays reproduces the construction of identity in the confidence game, a game that informs all of Mamet's writing. The theory of the "tell" requires that human beings give themselves away, revealing their true nature; the theory of the con requires that the tell can be consciously mimicked, suggesting that a true nature can be simulated and therefore, perhaps, does not exist. Consequently, there is in his plays a heightened awareness of the ways in which subject positions, including those marked by gender, are fluid and performed.

The femininity of Margaret and Karen is, of course, inscribed within power relations marked by gender, not least at the level of narrative. In interviews, and in the volumes of essays collected in *A Whore's Profession*, Mamet makes constant reference to Freud (*Whore* 351, for example), Aristotle (163), and Bruno Bettelheim (117). He also demonstrates a close interest in Joseph Campbell's "monomyth," in which "[a] hero ventures forth from the world of common day into a region of supernatural wonder: fabulous forces are there encountered and a decisive victory is won: the hero comes back from this mysterious adventure with the power to bestow boons on his fellow man" (Campbell 30). As Dennis Carroll has shown (91–106), Mamet's work appears to have been strongly influenced by this model. His constantly repeated dictum that "[t]he story is the *essential progression of incidents* that occur to the hero in pursuit of his one goal" (*Whore* 346) is comparable to Campbell's formulation, as is the structure of classical Hollywood cinema.

The structure of desire in such narratives has a psychological basis. Just as a play like Mamet's *Edmond* stages the structural drive whereby "every fear hides a wish" (68), or, in *House of Games*, Mike tells Margaret that her conversion to gun-toting kleptomaniac "is what you always wanted. . . . You sought it out" (70), so Campbell and Bettelheim see the world of the hero's adventure as a representation of the reader's or listener's unconscious fears and desires. For Campbell, by the end of the mythic adventure "we no longer desire and fear; we are what was desired and feared" (162), while for Bettelheim, "[i]n a fairy tale, internal processes are externalized and become comprehensible as represented by the figures of the story and its events. . . . The fairy tale is therapeutic" (25).

Campbell's monomyth was anticipated by Vladimir Propp's *Morphology of the Folktale* (1928). Propp argued that "[a]ll fairy tales are of one type in regard to their structure" (23), consisting of a selection of 31 possible "functions," performed in an invariable sequence by the dramatis personae, who occupy 7 "spheres of action" (villain, donor, helper, princess, dispatcher, hero, and false hero). When Mamet says that "the play should be about only one thing, and that thing should be *what the hero is trying to get*" (*Whore* 163), he like Propp is describing a subject-object division that assigns roles according to function and not to "character," which indeed "doesn't exist. The character is just habitual action. . . . The rest doesn't count" (*Whore* 354). In summary, Mamet's comments about dramatic form affirm a mythic model for the story that depends on structure rather than character, yet has a psychological draw provided by the emphasis on "habitual action," which suggests the Lacanian structure of a desire in perpetual pursuit of an Other to redeem the lack within the self.

Feminist criticism has argued that Proppian narratives of desire are inescapably gendered. "The 'quest,' the 'desire,' the 'action' are all male-determined and male-centred, and are privileged at the expense of the female" (Aston 40), who can be only the object of the quest and is thereby denied a subject position. Consequently, many have argued that an oppositional feminist drama requires quite different structures and emphases, "characterized by circular or spiraling patterns, involving a communal protagonist, employing comic devices of irony and festive license, but resisting the traditionally romantic resolution or, indeed, any clear-cut resolution" (Brown 15).

The apparently universal monomythical form should also be historicized. Propp's work after the *Morphology* "combines the synchronic or 'morphological' study of plot types and motifs with their diachronic or historical transformations" (de Lauretis 113); Campbell accepts that the monomyth presupposes a society that makes available the possibility of independent, autonomous, heroic action. In the modern world, however, "[o]ne does not know toward what one moves. One does not know by what one is propelled" (Campbell 388). This contemporary insecurity is exposed in the typical protagonist of a Mamet play, and to watch a Campbellian narrative unfold on Mamet's stage is to witness a situation of constant irony, of the discrepancy between the desire for structure and progress and the impossibility of their attainment.

Glengarry Glen Ross, Edmond, House of Games, Speed-the-Plow, and *Oleanna* have in common the same dialogic pattern. In all of these works there is a discursive hierarchy, in which an ostensibly privileged ideology (respectively capitalism, free will, psychoanalysis, Hollywood, and academic discourse) is undermined and ironized from within. This newly weakened ideology enters into competition with an alternative: pastoralism, determinism, the confidence game, high art, political correctness. By the end, this alternative has also been discredited. In the resulting aporia the plays seem either to fall between two stools or to occupy both stools simultaneously. On the one hand, the plays offer an Aristotelian resolution, a synthesis in which "what is revealed to have been the low objective is transmogrified into the high objective. And we realize that the high objective is carried in the low objective all the time" (Mamet, qtd. in Schvey 93). On the other hand, the plays present Mamet as confidence trickster, encouraging us to misplace our faith in one of two equally untenable propositions. This constant play of irony accounts for much of the tragicomic tension of his work.

In *Edmond,* for example, the eponymous hero embarks on a particularly dark variant of the quest and ends up sodomized in jail by a black prisoner, who becomes his lover. This story closely resembles the first part of *Speed-the-Plow*'s prison movie, which is clearly a parody of the 1980s "buddy movie": so predictable that Gould knows in detail what the storyline will be before Fox has had a chance to tell him. The element of irony and parody in *Edmond,* however, has less frequently been noted. McDonough argues that the ending is an affirmative recognition of the debilitating consequences of binary sexual stereotyping:

> If we view the masculine and the feminine, as Edmond seems to, as synonymous with domination and submission, then it is only through becoming feminized—something which Edmond had feared in previous scenes—that Edmond finds peace. . . . [I]t is here, after having all previous concepts of himself erased, that he at last is able to struggle toward a new sense of himself and of his position in society, to come to terms with what he accepts as inevitable. (200)

The playwright has similarly suggested that Edmond's "sexual identity, his social identity, his racial identity have been fractured and discarded. What he says is 'I didn't need them anyhow. I'm so happy that none of these things can be taken from me ever again'" (qtd. in Carroll 97). And for Dennis Carroll, by the end "community and a kind of reintegration are in sight" (99), as Edmond and the Prisoner "talk about special knowledge, special insights . . . no matter how ironically bestowed" (103). However, this "special knowledge" remains obscure, as would later be the case with *The Bridge* in *Speed-the-Plow*. We listen to two prisoners inventing theories about animals from space at the end of a play whose structure is ambivalent and cruelly ironic: Edmond "has simply reversed the roles of the first part of the play and is now more absolutely trapped in a smaller room than the one he had once sought to escape" (Bigsby 107). The play tends to confirm Campbell's own doubts about the validity of the monomyth in the contemporary world.

Edmond's connections with *House of Games* are equally strong. Like Edmond, Margaret Ford, author of *Driven*, seeks to uncover the determining influences that would account for compulsive behavior; as with Edmond, this culminates in a transformation in the final scene in which she, too, becomes problematically feminized. At the beginning of the film Margaret displays few of the conventional cultural markers of femininity: her hair is cropped short; she dresses austerely in trousers and jackets; she is the author of a book whose title recalls Freud's *Psychopathology of Everyday Life;* she is "a woman pretending to be a man" (Hall 144). At the end of the film, she has had her hair styled and wears makeup and a floral dress.

This ending is structurally related to the Aristotelian imperatives of recognition and reversal that Mamet insists are essential to drama. Three major implications of the reversal at the end of *House of Games* have often been noted. First, Margaret seems to have discovered her identity as a woman. Brewer calls the film a "female revenge play" in which, by the end, Ford "has finally chosen the real world, the world of women and of light" (23–24), and Van Wert notes that "[w]here before Margaret was dependent upon men to generate the thrill and excitement missing in her life, now she can generate her own pleasures and [live] quite comfortably in the company of other women" (9).

Second, the ending suggests that Margaret has successfully treated herself. Van Wert praises "the insightful way [the film] promotes psychoanalysis as a potent force for transformation (along the lines of a Lacanian replication of symptoms in lieu of a 'cure')," and suggests that by the end of the film, Margaret has learned to use her "impulse disorder . . . not as a sexual deficiency, which would guarantee further dependency upon a sexualized male other, but as a form of oblativity, or gift, to herself" (10).

Third, the ending compels us to reconsider the gender relations that throughout the film have been expressed in terms of power and knowledge. Although some have seen the triumph of the female in these climactic scenes, Laura Kipnis argues that *House of Games* maneuvers the spectator "into the position of a transvestite who ultimately renounces the female position and reclaims masculinity as the 'correct' way of seeing" (27). In support of this reading, she suggests that "Mike proceeds, in the film's climactic moment, to pronounce the *truth* of Ford's *pathology* (the truth of the woman's *essence*). Given his epistemological status [as 'epistemological hero'], there is no room for doubt—we are compelled to belief" (29). As in the previously cited readings of Karen in *Speed-the-Plow*, there is an assumption here that the film finally exposes something knowable about the character, closing the interpretive gap between spectator and screen image.

But *House of Games* prevents this relationship from cohering satisfactorily by consistently alienating the audience both from the protagonist and from the interpretive mechanisms of psychoanalytical interpretation. The final scene is not the first occasion on which Margaret has dramatically altered her appearance. After giving $80,000 to Mike, Margaret symbolically tears up her previous life by destroying her diplomas and replacing her androgynous professional outfit with an equally asexual red, hooded top. After her suspicions are aroused, she follows Billy Hahn to Charlie's Tavern and pulls the hood over her head. In the tavern, she for the first time sees the confidence men in a situation in which they are not trying to con her. The hooded top now signifies both a rejection of her professional past, and the motif of disguise. It may also carry a further connotation: she is Little Red Riding Hood confronting a wolf whose disguise she has now penetrated. In the following scene at the airport she is once again clothed in a relatively formal outfit, except that in wearing a skirt instead of trousers she has adopted a more conventionally gendered appearance. Presumably, she does not intend to arouse Mike's suspicions; the mask is no longer masculine, but feminine. In this context, it is hard to see her outfit in the final scene, a garish floral dress and enormous earrings, as revealing an unproblematic, newly found, liberating femininity. She is literally in fancy dress, wearing a disguise far more stylized, exaggerated, and unconvincing than any she has previously adopted. The ill-fitting dress seems to come from the 1950s, the earrings from the 1960s; the total effect is of a hurried parody of Doris Day. True, Margaret has become "cryptic," "the sphinx," "mysterious," "enigmatic" (Hall

144–45), but partly this is because her feminine guise is no more convincing than was her guise of masculinity.

As Kipnis observes, Margaret's transformations strikingly recall Mary Ann Doane's discussion of female spectatorship in "Film and the Masquerade." Doane notes that for Freud, there is an anatomically produced difference between the way in which male and female spectators look. For the boy, a first, irresolute interpretation of the female genitalia is replaced by a second once the boy feels threatened by castration anxiety. He re-reads, "is capable of a revision of earlier events, a retrospective understanding which invests the events with a significance which is in no way linked to an immediacy of sight" (Doane 80). As we shall see, this notion of re-reading is crucial to the strategy of Mamet's film. For the female, however, "[t]hat body which is so close continually reminds her of the castration which cannot be 'fetishised away'" (80). In feminist theory the feminine is often associated with touch, and the masculine with sight: hence the problem of female spectatorship in cinema, the result being "a tendency to view the female spectator as the site of an oscillation between a feminine position and a masculine position, invoking the metaphor of the transvestite" (80).

Doane draws a further distinction between transvestism and masquerade. While "it is understandable that women would want to be men, for everyone wants to be elsewhere than in the feminine position . . . [m]asquerade is not as recuperable as transvestism precisely because it constitutes an acknowledgement that it is femininity itself which is constructed as mask—as the decorative layer which conceals a non-identity" (81). In *House of Games*, Margaret's dual performance of transvestism and masquerade plays out these power relations. For most of the film, she occupies the transvestite position: the woman who wishes to be the masculine subject, the psychoanalyst, the one who is supposed to know. In the opening scenes she reinforces this role by her coolness toward strangers and her work-driven detachment from patients and friends.

However, what she conspicuously fails to achieve in her encounters with the confidence men is precisely the masculine analyst's retention of distance and the interpretive capability of looking again. In the poker scene, in which she is asked to watch the Vegas Man, the close-ups of his face and hands are shot from her perspective. She looks; she is our surrogate. Once the poker game is revealed as an attempt to con her out of her money, however, our reading of the scene has to change: retrospectively she must be seen as the object of a series of looks. Things have not been taken in by her gaze, she has been taken in by them: they have been staged by others for her to look at. During the argument in this scene as it appears in the film, although not in the published screenplay, Mike says

"Look," to which the Vegas Man replies: "I'll look later." This apparently innocuous exchange tells us something about how the film works: nothing in it can be taken for granted without a second look, a later look, and the question of who possesses the gaze at any given point can be resolved only retrospectively, if at all.

Perception, then, is fractured: although Margaret is our surrogate in a film that aims to con its audience, that identification is never total. If her masquerade in the final scene signifies her resistance to objectification by men, for the audience it represents the end both of our identification with her as protagonist, and of our objectification of her as a case study. "By destabilising the image, the masquerade confounds th[e] structure of the look" (Doane 81). Margaret's "non-identity" denies us the possibility of knowing her.

The masquerade is particularly powerful because certain aspects of the film have previously encouraged us to read her not as the passive female but as the active male, Mamet having inverted the conventional relations between the character's sex and his or her morphological or narrative function. As de Lauretis observes, in the Proppian model outlined in the first part of this essay, "the hero must be male, regardless of the gender of the text-image, because the obstacle, whatever its personification, is morphologically female and indeed, simply, the womb," while the hero

> crosses the boundary and penetrates the other space. In so doing the hero, the mythical subject, is established as a human being and as male, he is the active principle of culture, the establisher of distinction, the creator of differences. Female is what is not susceptible to transformation, to life or death; she (it) is an element of plot-space, a topos, a resistance, matrix and matter. (118–19)

There is a contradiction between this morphological structure and the film's iconography. Clearly "the night world of *House of Games*, its halls and parlors, is of and for men. The clinical daytime world, white, sterile, and joyless, is distaff" (Brewer 23). Yet Margaret fulfils a traditionally male narrative function, entering the womblike darkness of the House of Games and Charlie's Tavern from which she emerges as "the establisher of distinction, the creator of differences," no matter how untenable those differences finally appear.

More specifically, the film inverts some of the gender roles familiar from film noir, the genre that most strongly informs it and with which Mamet was familiar from his first film as screenwriter, *The Postman Always Rings Twice*. In many examples of the 1940s, such as *Double Indemnity*, *The Woman in the Window*, and *Scarlet Street*, a femme fatale lures the respectable, conventional, male protagonist into a dark, urban, underworld spiral of crime and murder. The protagonist discovers that he is driven by sexual motivations that contravene the societal norms he had previously accepted, while the woman, such as Barbara Stanwyck in *Double Indemnity* or Joan Bennett in *Scarlet Street*, is often the catalyst and possesses some of the attributes of the "vamp" of the silent era. As Doane notes, one form of "masquerade, an excess of femininity, is aligned with the femme fatale and . . . is necessarily regarded by men as evil incarnate" (766). Margaret performs an analogous role in the final scene of *House of Games*, and so adopts a different form of active femininity than that she had previously occupied, in a film that has already inverted the usual gender functions within noir by making the woman the protagonist and Mike the *homme fatal*.

The final scene also problematically shifts the focus back onto noir's interest in "the motives for and the psychological repercussions of the criminal act" as they are revealed within protagonists who "are not totally in control of their actions but are subject to darker, inner impulses" (Krutnik 46–47). Noir established popular psychology as a mechanism for exploring the mental landscapes of such characters. For example, in Fritz Lang's *The Woman in the Window* (1944), we first encounter Assistant Professor Richard Wanley delivering a lecture on "Some Psychological Aspects of Homicide." He asserts that there are homicidal "impulses of various degrees of culpability," so that "the man who kills in self-defence, for instance, must not be judged by the same standards applied to the man who kills for gain." Left to his own devices in his wife's absence, Wanley's attention is arrested by the picture of a woman in a gallery window, and he discusses with his friends at their gentlemen's club the pleasures and dangers of a "casual impulse" or a "forgotten natural tendency." Subsequently Wanley meets the woman, Alice, and is invited to her apartment. Their conversation is interrupted by the arrival of Alice's jealous lover, whom Wanley kills in self-defense. They hide the body, but the D. A. makes inexorable progress toward the exposure of Wanley as the killer, assisted by Wanley's frequent incriminating slips. Wanley takes an overdose, ironically at the very moment that the police are about to conclude that the murder was committed by another man. In a problematic happy ending, all of the episodes since Wanley and his friends met in the club are revealed to have been a dream.

Although there are many differences, the connections with *House of Games* are pervasive. In each film an overworked professional psychologist, who spends his or her time in predominantly same-sex environments, gives an unintentionally self-reflexive exposition on the hidden motivations of criminal acts. The protagonist's repressed desires, revealed through a series of slips and gestures, are aroused by a figure of the opposite sex. S/he is lured into danger and becomes involved in a killing that turns out not to have been a killing. The protagonist's world slowly but inexorably falls apart, and at the climactic moment s/he kills again: Margaret shoots Mike, Wanley commits suicide. The final scenes provide an unexpectedly happy ending: Wanley's adventure was a dream; Margaret forgives herself and discovers a new identity.

Such comparisons establish that Mamet's film is indebted to noir in its visual style and urban landscape, but more specifically in its interest in the psychology of the unwitting criminal. In other words, the film frames psychological readings not as a privileged hermeneutic device, but as a popular cinematic convention available for manipulation. Both *The Woman in the Window* and *House of Games* present pop psychology as a narrative and interpretive device within the film (an "object language") that we may or may not wish to treat with a certain degree of skepticism, and in addition bring a psychoanalytical "metalanguage" to the interpretation of the events in the film. (On object language and metalanguage, see Easthope 13.) To borrow Deborah Thomas's distinction in her discussion of noir, "we must look not at what the films are *saying* (in terms of overt Freud) but at what they *do*" (72).

House of Games undermines pop psychology both in its symbolism, and in its treatment of the figure of the psychologist. Some scenes and images appear to be staged for the benefit of the analysts in the audience, just as others are staged for the benefit of the analyst on the screen: a Borgesian trap to ensnare the unwary investigator. For instance, Margaret plays throughout with an almost comically large number of phallic symbols: guns, knives, combs, cigarettes, cigars, cigarette lighters. At one point, Mike holds up a door key and asks: "In or out . . . ?" (40). The camera lingers on the moment, before she takes the key from him. While thematically this gestures toward the lack Margaret apparently feels in herself as a woman, cinematically it suggests a deliberate foregrounding of obvious sexual signifiers.

The psychoanalytic interpretations staged within the film are equally nonrealistic. Near the beginning, Margaret interprets for her friend Maria the dream of one of her patients:

> Listen to this: in her dream: she saw a foreign animal. What is the animal? She cannot think of the name. It's saying, the animal is saying "I am only trying to do good." I say, "What name comes up when you think of this animal?" She says it is a "lurg," it is called a "lurg." So if we invert "Lurg," a "lurg" is a "girl," and *she* is the animal, and *she* is saying "I am only trying to do good." (7–8)

The "foreign animal" recalls Freud's difficulties with the "dark continent" of femininity. That the analyst is herself a woman signals, in Mamet's characteristically Aristotelian-Oedipal fashion, that Margaret's "goodness" and femininity will become the object of her own investigation, as do her Freudian slips, which are "surprisingly juvenile and suggestive of a personally unexamined life" (Brewer 7). She herself is a "lurg," a scrambled girl, and within her lurk both the male analyst and the female analysand of the original, and stereotypical, psychoanalytical relationship. Irresistibly, then, we recognize that Ford's analyses will tell us more about herself than about her patients.

In realistic terms, her unconvincingly pat decoding of the "lurg" indicates that she is "particularly unsophisticated as a clinical psychologist" (Brewer 7). Crucially, however, our recognition (confirmed by Maria) that Margaret is always giving away something about her sexuality repeats the reductive interpretive strategy for which we have just patronized her. In so doing the audience moves into the place of the "mark," which it has just assigned to Margaret, and like her we will be taken in by the film we thought we were decoding. In other words, *House of Games* provides a critique not only of its own psychological object language, but of its own psychoanalytical metalanguage.

To repeat, the con does not lie in persuading us to identify with or even understand Margaret: in all kinds of ways, the film prohibits such identification. The con works by first showing us that Margaret is not a realistically convincing character, and then persuading us to forget it, so that after seeing the film we become prone to reading her as a case study in precisely the ways against which we have been warned. The final scene is the crux: it appears to epitomize the classical Aristotelian reversal, in which the character's deep motivation is revealed, but simultaneously prevents us from reading the character satisfactorily. It is in this sense, arguably, that *House of Games* is truly feminist: it presents the structural disruptions of female power not as something to be exorcised through closure, but as creatively productive.

Speed-the-Plow seems more transparent, because it stages a confrontation between two ways of seeing in which the feminine perspective is finally excluded. Nevertheless, the relations between these ways of seeing are complex. At the start of *Speed-the-Plow*, Bobby Gould is "in the midst of the wilderness," and his opening line—"When the gods would make us mad, they answer our prayers" (*Speed* 3)—marks him as the paradigmatic Campbellian hero embarking on a mythic and spiritual quest. The object of that quest appears to be commercial and professional success, in the form of the surefire Hollywood hit brought to him by his associate, Charlie Fox. The complication comes with the entry of Karen, the temporary secretary and soon the object of a sexual quest when Gould bets Fox that he can get her into bed. By developing a sexual relationship with Gould, and insisting that he should greenlight the alternative text called *The Bridge*, Karen becomes the protagonist within, and champion of, what Nelson calls the play's "mistress plots," both of which disrupt the smooth operation of the two "master" plots, namely the Douggie Brown film and the relationship between Fox and Gould (Nelson 75). Fox finally persuades Gould that Karen seduced him to advance her career, and her expulsion at the end of the play carries with it the expulsion of the alternative narrative form and the reinstatement of masculine order and causality.

Agreeing with the kind of feminist analysis that "discusse[s] the rapport between narrative teleology and the reinforcement of male authority," Nelson suggests that Mamet has "only one way of reading. That is reading for the punch line, for the ending, reading for closure" (72). Nevertheless, she concludes that the resolution of *Speed-the-Plow* "could satisfy us only if we want to make her a prisoner of a representation that perpetuates the silencing of women. . . . [T]he incongruity of Gould's reversal makes evident the artificiality of th[e] ending" (81). If Mamet knows "only one way of reading," then Karen represents a blindness that escapes his modes of representation, modes that are outlined by Fox in suggesting that Karen "falls between two stools," being neither "a 'floozy,'" nor someone who "is so *ambitious* she would schtup you just to get ahead" (*Speed* 35).

For Fox, of course, Karen confirms rather than disrupts his view of the world. Fox sees all women in terms of their sexual availability: if there are two stools here, they are matching stools. This much is clear in his retelling of the action of *Speed-the-Plow* as a stereotypical Hollywood storyline: "A beautiful and an ambitious woman comes to town. Why? Why does *anyone* come here . . . ? You follow my argument? (*Pause.*) Everyone wants power. How do we get it? Work. How do they get it? Sex. The End" (71). Seen in these terms, Karen's confession that she would not have slept with Gould had he not greenlighted *The Bridge* places herself very firmly on one of the two stools: she *would* schtup you just to get ahead. As noted above, both Nelson and Hall suggest that this confession reveals Karen's sincerity, because she has nothing to gain from it. That it could be read differently, however, is apparent both in the reactions of Fox and Gould and in Karen's initial refusal to answer the question. The confession may be a sign of sincerity, but if so it is the paradoxical sincerity of the Cretan Liar. Moreover, following this admission Gould merely pronounces himself "*lost.* I have to think" (79). He does not actually reject her until she tells him "we have a meeting," immediately after which Fox can announce: "I rest my case" (79). Her blunder lies in adopting the language of male-dominated corporate business, to which she has previously seemed to offer an alternative both in her championing of *The Bridge* and in her repeated and, retrospectively, suspicious declarations of naivete throughout the first act.

This, perhaps, is a masculine argument, which has to be rejected by "the female reader of *Speed-the-Plow* who does not want to read as a man and who wants to resist the head-on collision with closure" (Nelson 73). Before discussing this female re-reading, however, it is necessary to insist upon the transparent irony that pervades the "master" narrative Mamet appears to privilege. This irony is everywhere apparent: in the send-up of the buddy movie, whose sequence of events Gould can describe even before it has been outlined to him by Fox; in the pile of scripts on Gould's desk bearing such legends as "The Story of a Horse and the Horse Who Loved Him" (6); and, in particular, in the structure of the dialogue:

> Gould: Fuck money.
> Fox: Fuck it. Fuck "things" too . . .
> Gould: Uh huh. But don't fuck "people."
> Fox: No.
> Gould: 'Cause, people, Charlie . . .
> Fox: People . . . yes.
> Gould: Are what it's All About.
> Fox: I know.
> Gould: And it's a People Business.
> Fox: That it is.
> Gould: It's *full* of fucken' people . . .
> Fox:And we're gonna kick some ass, Bob.
> Gould: That we are.
> Fox: We're gonna kick the ass of a lot of them fucken' people.
>
> (21–22)

There is something here of the circularity of *Waiting for Godot*'s dialogue, in which the end point of Vladimir's speculations is always the recognition that he and Estragon must continue to wait. Throughout, Fox and Gould signal their awareness of Hollywood's shortcomings and of their own roles within it: in such comic one-liners as Fox's "he takes his coffee like he makes his movies: nothing in it" (25), in their description of themselves as whores, and in Gould's assertion that "we're in business to . . . *[m]ake the thing everyone made last year*" (56). The repeated structure of comic bathos may indicate a degree of celebration, but that celebration is starkly ironized, not least in the ending, which as in *Godot* finds a character back within the kind of narrative structure from which he has attempted to escape. This ironic self-perception means that we cannot simply equate Fox and Gould with the Douggie Brown story: *Speed-the-Plow* is essentially a vicious satire of both Hollywood executives and Hollywood scripts.

But there are still more serious difficulties in associating Karen with *The Bridge*, and in regarding either as credible alternatives to the "master" plots. "The Bridge" is the title of a short story Mamet had already published in 1985, which closely resembles the novel of the same name in *Speed-the-Plow*: it, too, describes the end of the world in radiation or a nuclear holocaust that is seen as having a purpose. In the short story, the images and ideas take their place among the dreams and fantasies of a depressed man lying in bed. A recurrent motif concerns the man's attempt to find geometric order in the fuzzy shapes that surround him and in the apocalyptic thoughts that pass through his mind. Exactly the same motif is repeated in some of the early sections of Mamet's novel *The Village* (1994). The author of *The Bridge* in *Speed-the-Plow* and the centers of consciousness in the short story and in the cognate sections of *The Village* are male. Moreover, all of these scripts deal with experience in ways comparable to Fox's neutralization of Karen: they impose order upon potentially threatening and inchoate events. If anything, then, *The Bridge* is masculine. This lends some support to the view that Karen's championing of this text is opportunistic, and seriously challenges the argument that *The Bridge* is in some way generically interconnected with Karen's femininity.

Mamet has a close investment in the imagery, ideas, and structures toward which *The Bridge* appears to gesture. He has been reported as regarding Karen as a latter-day Joan of Arc; according to the director Gregory Mosher, the playwright "believe[s] in The Bridge"; and Colin Stinton, who has worked with Mamet on a number of projects and played Gould in the London production, has described the play as a "sermon" that offers Hollywood "opportunities for salvation" (Jones and Dykes 68–71). On the other hand, Mamet appears to have little time for the kind of "Eastern Sissy Writer" (*Speed* 23) who is supposed to have written *The Bridge*. As he put it in a recent essay, "I have always found the literature of our East effete . . . I am not interested in Art" (*Make-Believe* 89). As so often, his comments on his plays appear to be part of a gigantic confidence game, confounding obvious interpretations and even themselves in leading his audiences down the wrong tracks. What is clear, however, is that either Mamet knows more than "one way of reading," or his one way is broad enough to encompass both the Douggie Brown film and *The Bridge*.

Within the context of *Speed-the-Plow*, however, *The Bridge* resists any attempt to impose order upon its fragments, and fails completely: you can't believe it even if it's true. Nelson provides an extended interpretation, suggesting that, for example, "[r]adiation can be understood here as the inscription of Truth on the body of mankind" (79), while Hall asserts that, within *Speed-the-Plow*, *The Bridge* is "outlined, performed, and presented in great detail," and because of this "extended focus . . . the play appears to endorse the 'radiation' script" (154–55). Since there is no text of *The Bridge* for us to refer to, however, there is no way of establishing how extensively or reliably its ideas are presented to us or, indeed, of telling what else is in the rest of the book. It is far from monologic, as Karen discovers to her cost in picking out the wrong quotation with which to persuade Gould in her final stand. To demand a coherent argument from this material is to remasculinize it, to subject it to demands for order and interpretive closure that it cannot sustain.

Fox and Gould themselves expose the aridity of the Douggie Brown script, and Karen's exposition of *The Bridge* is similarly bathetic. This is particularly clear in her last-ditch attempt to persuade Gould to listen to her and not to Fox:

> One moment, Bob. Wait, Bob. The things we said last night. You called for help. Bob, you remember? Listen to me. (*She picks up the book and starts to read:*) "One bell was 'showers about us': two bells was 'showers across the Lake'; three bells was 'showers across the Ocean'; and four bells was 'showers across the World'. And he wondered how they had obtained that concession to rehearse the bells for the benefit of this instruction." No, that's the wrong bit. (80)

Every time anyone quotes from *The Bridge* the effect is the same, as we would expect of a text that does not even purport to be susceptible to paraphrase. Fox's statement that "[y]ou can't tell it to me in one sentence, they can't put it in T.V. Guide" (72–73) is doubly damning, condemning simultaneously the vacuity of Hollywood product and the attempt to film or condense a text that cannot be transposed either into film or into the medium in which it is presented to us.

Both *House of Games* and *Speed-the-Plow* demonstrate that the kinds of linear narrative within which Mamet works are far from monolithical or monologic. Nevertheless, the arguments for a predominantly masculine perception within them remain strong, and the women characters cannot simply be recuperated as convincing explorations of female subjectivity. Margaret retains many of the attributes and functions of the mythic male protagonist, while Karen remains a problem within masculine systems of signification, not because she is necessarily convincing as a woman but because she remains the object onto which the men project their lack. Although the role remains controversial, this is primarily due to the uncertainty concerning Karen's *function* in the drama: as catalyst, angel, whore, or feminist heroine. Within a linear narrative structured by the protagonist's acts of desire, this undecidability, this disruption and excess, perhaps signifies femininity; but the question of whether Karen is convincing as a *character* is secondary.

It is the focus on desire that foregrounds the problem of gender. For Mamet, desires are gender-specific: "try as one may to hew to the Correct Liberal Political Line of Equal Rights, and elaborate a moral imperative into a prescriptive psychological view (i.e., Men and Women are entitled to the same things, therefore they must want the same things), we know that such a view is not true" (*Whore* 279–80). Elsewhere, he writes that "[t]he difficulty, of course, is that one *wants* something from women: notice, sex, solace, compassion, forgiveness; and that many times one wants it sufficiently desperately that it clouds one's perceptions of what *they* want" (*Whore* 241).

This inquiry into what women want repeats the rhetorical move of Freud's lecture on femininity. "Throughout history people have knocked their heads against the riddle of the nature of femininity. . . . Nor will you have escaped worrying over this problem—those of you who are men; to those of you who are women this will not apply—you are yourselves the problem" (Freud 113; qtd. in de Lauretis 111). There is clearly a danger for the male analyst in both posing and answering a question concerning women. As Shoshana Felman comments:

> A question, Freud thus implies, is always a question of desire; it springs out of a desire which is also the desire for a question. Women, however, are considered merely as the objects of desire, and as the objects of the question. To the extent that women "are the question," they cannot enunciate the question; they cannot be the speaking subjects of the knowledge or the science which the question seeks. (qtd. in de Lauretis 111)

That Mamet engages in a repetition of Freud's circular approach to the question of femininity is perhaps significant, insofar as it reenacts the structure of mythic narrative desire that Mamet has always privileged. Like the hero in the quest story, both Freud and Mamet acknowledge a lack (in this case, a lack of knowledge about femininity), and a corresponding desire to make good the lack; a structure that corresponds to the Lacanian view of desire as a constantly thwarted attempt to rectify the loss or lack produced in the self when it enters the symbolic order.

But the acknowledgement of that lack produces another problem: if the object of pursuit is also a representation of a desire which cannot be satisfied, or is elided by a structure within which the subject answers his own question, then the object cannot simply be fixed within representation. In the Oedipal pattern typical of Mamet's works, the object of pursuit dissolves, disappears, or changes: for example, the "leads" in *Glengarry Glen Ross* lead only to people who "just like talking to salesmen" (62); the nonplot of *American Buffalo* turns out to have been generated by mistakes and lies; *Mr Happiness* is a catalog of unfulfilled wishes. Gould's *petit object a* in *Speed-the-Plow* is variously prestige, money, sex, the desire "to do good" (81), but ultimately it always returns to the self, to the protagonist's thwarted desire for self-completion. It is hardly surprising, then, that in the (relatively few) plays in which the object of pursuit is a woman, she always escapes capture, literally and metaphorically: at the end of *Sexual Perversity in Chicago,* Danny and Bernie are unacknowledged by the woman on the beach; at the end of *House of Games,* Margaret turns the tables on Mike; at the end of *Speed-the-Plow,* Karen is expelled, leaving some "unbalanced" critics in her wake (Mamet, qtd. in Jones and Dykes 114). This is one of the most significant ways in which Mamet ironizes the monomyth: there are no successful love stories anymore. His plays are masculine not because they objectify women but because they acknowledge their inability to objectify them; they question the validity of their own representations of women precisely because women are the objects of desire; they do not attempt realistic portrayals of women because such portrayals would always be an illusion masking the lack within the protagonist himself.

In 1990 Mamet appeared on BBC television's *Talk Show with Clive James,* and announced: "It's taken me a long time to figure out what I think it is that women actually want. And if you think I'm going to share it with your viewership, you're out of your mind."

WORKS CITED

Aston, Elaine. *An Introduction to Feminism and Theatre.* London: Routledge, 1995.
Bettelheim, Bruno. *The Uses of Enchantment: The Meaning and Importance of Fairy Tales.* London: Thames and Hudson, 1976.
Bigsby, C. W. E. *David Mamet.* London: Methuen, 1985.
Brewer, Gay. *David Mamet and Film: Illusion/Disillusion in a Wounded Land.* Jefferson, N.C.: McFarland, 1993.
Brown, Janet. *Taking Center Stage: Feminism in Contemporary U. S. Drama.* Metuchen, N.J.: Scarecrow, 1991.
Campbell, Joseph. *Masks of God.* New York: Viking, 1959.
Carroll, Dennis. *David Mamet.* Basingstoke: Macmillan, 1987.
Cinch, Minty. "Mamet Plots His Revenge." *Observer* January 22, 1989: 46–50.
De Lauretis, Teresa. *Alice Doesn't: Feminism, Semiotics, Cinema.* Basingstoke: Macmillan, 1984.

Doane, Mary Ann. "Film and the Masquerade: Theorising the Female Spectator." *Screen* 23 (1982): 74–87.

Easthope, Antony, ed. *Contemporary Film Theory.* London: Longman, 1993.

Fraser, C. Gerald. "Mamet's Plays Shed Masculinity Myth." *New York Times* July 5, 1976, sec. A: 7.

Freud, Sigmund. "Femininity." *The Standard Edition of the Complete Psychological Works of Sigmund Freud.* Trans. James Strachey. Vol. 22. London: Hogarth, 1964. 24 vols. 1953–73, 112–35.

Hall, Ann C. "Playing to Win: Sexual Politics in David Mamet's *House of Games* and *Speed-the-Plow.*" *David Mamet: A Casebook.* Ed. Leslie Kane. New York: Garland, 1992, 137–60.

Harriott, Esther. *American Voices: Five Contemporary Playwrights in Essays and Interviews.* Jefferson, N. C.: McFarland, 1988.

Jones, Nesta and Steven Dykes, eds. *File on Mamet.* London: Methuen, 1991.

Kennedy, Andrew K. *Dramatic Dialogue: The Duologue of Personal Encounter.* Cambridge: Cambridge UP, 1983.

Kipnis, Laura. "One Born Every Minute." *Jump Cut* 36 (1991): 25–31.

Krutnik, Frank. *In a Lonely Street: Film Noir, Genre, Masculinity.* London: Routledge, 1991.

Mamet, David. "The Bridge." *Granta* 16 (1985): 167–73.

———. *Edmond.* London: Methuen, 1986.

———. *Glengarry Glen Ross.* London: Methuen, 1984.

———. *House of Games.* London: Methuen, 1988.

———. *Make-Believe Town: Essays and Remembrances.* London: Faber, 1996.

———. *Speed-the-Plow.* London: Methuen, 1988.

———. *A Whore's Profession: Notes and Essays.* London: Faber, 1994.

McDonough, Carla J. "Every Fear Hides a Wish: Unstable Masculinity in Mamet's Drama." *Theatre Journal* 44 (1992): 195–205.

Nelson, Jeanne-Andrée. "*Speed-the-Plow* or Seed the Plot?: Mamet and the Female Reader." *Essays in Theatre* 10.1 (1991): 71–82.

Propp, Vladimir. *Morphology of the Folktale.* Tr. Laurence Scott. Austin: Univ. of Texas, 1968.

Ranvaud, Don. "Things Change." *Sight and Sound* 57 (1988): 231–32.

Schlueter, June. *Feminist Rereadings of Modern American Drama.* Rutherford, N. J.: Fairleigh Dickinson UP, 1989.

Schvey, Henry I. "Celebrating the Capacity for Self-knowledge." *New Theatre Quarterly* 13 (1988), 89–96.

Thomas, Deborah. "Psychoanalysis and Film Noir." *The Movie Book of Film Noir.* Ed. Ian Cameron. London: Studio Vista, 1992, 71–87.

Van Wert, William F. "Psychoanalysis and Con Games: *House of Games.*" *Film Quarterly* 43:4 (1990): 2–10.

Walker, Michael. "Introduction," in *The Movie Book of Film Noir.* Ed. Ian Cameron. London: Studio Vista, 1992, 8–38.

Prophecy and Parody
in *Edmond*

Richard Brucher

Gregory Mosher, David Mamet's longtime collaborator, remarked a few years ago that what was great about Eugene O'Neill was that he could "*see* the culture. . . . O'Neill couldn't write a line of dialogue if you put a gun to his head, but he sure looked out at America, and he said at the turn of the century, 'We blew it. It doesn't work. The American Dream failed. It's a tragedy, America'" (Kane 236–37). Mosher invokes O'Neill to make a claim for clairvoyance in *Edmond*, Mamet's 1982 play about (in Mamet's words) "a man trying to discover himself and what he views as a sick society" (Schvey, "David Mamet" 94). According to Mamet, the play addresses the social consequences of a capitalistic dream that has nothing left to exploit. "'All those considerable talents that the white race has been living by since the birth of Christ and before, the emotionlessness, the viciousness, and the acquisitiveness that have sustained them, they now turn against each other . . .'" (Leahey 3). In this version of the American Dream turned nightmare, Edmond Burke, a middle-class white executive, leaves his wife to seek validation among New York's conmen and whores. They cheat him and beat him, until he turns on a pimp who tries to mug him. Beating the black man mercilessly liberates Edmond; he picks up a waitress and gets the sex he's wanted, but then he kills her in a panicky dispute about honesty. He finally achieves peace in jail, after being sodomized by his black cellmate. Mosher contends that what seemed horribly exaggerated in 1982 turned out to be an accurate prediction of the racial strife at Bensonhurst and the "exploding hatred" of the 1980s (Kane 236).

Edmond has not been a popular or well understood play. Its characters' racism, misogyny, and homophobia are calculated to offend; and its attitude toward its protagonist is delightfully ambivalent. A 1982 reviewer remarked that Mamet "clearly sees [Edmond] as representative of an abused underclass" (Gussow C17), a notion that suggests the play's sustained irony. In partial defense of Edmond's homicidal degradation, Mamet has cited Jung's contention that sometimes society, not the individual, is sick (Schvey, "David Mamet" 94). On another occasion, with what I suspect was some disingenuousness, Mamet asked a hostile critic, a woman, "'Didn't you feel any compassion for [Edmond]?'" (Dean 188). Yet despite the sympathy he invests in Edmond, Mamet makes his protagonist highly culpable. As a middle-class white man, Edmond is heir to the American Dream and its fallout, a naive but by no means innocent victim of his race's success. As an Irish-American, Edmond Burke may be a fairly recent achiever of the dream, but that affirms the play's disturbing prophecy. The racial and ethnic violence for which Bensonhurst has become a code word can be read as white backlash against black predation in white neighborhoods. However, in Bensonhurst, Brooklyn, in 1989, Yusuf Hawkins, the young black man killed by whites, was innocent of criminal intent. He was looking for a used car in the wrong neighborhood (DeSantis passim). Backlash against intrusion becomes indistinguishable from racism, an expression of violent primitivism lurking beneath the surface of what purports to be a civilized society.

The persuasiveness of *Edmond*'s clairvoyance—its ability to see contemporary America so clearly that it seems prophetic—derives in part from its ironic affirmation of prophecies made by earlier social theorists and its witty appropriation of conventions used by earlier playwrights. The cultural degradation *Edmond* depicts can be traced to the breaking of social contracts that Edmond's namesake prophesied two centuries ago. According to Edmund Burke, the conservative political philosopher, "liberty without wisdom and without virtue . . . is folly, vice, and madness . . ." (373).[1] But if *Edmond* the play seems to insist on the consequences of violating Burke's principles of social order, Edmond the character seems to operate according to the premises of one of Thorstein Veblen's new aristocrats, parodic heir to the elite order presumably championed by Burke the conservative philosopher. Edmond's reversion to violence can be as easily associated with Veblen's leisure class as with Edmund Burke's anarchists and New York's predators. Veblen observes that fair-haired Europeans are particularly prone to reversion to barbarism.

It is a matter of common notoriety that when individuals, or even considerable groups of men, are segregated from a higher culture and exposed to a lower cultural environment, or to an economic situation of a more primitive character, they quickly show evidence of reversion toward the spiritual features which characterize the predatory type; and it seems probable that the dolicho-blond type of European man is possessed of a greater facility for such reversion to barbarism than the other ethnic elements with which that type is associated in the Western culture. (136)

Mamet has called *Edmond* "a morality play about modern life" (Schvey, "David Mamet" 94), a description with which many of its commentators would agree. As a morality, "it reveals with a frightening explicitness Mamet's apocalyptic vision of a society bent upon self-destruction" (Schvey, "Power Plays" 99). But as one reviewer noted in 1982, "Where conventional morality plays (or even moralistic ones) attempt to soothe or educate, *Edmond*, until its final, oddly blissful scene, is a continuous affront," making it seem "like a grotesque parody of a morality play" (Kissel 160). In 1982, *Edmond* tended to be described, even by those who liked it, as "a brutish, unsparing" play, one "squeezed . . . almost dry of humor and color" (Gussow C17). In its New York revival in the fall of 1996, at Mamet's Atlantic Theater, *Edmond*'s violence seemed less shocking than in 1982 (because of Bensonhurst?); but its tone and attitude still divided viewers. One 1996 reviewer noted a "seriously comic interpretation that [gave] new credence to a much maligned play" (Brantley C13). Yet charges of implausibility have persisted. Edmond's "descent, from collected man in a conservative suit to ferocious killer, feels forced," another critic complained. His "transformation at the end is not credible," and his "sophomoric conversation about life's meaning" with his black cellmate is "weak" (Greene 12).

The problem with the charges of implausibility is not that they seriously undervalue *Edmond*. Rather, they betray a yearning for a naturalism or psychological realism that would offer a full accounting of Edmond's journey into squalor, crime, self-discovery, and redemption. *Edmond* supplies no such reliable causality. "And you are unsure what your place is," a Fortune Teller assures Edmond in the opening scene, "To what extent you are cause and to what an effect" (scene 1, 16). Her remark, calculated to aggrandize her client, poses the play's dilemma fairly well, but Edmond never seems to get it. He may see how his savaging experience can be construed as an effect of a civilization that has lost its bearings. "Do you want to live in this kind of world?" (scene 11, 51), he justifiably wails at a hotel clerk who refuses to help him after he's been beaten and robbed. His incarceration may appeal to his liberal sense of inevitability. "You know, I always thought that *white* people should be in prison. . . . To be with black people," he remarks naively to his cellmate just before he is sodomized (scene 20, 90). But he never quite sees how he may also be cause. Consequently, the psychological justification for his murdering Glenna, the waitress he picks up, may be difficult to perceive. The situation is absurd, a moment of high cultural satire rather than of psychological clarity or melodramatic plausibility. Similarly, the philosophizing between Edmond and his cellmate, leading up to their goodnight kiss that ends the play, fails to resolve matters because Mamet intends the talk to be superficial and disconcerting. What appears to be sophomoric, a barely credible parable of the achievement of racial and sexual harmony, is parodic, a travesty of the sort of recognition we expect to experience in moralities and tragedies. *Edmond*, for all its nasty seriousness, may be another of Mamet's oblique comedies. That is, Mamet offers a scathing indictment of late-twentieth-century American society, and perhaps even the possibility of a middle-class tragedy, except that he keeps turning the play back in on itself, distancing us from Edmond as self-conscious victim, and so deflecting the tragic gesture with ironic comedy.

At least that's a proposition I'd like to test by looking at several of *Edmond's* scenes in light cast by Veblen's *The Theory of the Leisure Class* (1899) and by *The Hairy Ape* (1922), another play, despite O'Neill's subtitle, that almost no one credits as a comedy. Mamet's fondness for Veblen is well known. Veblen's skepticism about social progress and his insistence that capitalist behavior is essentially irrational and hedonistic—"an almost atavistic phenomenon reflecting not so much the cool prudence of bourgeois man as the residual habits of primitive societies" (Diggins 18)—resonate in *Edmond*. So does Veblen's deadpan, high comic style inform the sustained irony of Mamet's observations of late-twentieth-century yuppie ennui. The O'Neill connection is more tenuous. I don't mean to offer *The Hairy Ape* as a rival source for *Edmond*, although the two models for *Edmond* most often cited—Georg Buchner's *Woyzeck* (1836) and Georg Kaiser's *From Morn to Midnight* (1912/1916)—have also been cited as influences on *The Hairy Ape*.[2] I would like to invoke the Emersonian license implicit in a remark on intertextuality by Stanley Cavell: "When a given text is claimed to work in the light, or in the shadow, of another—taking obvious extremes, as one of a given work's sources or as one of its commentaries—a measure of the responsibility of such a linking is the degree to which each is found responsive to the other, to tap the other, as for its closer attention" (1). Whether or not Mamet had O'Neill's early radical play in mind when he wrote *Edmond*, the two plays tap one another responsively.[3] Both plays use episodic structures to reveal absurdly causal worlds and to satirize inhuman modern life, and both plays invoke and resist naturalistic determinism as a way to explore will and culpability. Both plays pursue paradoxical impulses to rediscover roots in nature and to belong to human communities, impulses presented with particularly American notions of privilege. Part of the mutual responsiveness, then, has to do with O'Neill's ability to "*see* the culture," as Mosher put it. O'Neill thought *The Hairy Ape* was "a surprisingly prophetic play. Not superficially, about labor conditions," he wrote Lawrence Langner in 1941, "but about Man, the state we are all in of frustrated bewilderment." The war in Europe affirmed for O'Neill that "we have certainly failed to 'belong' and then unlocked the cage and turned the Gorilla loose." O'Neill thought the play's symbolism and meaning would be clearer in 1941 than in 1922. "Very few got it then," he complained to Langner (Bogard and Bryer 522).

Incidental cultural and sociological details may have proved more prophetic than universals. Yank champions his labor as a vital force, dismissing as irrelevant the class of owners and their factotums, but conversion to diesel engines on the ocean-going liners would soon make stokers extinct. By converting Yank from a Liverpool Irishman to a New York tough, O'Neill capitalized on a cult of male primitivism and anticipated problems of mobility and assimilation that dominated American culture in the twentieth century.[4] Certainly Yank anticipates Mamet's boisterous, baffled males, both in their need to belong and in their obscenity, which is usually vented at women when social pressures become strong and dislocating. Yank's animus toward "Fif' Avenoo" mannequins—"Bums! Pigs! Tarts! Bitches!" (scene 5, 209)—is only slightly less vicious than Edmond's rage against a woman in the subway who views him as a pervert when he gets nostalgic about his mother's hat: "I'm *talking* to you . . . What am I? A *dog*? I'd like to slash your fucking *face* . . ." (scene 13, 58). Yank's eventual envy for the gorilla in the zoo—"Youse can sit and dope dream in de past, green woods, de jungle and de rest of it" (scene 8, 230)—echoes back to us in Edmond's conversation in a bar. "I'll tell you who's got it *easy*," a Man explains. "The niggers. . . . Northern races *one* thing, and the southern races something else. And what *they* want to do is sit beneath the tree and watch the elephant. (*Pause.*) And I don't blame them one small bit" (scene 3, 22–23). Remarks from the beginning of *Edmond* seem to pick up where *The Hairy Ape* leaves off, as Yank's existentialism collapses into the Man's wistful, casual racism. This example illustrates my idea that the plays respond to one another's anxieties in particularly apt and disturbing ways. Especially interesting, in this context, is the relationship between comic-ironic form and the characters' "not getting it," notably in the plays' controversial final scenes.

The subtitle of *The Hairy Ape*—"A Comedy of Ancient and Modern Life in Eight Scenes"—suggests O'Neill's intended universalism and reflects the "tone of hard-boiled irony" he cultivated as a hedge against the sentimentalism to which Smitty was prone in the earlier sea plays (Engel 54–55). But O'Neill was not being purely ironic or coy, as if we are to understand "tragedy" for "comedy." Comic form pervades the play, especially in Bergson's sense of the mechanical encrusted upon the human. Dehumanization is most explicit in the ape-like stokers' robotic movements and metallic choruses—as if this is the mechanical encrusted upon the subhuman. Mechanization pervades Yank's words and gestures, too, even as he asserts his dominance over machines and men. Yank boasts of his union with steel, and his crudely sexual language suggests that shoveling coal has displaced his urge to have sex with women. "Dat's de stuff! Let her have it! All togedder now! Sling it into her! Let her ride! Shoot de piece now! Call de toin on her! Drive her into it! Feel her move!" Yank chants, shoveling, "*His voice rising exultantly in the joy of battle*" (scene 3, 189). The stokehole scene offers a lurid "condemnation of the whole structure of machine civilization, a civilization which succeeds only when it destroys the psychological well-being of those who make it possible" (Winter 196). Still, the scene reproves Yank for so willingly perverting his own vitality. Yank would do well to heed Bernie Litko's advice to his friend Danny Shapiro (in Mamet's *Sexual Perversity in Chicago*): "Dan, Dan . . . don't go looking for affection from inanimate objects" (53).

Disjunctions between characters' assumptions about control and what actually happens to them create comic, alienating effects and patterns in *The Hairy Ape*, subverting romantic and melodramatic conventions, and preventing us from sentimentalizing the action. The sight of Yank, furious in the stokehole, knocks Mildred unconscious and out of her liberal posing. The sight of her—a ghostly sign of his own expendability—emasculates Yank, although he's slow to understand the effect her shock ("Oh, the filthy beast!" 192) has on him. He will eventually glean some irony in his condition. "Sure dere was a skoit in it—but not what youse mean, not dat old tripe" (scene 6, 213), he says by way of accounting for how he lands in jail. Initially, though, Paddy's sarcastic rendering of the perverted romance baffles Yank: "And there was Yank roarin' curses and turning around wid his shovel to brain her. . . . 'Twas love at first sight, divil a doubt of it!" (scene 4, 197). Paddy's mocking enrages Yank, precipitating a beating that initiates a recurring pattern of physical and psychological humiliation. All hands pile on Yank as he rushes for the door, "*and, after a fierce struggle, by sheer weight of numbers,*" the stokers bear him to the floor (scene 4, 201 s.d.). In subsequent scenes Yank is "*clubbed to the pavement and fallen upon*" (scene 5, 210 s.d.) for inconveniencing a Gentleman at a bus stop, hosed down (and probably straight-jacketed) in jail for inciting a riot (scene 6), and tossed into the street, "*with gusto and éclat*" (scene 7, 225 s.d.), for seeming to be a police informant at a Wobblies' local. The sequence isolates Yank poignantly, taking him deeper and deeper into his existential angst. "Say, where do I go from here?" he asks a cop, in "*a vague mocking tone,*" after his ejection from the union hall, to which the cop answers, "Go to hell" (scene 7, 227). The humiliating pattern is nonetheless comic in its redundancy (a manifestation of his mechanization), comic in its irony (he's supposed to be so tough), and comic in its exasperating wrongheadedness. By the time Yank arrives at his rendezvous with destiny at the zoo, he has tried four times to secure his place in the world by avenging himself on that skinny, white-faced tart; and he has been beaten up and tossed in jail or out on the street four times for his efforts.

The routinization of the action contributes to the bizarre quality of the final scene at the zoo. Yank has tried valiantly to "tink" and to discover a language that articulates his increasing alienation. Yet he has misread the situation every time, and so has learned almost nothing, except, perhaps, to seek affection from animate objects. But he offends the gorilla, too, whom he wishes to befriend and liberate. His language, groping back toward Paddy's lyrical evocation of an idyllic life on the sea, envies the gorilla's natural primitivism. Mockery in Yank's voice insults the gorilla, and it kills Yank for it, tossing him, in a now familiar gesture, to the floor of the cage. Perhaps Yank has achieved peace, as O'Neill's closing stage direction suggests; but it's not a peace in which an audience can take solace. The gorilla's opportunism, shuffling "*off menacingly into the darkness*" (scene 8, 232 s.d.), Yank's contributory aggression, his mocking tone, and his objectifying himself as a side-show attraction—all mitigate against the empathy associated with Aristotelian (or even working-class) tragedy. One of the great things about *The Hairy Ape* is not that O'Neill dared to make a tragic hero out of a stoker, but that he resisted the urge.

This may be a way of agreeing with Joel Pfister's recent, controversial reassessment of O'Neill's art as a staging of middle-class cultural identity for middle-class audiences. Although appreciative of O'Neill's depiction of working conditions in *The Hairy Ape*, Pfister argues that "O'Neill's deep interest seems to be in creating a working-class seaman who has been converted to professional-managerial-class angst" (119). Even so, there's little flattery in the transmutation because Yank, like the original critics and audiences (who according to John Styan probably identified with Mildred [107–08]), never quite gets it. He's a "bonehead," the Secretary of the Wobblies says (scene 7, 225), and so the analogy insults managers as well as workers. The point I wish to carry over to *Edmond* is that resistance to tragic empathy keeps the social criticism alive. "[A] dollar more a day . . . and cauliflowers in de front yard—ckal rights—" (scene 7, 225) won't fix Yank for Jesus, but neither will nostalgia for the good old days in the jungle. Nor will the brute power Yank still celebrates in the gorilla, and with which the gorilla kills him.[5]

Mamet tests this premise in *Edmond*, using comic-ironic devices similar to those deployed by O'Neill. Edmond Burke is the sort of egotistical, alienated "professional" that Yank, in Pfister's argument, is supposed to represent. Yet I doubt if Edmond would "get it." He might identify with Yank's sense of victimization—"I ain't on oith and I ain't in heaven . . . I'm in de middle . . . takin' all de woist punches from bot' of 'em" (scene 8, 230–31)—but it's less likely that he would see the irony in the failure of Yank's primitive strength. As Christopher Bigsby has argued, Edmond imagines his reversion to primitivism to be therapeutic (103). Beating the Pimp liberates him from 30 years of racist guilt and gets him laid, to boot, which is more than Yank manages. It's as if this beating solves for Edmond the centuries-old problem of Hamlet's liberal paralysis, an anomie Yank tries to overcome with physical power. "That fucking nigger comes up to me, what am I fitted to do. . . . Thirty-four years fits me to sweat and say he's underpaid. . . . Eh? That's what I'm fitted to do. In a mess of intellectuality to wet my *pants* while this *coon* cuts my *dick off*. . . eh? Because I'm taught to *hate*" (scene 16, 68).

The beating, though, is highly problematic. Edmond presumably beats the Pimp because the attempted mugging is one too many violations. Civilization, as Edmond thinks he understands it, has collapsed. He has just been rebuffed by the woman in the subway, with whom he tried to make human contact: "My mother had a hat like that" (scene 13, 58). Her refusal to be drawn into his nostalgia replays the rebuff he received from the Hotel Clerk. She regards Edmond as strange, perhaps demented, and certainly dangerous, especially after he grabs her and threatens her with his survival knife. His response to her fear only affirms her suspicions: "Is everybody in this town *insane?* . . . Fuck you . . . fuck you *all* . . . I don't *need* you . . . I worked all my life!" (scene 13, 59). It's not clear what kind of dispensation Edmond expects to receive for that last assertion; it's as if he's back in the bar, insisting on his privileges as one who has accepted his white, middle-class, professional responsibilities and now expects to be ratified for it. That truculent plea carries Edmond into his encounter with the Pimp, who gains Edmond's confidence only to break their implied contract by taking Edmond's money without supplying the agreed-upon service (Tuttle 159). Scene 14, then, enacts both white, middle-class anxiety and its fantasy of revenge, but it does so on a professional as well as a moral and ethical frontier. Edmond has been soliciting sex for money, and he may be violating his own professional code by inhibiting the Pimp's work. In any case, and in a replay of the subway-hat scene, Edmond's righteousness quickly turns vicious: "You *fuck*. You *nigger*. You

dumb *cunt*," he screams as he kicks the man (scene 14, 65). The Pimp becomes the scene's baffled victim: "Hold on. . . . I . . . I . . . Oh, my
God . . ." (64).

Obviously this scene shows how savagery can lurk in all of us and that
Edmond may be as bad as his predators. That ambivalence perfectly captures the "exploding hatred" of Bensonhurst and Howard Beach; it nails
an audience's ambivalence, too, as we delight in Edmond's rebellion and
recoil at his extra kicks. But white backlash against urban predation does-
n't fully account for the beating, especially as a context for the dispute
over personal liberation and professional identity that results in Glenna's
death. The chain of causation is indirect. The beating doesn't justify or
even explain Edmond's descent into barbarity so much as it observes an
anthropological phenomenon and offers an episode in Edmond's parodic
self-creation. Edmond quite literally *imagines* his therapeutic liberation.
Beating the Pimp frees Edmond to eschew coffee for Irish whiskey and
beer, to resee his previous life as fog-bound, and to proposition the white
waitress boldly. However, after sex with Glenna, he invents the beating as
liberation. The story he tells Glenna, as he brandishes the survival knife,
is not much like the incident we witnessed.

> I want to tell you something. Something *spoke* to me, I got a *shock* (I don't
> know, I got mad . . .), I got a *shock,* and I spoke *back* to him. "Up your *ass,*
> you *coon* . . . you want to fight, *I'll* fight you, I'll cut out your fuckin' *heart,*
> eh, *I* don't give a fuck. . . ." Eh? I'm saying, "*I* don't give a fuck, *I* got some
> warlike blood in *my* veins, too, you fucking *spade,* you coon. . . ." The *blood*
> ran down his neck. . . . (scene 16, 68–69)

In one sense, Edmond is cheering himself up, aggrandizing his action,
converting what appeared to be an act of frustrated rage and terror into a
political act, a declaration of race pride. At the same time it is a clever act
of parody, as Mamet has Edmond lay claim to the language and values of
Veblen's warrior-sportsman and O'Neill's waterfront toughs, values Veblen and O'Neill have already discredited. Veblen calls this celebration of
violence a "common-sense barbarian appreciation of worth or honor."
This "high office of slaughter, as an expression of the slayer's prepotence,
casts a glamor of worth over every act of slaughter and over all the tools
and accessories of the act." Hence Edmond's pride in the acquisition of
the survival knife. At the same time, common labor becomes "odious" and
"irksome" (31).

Edmond kills Glenna, in effect, because she refuses to admit she's a
waitress. Still trapped by the assumptions of the consumer society he
thinks he has escaped, he won't allow her claim to be an actress because

she's never acted before paying customers. In this sense, Glenna proves to be just as expendable as the poseur Mildred, and, ironically, in similar socio-economic terms. Anemic Mildred, by her own admission, is "a waste product in the Bessemer process" (scene 2, 183) from which her grandfather, an Andrew Carnegie avatar, made his millions. Useless and unnatural—she doesn't even like sports—Mildred disappears from the play, as if to affirm Veblen's theory of the leisure class, a class defined by its incapacity to do productive work (Veblen 24–25). Glenna, on the contrary, is a working woman, a role Edmond both denigrates and sentimentalizes. In the coffeehouse, he exhorts her to reject subservience: "you can do anything you *want* to do, you don't sit down because you're '*working*,' the reason you don't sit down is you don't *want* to sit down, because it's more comfortable to *accept* a law than question it and live your life" (scene 15, 67). In her apartment, Edmond needs to behold Glenna as worker to affirm what he believes is his new commitment to living life honestly: "I loved a *woman*. Standing there. A working woman. Who brought life to what she did. Who took a moment to *joke* with me. That's . . . that's . . . that's . . . god *bless* you what you are. Say it: I am a waitress" (scene 16, 75). Like the story of the beating, this version of their meeting distorts and sentimentalizes the scene we witnessed. Edmond rebukes Glenna for betraying her honest productivity with pretense. More fundamentally, though, he objectifies her as his prize for beating the Pimp. As warrior's booty, she too plays out a favorite Veblen metaphor for the unproductive wealthy, their possessions, and their imitators. Mamet sacrifices Glenna to his cultural analysis more ruthlessly than O'Neill expends Mildred.

Glenna demonstrates the "incentives," as Veblen calls them, for acquiring women as property: She gratifies Edmond's propensity for coercion, she verifies his prowess as owner, and she provides sexual and other utilitarian services (Veblen 52). I think it is probably this sense of "possession" that Mamet had in mind when he suggested to a British audience its centrality to dislocations in American culture. According to Carla McDonough's summation, "Mamet describes how the continuity of relations between men and women has always been upheld 'by the possession of woman' so that having women in the market place vying for equal positions in a 'man's world' seems the reason that the old value system in this country is breaking down" (197). Mamet's social criticism seems to me to be deeper, more playful, and perhaps more rueful than this summation suggests. The "old value system" is itself a travesty, a higher form of barbarism masquerading as civilized progress, as Mamet would understand from his reading of Veblen. This is not to say that male anxieties are not real, and it's not to say that the anxieties, however false the premises may be that rouse them, do not result in real violence against women. But Veblen provides a useful gloss on the gender and race issues that McDonough notes in *Edmond* (and that are similarly vexed in *The Hairy Ape*). When, after providing sex, Glenna refuses to define herself by her productive labor, but rather by creative or professional pretension, she is annihilated by Edmond's crazy reformist zeal. Her gesture toward self-preservation refutes the presumptions of consumerism that have driven Edmond from bar to peepshow to whorehouse to pawnshop. "Get out!" she shrieks. "GET OUT GET OUT! LEAVE ME THE FUCK ALONE!!! WHAT DID I DO, PLEDGE MY LIFE TO YOU? I LET YOU FUCK ME. GO AWAY" (scene 16, 77). In a now familiar pattern, Edmond displaces onto her his own rising hysteria. As "*He stabs her with the knife,*" he accuses her: "Are you *insane?* Are you *insane,* you fucking *idiot? . . .* You stupid fucking *bitch. . . .* Now look what you've blood fucking done" (scene 16, 78). The scene is terrifying in its depiction of the hazards of reading feel-good-about-yourself manuals and of consenting to casual sex, and yet it's absurd in its logic. Is being a waitress who studies acting an offense against society (or art?) punishable by death? The enormity of the act never dawns on Edmond. His presumptuousness contributes to the scene's sardonic humor, as the play sacrifices Glenna to its analysis of primitivism, solecism, and professional prerogative. This is what I meant earlier when I suggested that this murder scene, building on painful comic disjunction, succeeds as travesty and social satire rather than as psychological analysis or melodrama.

The impulse toward primitivism and the critique of middle-class anxiety come full circle in the play's final scene, although how we're to take the scene is much debated. Dennis Carroll, for example, argues that Edmond's "new-found vulnerability . . . indicates further growth in him." His relationship with his cellmate, although begun in rape, is now "marked by genuine rapport" (103). Characteristic of the play's ambivalence, there appears to be some truth in this. "Every fear hides a wish" (scene 20, 89), Edmond remarks hopefully to his cellmate when he first arrives in jail; by the end of the scene Edmond will be sodomized. Edmond—misogynist, racist, and homophobe—becomes "wife" to his black cellmate; and he seems, by the end of the play, to be reasonably happy with his turn in fortune. His language loses its hostility and obscenity, which implies some personal and social progress. I'm tempted to say that the final scene in prison replays and "improves" O'Neill's ending to *The Hairy Ape.* Edmond's affectionate goodnight kiss with his black cellmate recalls and transcends Yank's murderous embrace in the zoo cage with the gorilla, suggesting that the primitivism is domesticated rather than loosed. It's characteristically bold and witty of Mamet to literalize

O'Neill's metaphors to confront and transcend late-twentieth-century racial and homosexist fears.

The ending of *Edmond*, however, resonates well beyond *The Hairy Ape*, although it, too, can be said to mock its protagonist the way Yank's encounter with the gorilla mocks him. As Christopher Bigsby has argued, banal philosophical musings, of the sort popular in the 1970s, hardly compensate for the radical circumscription Edmond's life has undergone. Desiring freedom, he's achieved prison, where sodomy "happens" (scene 21, 94; Bigsby 107).[6] This may be a morality play in the manner of Marlowe's *Edward the Second*, with its sardonic, deeply disturbing insistence on poetic justice. And yet it's *Hamlet*, that great, troubled document of secular humanism, to which *Edmond* seems parodically to aspire at the end. "There is a destiny that shapes our ends," Edmond muses, "Rough-hew them how we may." "How e'er we motherfucking may," the Prisoner adds (scene 23, 100). Perhaps Edmond has "adopted a Hamlet-like position of acceptance" (Schvey, "Power Plays" 100), but what strikes me is how un-Hamletlike the posture is. "Divinity" shapes Hamlet's end (5.2.10); and that signals, at least in a traditional humanistic reading, his acceptance of and responsibility to a moral order beyond himself. Edmond and the Prisoner cast about for some "destiny" to shape their ends, in effect exonerating themselves. Edmond expresses some remorse for killing Glenna, but he never quite assumes responsibility for the act. "I think I'd just had too much coffee," he explains to his estranged, unsympathetic wife (scene 19, 87). "O Hamlet, what a falling-off was there" (1.5.47), we might say with the Ghost of King Hamlet. Travestying Hamlet's recognition doesn't make a strong case for providential redemption. About the best Edmond and the Prisoner can do is hope that someone understands—"Some whacked-out sucker. Somewhere. In the Ozarks?"—and admit that maybe *they* (we) are the animals (scene 23, 102, 105). That is not a lot of progress in the 60 years that separate *Edmond* and *The Hairy Ape*, let alone in the four centuries that separate *Edmond* and *Hamlet*.

If *Edmond* did see the early 1980s so clearly that it predicted the exploding hatred of the middle- and late-1980s, it seems to me to be less willing to prophesy lasting reconciliation. Its parodic attention to earlier texts—by Veblen, O'Neill, and Shakespeare, in my brief analysis—underscores the human propensity for self-delusion that makes reconciliation so necessary and difficult. That admission, I suppose, places me with those who read *Edmond* pessimistically, as Mamet's journey to the heart of darkness.[7] Nonetheless, I wish to recognize a serious comic technique at work in the play that resists wishful thinking and melodramatic gloom. Echoes of Veblen and O'Neill help us see that Edmond's problems are not the product, in any simple way, of recent encroachments by women, blacks, and others into the provinces of white males. Admittedly, the *Edmond-Hairy Ape* connection may be far-fetched. As a pair, though, the plays analyze problems of identity and belonging in American society that arc over the entire century. *Edmond* literalizes the middle-class angst that finds incipient expression in O'Neill's alienated stoker. (The recent Wooster Group production of *The Hairy Ape* in New York gave astonishing expression to Yank's energy and diminishing power, as if he were one of Mamet's street people.) Both plays create persistently materialist environments that account for their characters' baffled rage and yet also reveal them to be surprisingly culpable for not understanding more clearly their choices within those environments. *The Hairy Ape* and *The Theory of the Leisure Class* are part of the cultural critique that *Edmond* reexamines, and comic-ironic dramatic form—comedy of ancient and modern life—is crucial to that enterprise. These texts tap one another as if for closer attention, especially in these times of rampant, self-deluding capitalist behavior.

NOTES

This essay is dedicated to the memory of John Sekora.

1. Jon Tuttle, in "'Be What You Are'" (158), and Henry I. Schvey, in "Power Plays" (101), discuss Edmund Burke's presence in *Edmond.*
2. C. W. E. Bigsby discusses the *Woyzeck* influence in *David Mamet,* 103–04, as does Schvey ("Power Plays" 100–101), and a number of reviewers. Jon Tuttle makes a persuasive case for *From Morn to Midnight* in "'Be What You Are'" (158–9).
3. Marcia Blumberg argues that "*Edmond* traces the O'Neillian dive to the gutter" but associates Edmond with Edmund Tyrone (107).
4. Jon Curry discussed this socio-economic issue and the pertinence of *The Hairy Ape* in "'Men of an Entirely Different Grade': O'Neill's Laborers," a paper presented at the Conference on O'Neill's People, Boston, MA, May 12, 1995. On the masculine primitive, see James A. Robinson, "The Masculine Primitive and *The Hairy Ape.*," and Carla J. McDonough, "Every Wish Hides a Fear."
5. Although the program notes don't verify it, it appeared to me that in the recent (Spring 1997) Wooster Group production of *The Hairy Ape* in New York, Kate Valk, who played Mildred Douglas, re-appeared in a monkey-fur coat to play the gorilla. It was a witty detail in this brilliant interpretation, directed by Elizabeth LeCompte.
6. Bigsby uses Christopher Lasch's *The Culture of Narcissism* (1979) effectively to contextualize Edmond's solecism in *David Mamet* (101–10).

7. Tuttle invokes Conrad's *The Heart of Darkness* in "'Be What You Are.'"
Schvey, "Power Plays," and Bigsby are also persuasive on the darkness of
Edmond.

WORKS CITED

Bergson, Henri. "Laughter" (1900). *Comedy.* Ed. Wylie Sypher. Garden City, NY:
Doubleday Anchor, 1956.

Blumberg, Marcia. "Eloquent Stammering in the Fog: O'Neill's Heritage in
Mamet." *Perspectives on O'Neill: New Essays.* Ed. Shyamal Bagchee. Victoria,
BC: U of Victoria P, 1988, 97–111.

Bogard, Travis, and Jackson R. Bryer, eds. *Selected Letters of Eugene O'Neill.* New
Haven: Yale UP, 1988.

Brantley, Ben. "In Mamet's 'Edmond,' a Man on Empty." *New York Times* October 2, 1996: C13-C14.

Burke, Edmund. *Reflections on the Revolution in France.* Harmondsworth, England: Penguin Books, 1969.

Carroll, Dennis. *David Mamet.* New York: St. Martin's, 1987.

Cavell, Stanley. "Macbeth Appalled (I)," *Raritan* XII:2 (Fall 1992): 1–15.

Dean, Anne. *David Mamet: Language as Dramatic Action.* Rutherford and Madison, NJ: Fairleigh Dickinson UP, 1990.

DeSantis, John. *For the Color of His Skin: The Murder of Yusuf Hawkins and the
Trial of Bensonhurst.* New York: Pharos Books, 1991.

Diggins, John P. *The Bard of Savagery: Thorstein Veblen and Modern Social Theory.*
New York: Seabury Press, 1978.

Engel, Edwin A. *The Haunted Heroes of Eugene O'Neill.* Cambridge: Harvard UP,
1953.

Greene, Alexis. "Theatre Reviews." *Theater Week* 10:12 (October 21 1996):
12–13.

Gussow, Mel. "Stage: Mamet Explores the Fall of 'Edmond,'" *New York Times*
June 17, 1982: C17.

Kane, Leslie. "Interview with Gregory Mosher." *David Mamet: A Casebook.* Ed.
Leslie Kane. New York: Garland, 1992, 231–47.

Kissel, Howard. "'Edmond.'" *Women's Wear Daily* October 28, 1982; reprinted in
New York Theatre Critics Reviews 43 (1982): 160.

Leahey, Mimi. "David Mamet: The American Dream Gone Bad." *Other Stages*
(November 4, 1982): 3.

Mamet, David. *Edmond.* New York: Grove, 1983.

———. *Sexual Perversity in Chicago and The Duck Variations.* New York: Grove,
1978.

McDonough, Carla J. "Every Wish Hides a Fear: Unstable Masculinity in
Mamet's Drama." *Theatre Journal* 44:2 (May 1992): 195–205.

O'Neill, Eugene. *The Hairy Ape. "Anna Christie," The Emperor Jones, and The Hairy
Ape.* New York: Vintage, 1972.

Pfister, Joel. *Staging Depth: Eugene O'Neill and the Politics of Psychological Discourse.* Chapel Hill: U of North Carolina P, 1995.

Robinson, James A. "The Masculine Primitive and *The Hairy Ape.*" *The Eugene O'Neill Review* 19:1 & 2 (Spring & Fall 1995): 95–109.

Schvey, Henry I. "David Mamet: Celebrating the Capacity for Self-Knowledge." *New Theatre Quarterly* 4:13 (February 1988): 89–96.

————. "Power Plays: David Mamet's Theatre of Manipulation." *David Mamet: A Casebook.* Ed. Leslie Kane. New York: Garland, 1992, 87–108.

Shakespeare, William. *Hamlet.* Ed. Edward Hubler. New York: New American Library, 1963.

Styan, J. L. *Modern drama in theory and practice, volume 3: Expressionism and epic theatre.* Cambridge: Cambridge UP, 1981.

Tuttle, Jon. "'Be What You Are': Identity and Morality in *Edmond* and *Glengarry Glen Ross.*" *David Mamet's "Glengarry Glen Ross": Text and Performance.* Ed. Leslie Kane. New York: Garland, 1996, 157–69.

Veblen, Thorstein. *The Theory of the Leisure Class.* Ed. C. Wright Mills. 1899; New York: New *American Library, 1953.*

Winter, Sophus Keith. *Eugene O'Neill: A Critical Study.* New York: Russell & Russell, 1934.

Demotic Male Desire
and Female Subjectivity
in David Mamet

The Split Space of
the Women of *Edmond*

Imtiaz Habib

In the inaugural issue of *The David Mamet Review*, Leslie Kane has described in detail the intense acrimoniousness that attended the discussion of gender issues in David Mamet's plays at the 1994 MLA convention in San Diego (7). Not too long ago, Ilkka Joki cataloged extensively the chorus of bitter complaints that have been heard over the last decade regarding Mamet's alleged misogyny and outrageous gender representations (11- 13). Some years ago, Bharati Mukherjee, a respected and influential minority novelist, inscribed prominently—in the opening section of one of her short stories, "A Wife's Story"—Mamet's supposed gender as well as racist slurs in *Glengarry Glen Ross* (25–27). One of Mamet's later plays, *Oleanna*, ends disturbingly with a women being beaten on stage. Some of Mamet's own spare remarks—that he prefers to write about men (Fraser 7)—may be seen only to confirm the feeling that often surfaces in popular responses to Mamet's plays that this is a playwright with an anachronistic hostility to, or apathy for, women.

Such a conclusion, however, misreads both the playwright and his dramatic discourse. In fact, some current postfeminist studies of Mamet make possible a contrary perspective. Mamet's women, Ann Hall has suggested in an important essay, are figures who subvert male structures of knowledge and action in the plays, specimens of femininity that,

Charlie Fox in *Speed-the-Plow* says, "[fall] between two stools"; Mamet's ambiguous women are the source of conflict for men. By "falling between two stools," that is, "by constantly moving out from under the labels, [they] expose the male system of oppression as a house of cards" (137–38). Citing the theories of the French psychoanalyst Jacques Lacan, Hall points out that whereas women are in touch with intrinsic human fragmentation, men strive to write a delusional self-reliant autonomy that becomes "a confidence game" and "leads them to objectify and oppress women in order to support their existential illusions," to construct "an Other . . . in order to feel complete" (138–39).

Women embody the site "onto which [male] lack is projected," and in that fashion they are constructions of male desire. In this Lacanian scheme, however, Hall observes that women's unpredictability and refusal to stay fixed is a strategic advantage because it constitutes a "*jouissance*, a disruptive excess" (139), which converts female subjectivity, even if blocked or cancelled, into a subversive force. Using these Lacanian assumptions and some ideas from the French feminist philosopher Luce Irigaray, Hall argues that Mamet's women are not only "mirrors . . . [or] objects of male desire; they have access to a revolutionary method which violates the dialectic designs of their male oppressors. By challenging the power structures established in the plays, and . . . the expectations of the other characters and their audiences, . . . [they] embody this revolutionary femininity" (139). Applying these ideas to Karen and Margaret in *Speed-the-Plow* and *House of Games*, Hall concludes that Mamet's texts "*mimic* the patriarchy and the role of women in them," and even if the upsets they create are under suppression in their play's total action, they do succeed in making us "return, rethink and reconsider" (158).

Elsewhere in Mamet too, this same perspective applies, as Dorothy Jacobs has more recently demonstrated in her study of the effects of women in *Glengarry Glen Ross*. Within the verbally abusive, sexually demeaning, homosocial universe of the scam salesmen of the play, Jacobs outlines two pointed instances in which women resist and disturb the male ideology of the play. The first is Shelly Levene's reference to his daughter, in his unsuccessful plea to Williamson to give him good leads to prospective clients, in which the daughter's momentary floating presence is marked by a linguistic inability in the speaker that produces only an incomplete sentence phrase, "John, my daughter," and a near incoherent reference to a child he dreams of educating fully (45). The second and more potent instance is Jinny Lingk's successful refusal to let her husband close the land deal that the predatory Roma had talked him into and that James Lingk brokenly but insistently recounts (52–54).

Both of these, Jacobs shows, are temporary but telling moments of a female Mametian presence that even from its totally marginalized off-stage presence obfuscates and radically thwarts the play's rabid imperial patriarchy, suggesting another order that becomes instantly a radical critique of the former. Even though that male order is not finally discursively displaced, and even though it seems to reflect Mamet's own apparent enjoyment in his essays of the sociolinguistic pleasures of a male world, Jacobs, citing C.W. Bigsby, points out that the cancelled female presence inflects a loss in that dramatized male order and exposes it as one that "substitutes expletives for needs and bluster for insecurity" (119). It writes that male world as an unstable exclusionary social imaginary and through that writing "Something revelatory is gained"(120). In Jacobs' view such counter-inscription of contemporary patriarchy occurs throughout Mamet's works. In Irigaray's terms, Mamet's female characters, like Jinny Lingk, by "break[ing] the silence and assert[ing] the power of the female voice," disconnect "a staging of feminine representation and modif[y] the phallocentric order" (115).

Hall's and Jacobs' essays establish a plausible heuristic for reexamining the treatment of women in Mamet's plays. Neither critic loses sight of the patent homosociality of Mamet's dramatic discourse but both position his women characters within a renitent counter-dialogue. Mamet's textual liability follows ipso facto from the one to the other. Carla McDonough, and, before her, David Radavich, have shown the instability of masculinity and homosocial order in Mamet's plays, in which Mamet's characters are "frustrat[ed] with traditional masculine identity" and undertake a "search for a new identity" that they "usually fail to complete" (McDonough 196–97). Radavich describes this phenomenon as Mamet's enactment "of a searching, multivalent American drama of homosocial desire questioning and assessing itself" (134). In the endplay of its performance this is the Foucauldian splitting of discourse into its own contra objective, its deconstructive twinning into a sly alterity.[1] This translates into a perspective that frames his dramatic women in a divided space, as both participants in and critical antagonists of, the value system that constructs them. In this powerful dual function they are a key element in the playwright's reconfiguration of an exhausted urban landscape. Rather than simply representing a gender antagonism, Mamet's women characters, I wish to argue, are important dramatic presences who interrogate demotic male desire, and through that, function as agents of recovery in a fragmented postmodern wasteland.[2]

Mamet's fictional women comprise a varied range. They include women who are defiant resisters of male hypocrisy and manipulation such as Cora in *The Postman Always Rings Twice* and Mary Rooney in *The Verdict;*

women who are puissant, insistent cavilers of male failures, such as Joan and
Deborah in *Sexual Perversity in Chicago* and Ruth in *The Woods;* and the
powerful, agile learner-instructor women who both are acted upon and act
in a sterile male world, such as Karen in *Speed-the-Plow* and Margaret in
House of Games. Yet it is paradoxically the women who suffer most and are
the most oppressed who are the most effective vehicles of Mamet's brilliant
inquisition of male self-aggrandizement and of his agenda of contemporary
spiritual reparation. The fictional women of this rare group, such as the
women of *Edmond,* exemplify a clever Mametian process that converts
male triumph into male tyranny and self-destruction, and that encourages
male aggressive desire only to undermine and subvert it.[3] These women are
the catalysts of the action in the sense that they are what implicate the male
discourses of their plays and in their own venalities. In being at once figures
of an oppressed female selfhood and elements of a male critique, they occupy a unique split space in Mamet's art.

The atypicality of *Edmond* in the Mamet oeuvre, a critically neglected,
masterful postmodern parable of the search for self-meaning, issues from
the singular fractured roles of its women characters. Mamet's own thematic explanations of *Edmond,* that it "is a morality play about modern
society," "about someone searching for truth" (Jones and Dykes 51),[4] construct the play's allegorical paratext as a prefigurative archetype of contemporary redemptive self-immolation, with the intertextual links to
both Georg Buchner's *Woyzeck* and Joseph Campbell's *Hero with a Thousand Faces* that early neoformalist Mamet studies identified (Carroll
98–100).[5] This paratextual construction is not, however, an undifferentiated Mametian tropic replay of the regenerative urge within the detritus
of contemporary urban underlife that we see elsewhere in the playwright.
It is also a complicative deployment of the culture/gender politics inherent in that trope. In a fashion unmarked up to this point in Mamet's
work, *Edmond* positions woman as the catalytic avatar of man's failed self-
education, at once its agent and its object.[6] It does so not despite but because of the textual marginality of its women characters, who enable the
play's dominant discursive machinery by also jamming it.

Mamet's men don't only need approval by men, as Jacobs emphasized (112), but also, and more importantly, as *Edmond* shows in a manner that is still exegetically unremarked, by women.[7] In the play it is
women whose direct or proxy validation the title character seeks. Scattered across the sterile urban playscape in which Edmond sinks are
pointillist female presences, each of whom drives forward his social/
individual incompletion. These are the most pungent of the play's brilliantly staccato, micro-episodes, and they each constitute an elliptical
script of female obfuscation of male psychological/sexual autonomy. In

the play's second scene, the failure of affirmation that catapults the middle-class suburbanite male yuppie to terminate his marriage is not articulated, but it is the final initial of male insecurity in the history of an undramatized relationship in which the woman has not embodied the man's self-energizing powers of domestication.[8] In the taut conversation between Edmond and his wife, in what serves as a symbolic intratext, the unnamed "girl" who has "broken the lamp" is also the unnamed "Wife" whose self-authority in the relationship matches his to the point that *her* dissatisfaction with him exceeds his with her: "You idiot . . . *I've* had enough . . . to see you passing *judgment* on me all this time . . . and then you tell me 'you're leaving.'"[9] Edmond's callous walking out on her is also her throwing him out: "Go. Get out of here. Go . . . And don't you *ever* come back" (14). Arguably, the man's persecutory abandonment of the woman is at once, and because of, her antecedent dismissal/cancellation of him. In effect this brief scene counterpoints her terminal refusal to acknowledge his dominion over her. Within but against the fantasy of male desire of power, and confirming the Fortune Teller's prognosis in the preceding scene, she blocks him from being in the game of sexual politics where he wants to "belong," making him an "effect" rather than a "cause" (scene 1, 11–12).

That an unsubordinated female subjectivity simultaneously powers and undercuts the play's archetypal postmodern male drive for a recoverable self-entity is underlined by the fact that it is a female fortune teller at the play's very beginning who (presumably instead of announcing his successes in life) conceptualizes Edmond's failures for him and starts him off on his self-expurgating journey. It is also indicated by what the man in the bar urges Edmond to do, and by the several disempowerments that the play's other women inadvertently and deliberately inflict on him. If, as the bar man theorizes, the source of contemporary man's malaise is an emasculatory powerlessness, "Like your balls were cut off," the solution is to "get laid" (scene 3, 16). In the demotics of male desire, "A man's got to get away from himself," and the path to "*Power*" is through "*Pussy*" (scene 3, 15). The ordering of "pussy" is Edmond's buying of sex, subsequently at the *Allegro,* the peepshow, and the brothel, the achievement of instant anonymous sexual gratification becoming for him a surrogate for male self-aggrandizement.[10]

The bar girl, the peepshow girl and the prostitute are all located within a contemporary materialist and symbolic patriarchal capitalist economy of sexual objectification, but from inside this location they each enact a systemic disruption that denies the play's male purveyor his enjoyment of the system. They do this paradoxically by using the system and holding on to it to resist the man's freedom inside it, that is, to maroon him within it. Since the availability of the bar girl at the *Allegro* operates only within the specific transactional space that the sexual commodification system gives her, she will not exist for Edmond outside that system. His proposal to her—"I'll give you the five you'd get for the drink if I gave them ten. But I'm not going to give them the ten"—produces from her the response, "I got to give him the five" (scene 4, 17–18). The peep show girl in scene 5 insists on being for Edmond only an anonymous body part behind an irremovable glass panel because that is all that the male material and symbolic sexual economy he is relying on has contracted her to be. In scene 8, the prostitute's polite but firm refusal of Edmond's plastic money confirms the materialism that has constructed her, to lock him out, effectively rendering impotent the very currency of the male purchase of female gratification.

The bar, the sex arcade, the brothel, these typical urban playscapes that Matthew Roudané, using the ideas of the French semiotician Roland Barthes, has identified as the dramatized sites of Mamet's recovery of the contemporary wasteland (and that are the carnivalesque semiotics of postmodernity's locations), are also the locales of demotic male desire's conflicted self-engendering (9–10). In another disjunctive metropolitan venue in the play, an uncooperative female agency further marks Edmond's failing urge toward a lost manly dominance. The woman in the subway that Edmond accosts in scene 13 functions within the anonymity of city populations and the exotopic dysphoria that is the signature of postmodern experience. As a typical subway commuter she is positioned within a nameless ungendered collectivity that, while flattening her sexual-psychological individualism, gives her an impersonal belonging. Her resistance of the personal space that Edmond tries to appropriate in her, by his individuation of her hat as resembling one that his mother used to have, reiterates the impersonality that defines her by refusing the free personalism that Edmond seeks with her. This effectively confines him in the very sterility that he has been struggling to leave: "who the fuck do you think you are? . . . what am I? A stone . . . A dog? . . . You don't know who I am? . . . Is everyone in this town *insane?*" (scene 13, 31- 32). If naming is power, and in the text of patriarchy a quintessential exercise of self-agency, the blocked grammar of its inherent violence explodes in Edmond's manhandling of the woman. A similar blockage, by the unreachability of a purchasable female and the consequent denial of sexual power that it spells, fuels Edmond's murder of the Pimp in the street outside the peep show in scene 14.[11]

However, the clearest and most complex instance of the double play of recusant female subjectivity's simultaneous acknowledgment and contravention of contemporary fantasies of masculine power in *Edmond* occurs in Scenes 15 and 16, in Edmond's violent encounter with Glenna, the waitress at the coffee shop. Located in the approximate formal center of the play, and identified early as the play's "centerpiece" (Carroll 100), these scenes climax the ruptured role of women in the play. They consolidate the play's bifurcated performance of female subjectivity to both enable and pervert the male instinct to power, and they do so by marking Edmond's sole moment of achievement of power reflexively as also the beginning of his true education in powerlessness. As the only woman who is named in the play, and as the only woman with whom Edmond consummates a relationship, Glenna is the play's archetype of a contemporary female subjectivity that is both connected to and independent of the demotic male desire that it constantly has to negotiate.[12] She is also the play's final instance of the violence that accompanies Edmond's knowledge of a male self-agency, but in a manner that makes the episode of her killing and that of the Pimp's murder a contrasting pair.

As the play's ultimate female authenticator and invalidator of demotic male desire's self-aggrandizement, Glenna is both the student and the teacher of the meaning of Edmond's murderous act of self-assertion. Initially, she is the cheerful female witness of his ideological construction of self-power:

Glenna: You're in a peppy mood today.
Edmond: You're goddam right, I am. And you know *why?* Because I'm *alive.*

Glenna responds supportively, through clarificatory questions such as, "Who is?" (in response to his statement "You know, you know, we're *sheltered*"), and varyingly cooperative replies such as "I can't, I'm working" (in rejoinder to his teacherly invitation to her to sit down), and "Twenty-eight" (in answer to his demonstrative question to her about how old she is) (scene 15, 35–36). These implicitly compliant rhetorical postures of Glenna help Edmond's explanation of why he is "*alive*" grow in philosophical abstractions, even though it comes to complete fruition only in the next scene. Her interested hearing of his self-teaching affirms for him its psychological potential, and through that bolsters his ongoing but faltering male search for unimpeded self-action as the source of power: "You know how much of our life we're alive, you and me? *Nothing* . . . the reason you don't want to sit down, because its more comfortable to *accept* a law that questions it and live your life . . . We've bred the life out of ourselves . . . we're dead . . . And you know what the answer is? To *live* . . . Our only treasure is to act" (scene 15, 35–36).

Her unspoken acquiescence in his sudden but now logical need for palpable sexual conquest confirms his evolving text of self-authorship:

Edmond: I want to go home with you tonight.
Glenna: Why?
Edmond: Why do you think? I want to fuck you . . . What's your name?
Glenna: Glenna. (*pause*) What's yours?
Edmond: Edmond.

(scene 15, 36)

The mutual act of naming with which the plan of their sexual tryst is sealed, and that marks a pointed movement forward from Edmond's failed attempt earlier with the woman in the subway, is Glenna's participatory reward of Edmond's striving for a self-serving manhood that can freely write itself on the world. Within this supportive cross-play, however, Glenna's own self sovereignty is not infarcted but merely conjoined to the male play for power. Its own agenda, which signally formats the angular spaces of this conversation, makes his teaching and prospective sexual writing of her also her leading of him how to do those things.[13] This is to say her studentship underwrites his teachership, teaches him how to teach them both. By extension, she is the desirable object of the male will to power as much as she is the desiring subject itself.

It is within these tensions and limits of her splayed self and her consequentially uncertain relationship with Edmond that Glenna in the next scene bolsters, circumvents, and undermines Edmond's new-found masculine self-being, ultimately even through the reflux of her own extinction. As the student who is teaching the teacher, she initially helps Edmond consolidate the "lesson" of his recent violent self-avowal:

EDMOND shows Glenna the survival knife
You see this? . . . That fucking nigger comes up to me . . . "Give me all your money" . . . he's a killer . . . so he'd do anything . . . Something spoke to me . . . I came out there with my knife, and stuck it in his neck . . . if you are a man you should be feared. (*pause*) You should be feared. . . .

(scene 16, 36–37)

The series of credulous gestures with which Glenna helps this excited confession—"Yes," "Yes," "Did you kill him?" (37)—reinforces the charge and force of Edmond's strident self-construction and leads it to its completion. Her (affirmation) of his vicious racial hatred here ("That's wonderful"), and her furtherance of that hatred onto sexual domains a little later in the articulation of her hostility to gays, is complicit in the hegemonic violence of a prejudicial patriarchy because she exists within its demotic constructions and is a part of it. But it is also an element of a contingent exposure of how intolerance merely breeds intolerance and masks insecurity. Her hatred of gays highlights the hatefulness of hating women ("I hate them cause they don't like women") and through that, spotlights patriarchy's fear of femininity and of the instability of its sexual self-construction. The latter is pointed up in Edmond's explanation of why *he* hates gays: "They suck cock" (37). Such lessons trace the inverse relationship that underlies and distends Glenna's pupilage with Edmond. They also set up the strong undertow of Edmond's headlong rush to a false self-knowledge within which he is ultimately caught.

In the latter half of this scene Glenna not only helps Edmond's celebratory development of his inchoate knowledge of the power of a self-authored being but also radically problematizes it. She plays back to Edmond his transgressive shift from the assurance of the rightness of one's self-authoring to the oppressive projection of that self-authoring onto others, that is, the slide from male self-agency to self-aggrandizement, in three progressive critical movements the last of which costs her her life. In the first movement, her cooperation with Edmond's insistence to her to instantly articulate empowering self-affirmations, so as to aver the power of self-speech (and which is, like his earlier demand for sex, a reiterative instinct to objectively manifest his new self-authority and indulge it), "Then *Say* it. If it makes you feel whole. *Always* say it. *Always* for yourself," is in the form of asseverations about the verbal release and emotional self- fulfillment of acting: "That's why I love the Theatre . . . Because what you must ask respect for is yourself . . . When you're on stage . . . For *your* feelings . . ." (38).

The rhetorical overshot of this response, that is, the way in which it meets and slightly exceeds/misses Edmond's expectations (he had wanted an egotistical affirmation of self-belief as self-projection, she gives him a declaration of the sanctity of self-respect and personal feelings), provides Edmond the exact stimulus for further growth. It does so by accelerating the skid of his unstable self-power and making him try, in the next movement, for a tighter approximation of what he wants her to be. Her response in this first movement, thus, both feeds his craving for self-power and discreetly turns it back on himself.

In the second movement, which follows immediately from the first, Glenna functions in widening the slippage between the thrust of Edmond's self-power and its incremental catachrestic failures, through her willingness to enact for him her authorship of herself but not his of her. She accedes to his power of naming by enunciating the mandate of her subjectivity to perform herself. Her consent to Edmond's demand that she act something for him (and that again repeats his reiterative instinct to objectively manifest his new self-agency and indulge it)—"Do something for me . . . Act something for me"—reciprocally strokes the flattery of his interest in her and nourishes his enjoyment of his manipulative freedom with her: "Would you really like me to?," and "What would you like me to do?" (39). Concomitantly, however, the ideological underlay that is the tactical destination of this encouragement is the sovereign truth-value of her own self-writing, the inviolable mandate of her definition of her actress-ship. The corrective collision that her encouragement of Edmond's aggressive pursuit of self-performativity facilitates, between her construction of her performative *Ur* identity ("I am an actress") from her classroom performance of scenes from Shakespeare in college and Edmond's imperial denotation of actress-ship ("Not, not for a paying group . . . Then you are not an actress" [39]), allows for the presentation of a self-authority that Edmond cannot overwrite: "I am what I am" (41). This "lesson" about the limits and losses of Edmond's pursuit of an overarching self-authority carries forward significantly from the first movement and from the earlier part of the scene, Glenna's subversively dialectical education of him.

The third movement, which overlaps with the second, climaxes the implicitly retaliatory renitence of Glenna's education of Edmond, not just through now-unassailable postures of resistance but also through the catastrophic irreversibility of her death. The rhetorical moment that is the beginning of the third movement is comprised of Glenna's querying of the grammar of Edmond's renewed expression of nomenclatural power: "You're a beautiful woman . . . Be what you are. God bless you what you are. Say it: I am a waitress. Say it . . . Say it with me . . . 'I am a waitress.'" Unlike earlier in the scene, her interrogative responses now—"What does it mean if I say something? . . . I don't know what you're talking about" (41)—are divisive rather than ambiguously convergent, and bluntly oppositional. They leave in place, by default, the operation of an existing verbal economy but without the obligation of agreement or support. In conjunction with some denotatively independent physical actions—"(*She takes out a vial of pills*)"—they announce the withdrawal of a previously offered community and the affirmative return of an autonomous privateness disinterested in social commerce:

> Edmond: . . . What are those?
> Glenna: Pills.
> Edmond: For what? Don't take them.
> Glenna: I have this tendency to get anxious.

>   (41)

This indulgence of her subjectivity follows her earlier emphasis on its inviolability ("I am what I am"); if the earlier had pronounced it, this performs it. The aggressiveness of this performance of the inviolability of her subjectivity parallels her first active (as opposed to *re-active*) statement in the entire episode: "I think you better go" (41). These retrogressive verbal and physical signals propel Edmond to an even more desperate recovery of dominion than before, and rapidly to the same urgent violence as in the scene with the Pimp, but from an opposite direction and with a totally different result: there his violence was the product of his attempt to acquire self-power whereas here it is the result of his trying to hold on to it, and if then it created in him a false sense of self-power, here it leaves him with a true feeling of powerlessness. Glenna's suddenly stiffening positions are here the necessary concluding elements of a subtle epistemological pedagogy that forms Edmond's ultimate, harrowing self-knowledge by breaking him.

Glenna's "anxiety" leads Edmond's to establish in a combinatory symbiosis both the fear of self-suzerainty's contravention and the violence of its survival struggle, the fear and the violence together describing the unavoidability of the self's location as both object and subject. Glenna's "anxiety," coming off Edmond's continuing efforts to write his being on her ("*Be* with me . . . I want you to change your life with me") and already presented in her stipulation to him to leave, in turn powers his anxiety about unsuccessful self-authority toward aggressive efforts to control her physically: "(*He knocks them from her hand*) . . . Don't take them. Go *through* it. Go *through* with me" (41). Correspondingly, as Glenna's fear ("You're scaring me") hardens into the contained energies of a rigid position ("Get out . . . I told you go away") and explodes into the violence of hostile language ("GET OUT GET OUT! LEAVE ME THE FUCK ALONE!! WHAT DID I DO, PLEDGE MY LIFE TO YOU? I LET YOU FUCK ME. GO AWAY"), Edmond's terror of having lost escalates into deliberate physical violence: "(*He knocks the phone from her hands. She cowers*)" (41–42). In a kind of bizarre reflex, her pleas to him not to hurt her ("Don't hurt me, . . .") and her defiant self-assertion ("you can't kill me") trigger his stabbing her as his last attempt to regain control.[14] That the psychological whiplash from her perceived victimage objectifies him is implicit in his cry just before he stabs her ("What the fuck are you trying to *do?*") and in his incredulous utterance right after the deed ("Now look what you've bloody fucking done") (42–43).

In other words, the moment in which Glenna is killed by Edmond is also the moment in which her actions inhere in him, and as she is "written out" by him she also "writes" him. As he tests the power of his "authoring" by authoring her "waitressing," she conversely exercises *her* self-authoring by writing him as a brutalizer and murderer. Her death serves almost as her final teacherly lesson to Edmond about the losses of

self-authority that are the inevitable reverse accompaniments of the urge
to an uncompromised self-power, and about how true self-authority is
implicated in the authority of others over oneself. It can only be a sharing act between oneself and the world. Since, arguably, Edmond's situation at play's end—that he is lost—is not intrinsically different from
where he was at the play's beginning—also lost—the essence of Glenna's
"lesson" is a valorization of his "lostness," a teaching of the necessity of
our dependence on others that the ineradicable desolation of our lives require. In participatorily performing this difficult "lesson" overall, Glenna
is caught between man's desire to *be, on her,* and the promptings of her
own selfhood to achieve a being that cannot be written by another. Her
wholeness is both connected to man and inimical to him.

Glenna's "lesson" to Edmond is not of course a phenomenon of syn-
optic neatness or summarizing cogency. It is at best an expositional discursive construction that in the play's ongoing dialogue performs
retroactively and in discrete effect. Its consequential life is nevertheless
visible in Edmond's residual dramatic career. The cognitive backflow of
Glenna's murder sets up in Edmond a confessional current that in the
next scene washes him up against a mission preacher's exculpatory exercise and prompts in him a self- effacing impulse to state publicly his personal insufficiency and need for redemption: "I will testify" (scene 17, 44).
This same note, which is markedly a new one for Edmond since Glenna's
interaction with him, carries his admission of visceral disrepair and struggling recovery in his interrogation by the police:

> Edmond: I don't know . . . I've been unwell. I'll confess to you that I've been
> confused, but, but . . . I've learned my lesson. . . .
>
> (scene 18, 47)

The "confusion," and the self-disavowal ("I don't know"), which are
the signs of the novel auto correctiveness that Glenna has inflected in
him, are elements of the "learned lesson" that he will try to piece together
more fully later. In the meantime, they also direct his part-nostalgic regret for his failed marriage and his yearning for a now-lost human support and closeness, when his wife comes to visit him in jail in the
following scene: "I know at certain times we wished we could be . . .
closer to each other. I can say that now. I'm sure this is the way you feel
when someone near you dies. . . ." (scene 19, 48–49).

The possible duplicitousness of this awkward outpouring cannot erase
its evident vulnerability and need for an unavailable human upholding,
because such declared inadequacies also lace his conversation with the
Chaplain in scene 21: "I feel so *alone* . . . so *empty* . . . Let him [God]

cause a new day . . . Where we grow up in love, and in security we're *wanted* . . . Tell him to do that . . . I'm *begging* you" (52–53). The conversation is cued by Edmond's rape by his cellmate, but that event and its philosophical fallout, as well as the foregrounded abnegation and humility of these remarks, reflect the kind of changes that the experience with Glenna has brought about in him.

It is in Edmond's scenes with his cellmate, though, that Glenna's "education" of him lives most strongly. The dialog and action in Scenes 20 and 22 contain radical departures from the ideological assumptions that the play had previously furthered through Edmond, and while their provocative value has been generally noted, their implications have not been fully spelled out. Edmond's tortuous discussion of "anxiety" and "fear" is his attempt to confront the instability of popular male drive in himself. In discursive terms this is male demotic desire's self-critique, patriarchal sexuality's own deconstruction, that the episode with Glenna has brought about. His repeated statement, "Every fear hides a wish" (49), is a verbal icon of both an acknowledgment and an abrogation of the apprehension of the loss of power that feeds male self-construction and its proprietorial drive to subjugate and dominate. That the acknowledgment and abrogation have seminal emancipatory intentions is advertised in his assertion, "I think the first time in my life (*pause*). In my whole adult life I don't feel fearful since I came in here" (50). They are predicated, through his immediate incarceration, on his general acceptance of powerlessness ("I think I am going to like it here. . . . Do you know why? It's simple. That's why I think that I am" [49–50]), and they are aimed at controverting the self-perpetuating misogyny and sexual and racial bigotry that pressured him earlier. His indictment of whites may seem over easy and specious ("I always thought that *white* people should be in prison. I know it's the black race we keep there" [50]), but it is the apotheosis of his fleeting, inchoate recognition with Glenna of his own racism ("For the first *time*, I swear to God, for the first *time*, I saw: THEY'RE [Blacks are] PEOPLE TOO" [scene 16, 37–38]), and it is materially powered by his cohabitation with his black cellmate.

The most important educative result of Edmond's failure with Glenna is the achievement of a transformative function that skewers the conventionally male line of power between gender, race, and sexuality in him. The feminization of ethnic minorities, like the subordinating other-ing of women, is a script of power that is manifest in popular male notions of the sex act itself. As has been remarked, sexual expletives in the overall discourse of Mamet's oeuvre semiotically replicate homophobic convictions of the male's superior position in heterosexual sexual intercourse, *taking, penetrating, possessing,* as opposed to *giving, being entered,* or *being possessed* (McDonough 199, Cohn 117–18). The aftereffects of the Glenna episode delegitimize this conviction by reversing the play of power in it. The sexual ramifications of the failure that Glenna imposes on Edmond has an emasculatory undertext that surfaces in Edmond's acceptance of his sexual subordination by his powerful black cellmate. If the theoretically illustrative point of Glenna's reverse inscription of Edmond as a brutalizer at the time of her death at his hands is the inherent cruelty and violence of imposing one's will on others, then the experientially demonstrative follow-through of that point is Edmond's sufferance of his black cellmate's imposition of his sexual will on him: "you should get on my body now . . . you going to try it or you going to die . . . The mother-fuck you can't. Right now, missy.(*The Prisoner viciously slaps Edmond several times*). . . ." (scene 20, 51–52). Edmond's later acceptance of this in his reflective comment in scene 23, "You can't control what you make of your life," in agreement with the Prisoner's statement that "what we [mankind] have done is to disgrace ourselves" (56–57), is not the play's discursive condonation of sexual violence but a highlighting of Glenna's education of Edmond in the need for gender, racial, and sexual compassion. As Edmond voluntarily kisses his black sexual partner goodnight at scene's end he completes, on Glenna's behalf, the play's subversion of the sexist-racist agenda of demotic male desire.

Glenna and the women of *Edmond* work in a fissured textual and discursive space. Numbering eight out of twenty-eight characters in the play, and, with the exception of Glenna, constituting a fleeting and often nameless presence in the action, they are textually marginal. But they have, as this chapter has shown, a central role in that action as they reactively catalyze its discursive conflicts and determine their outcome. Discursively, they deconstruct demotic homosocial desire even as they are located within it and are constructed by it. In this, they are both its agent and its object. They are simultaneously the object of male power and the subjective agency of male ethical disempowerment. At the same time, they exist in the liminal zone of their own subjectivity, struggling forever on the edge of a becoming determined by men but also aimed oppositionally at them. They function under a double jeopardy, having to walk a fine rhetorical line between being unresisting figures of persecution and traditional patriarchal icons of female manipulation of men. They can succeed only by failing convincingly. These complex and powerful responsibilities, particularly as in a character like Glenna, show an early new preoccupation in Mamet's drama that leads to concentrated, single male-female engagements as in *Oleanna* and to adversarially brilliant destroyers of male self-complacency as Carol. Glenna is the prototype of the teacherly female subject that Carol will become, who discursively instructs the popular male imagination about mediating and reconstructing the dangerous conjunction of patriarchy and authority in contemporary culture. If the ending of *Oleanna* can be used to view the denigration of women in Mamet, the ending of *Edmond* can be used to (re)view the necessary disempowerment of men that is also present in Mamet. This retrospective critical correction is a unique contribution of the women of *Edmond*.

In the broadest hermeneutic terms, the physical and verbal abuse of women by men, and the sexual and racial prejudice that are its accompaniments in the culturally dominant class of white men, are the demotic desires that Mamet cathartically ferrets out and purges in plays like *Edmond*. Through their splintered dramatic existence, the women of *Edmond* help to make Mamet's point about the recognitions necessary for the community of urban renewal. In their riven role they are Mamet's emblems of the regenerative urgencies of a lost worldscape. As Mamet has said in a recent essay, "In misery we strive to be or find a victim" ("Between Men and Women" 115). To realize the complex role played by Mamet's dramatic women is to understand his vital interest in the reclamation of a truly meaningful human community, again best described by Mamet himself: "What could be more lovely than two folks in love . . . who demand that not only their partners but the community make them complete. . . . As one is. For it is the Group that gave us our choice, and if we are, as we are, fated for bliss, then surely the group, in large or small, must bear the fault" ("Between Men and Women" 113).

NOTES

1. See Michel Foucault's *The History of Sexuality*, vol. 1, 102; cited by Richard Dellamora, "Textual Politics/Sexual Politics," on 148. Dellamora uses this Foucauldian idea to point to the homosexual counter-discourse within E. M. Forster's heterosexual novelistic world.

2. I am using the expression demotic desire as a compound critical-poetic metaphor of what might be called the contemporary male sexual imaginary, the unformalized convention of male fantasy that fetishistically constructs women as objects of sexual gratification and control and that differentially writes male self-identity itself. It is obviously deeply implicated in the operation of postmodern patriarchal culture. My cue for the term "demotic" is specifically from Ilkka Joki's socio-linguistic use of it, in the light of the cultural-linguistic semiotic theories of the Russian Marxist literary critic M. M. Bakhtin, to study the play of popular public address in Mamet's work. Joki uses the term to denote the "sociolinguistic dimension" of "the symbiosis of 'life' and 'art'" in a fashion that he thinks Bakhtin would have approved. The term, as he points out in a citation

from *The International Encyclopedia of Linguistics*, comes from the Greek word *demotikos*, meaning "'popular,' 'of the people'"; see *Mamet, Bakhtin and the Dramatic*, 4.

3. I am appropriating this critical trope from Christopher C. Hudgins' use of it in his essay, "Comedy and Humor in the Plays of David Mamet."

4. Interview in *New York Times*, October 24 1982; extracted in Jones and Dykes, ed., *File on Mamet*, 51.

5. Joki has also comparatively connected the play to Brecht's *Baal*; "egoistic hedonism," and "excesses lead[ing] to disaster," according to Joki, are common to both plays. Citing Robert Cunliffe, he also points out how the play can be seen as "a reversed *Pygmalion* (35).

6. My assertion modifies Radavich's observation (131) that this "new" shift "beyond homophobia" is a late phenomenon in Mamet, occurring only as late as *Speed-the-Plow*.

7. The few discussions of this play include Dennis Carroll's study cited before, C.W. Bigsby's, *David Mamet*, and *A Critical Introduction to Twentieth Century Drama* vol. 3; Edward Lundin's "Mamet and Mystery;" and Carla J. McDonough's "Every Fear Hides a Wish: Unstable Masculinity in Mamet's Drama." The last essay in its sketchy but useful exploration of unstable masculinity in the play echoes some points I make later in this chapter. But its underlying rhetorical assumption, contextualized by some of Mamet's remarks on British television, that the playwright's concept of women and of marriage "has much in common with the usual position (that of subjugation) of women in patriarchal society" (197), is at basic variance with mine. The remarks of Mamet that McDonough cites here need to be balanced by other statements that he has made, such as the following (on the occasion of the hostility of New York reviewers and audiences at the play's first performance): "[The play] is talking about a lot of things that really get under the skin. When people have suspended their conscious process of ratiocination by indulging in a theatrical thing, and you start talking about racial guilt, homosexual panic, impecuniosity, and misogyny in a way that's fairly clear, it's naturally going to upset a lot of people who are anxious about those things." *Chicago Tribune Calendar*, June 17, 1984; extracted in Jones and Dykes ed. *File on Mamet*, 51. Mamet's comment suggests the possibility of critics mistaking dramatic characters' views for their playwright's and of assuming dramatic discourse to be univocal and immune to its own deconstructive alterities. As I have said above, we need to problematize Mamet's male dramatic discourse as a divided performance that contains its own critique.

8. David Savran, in his book *In Their Own Words*, has called Edmond "an American urban, white, middle class Everyman" (133).

9. This is true even if the "girl" is later (in scene 16, 37), identified as the black cleaning girl. My textual citation, here and throughout this essay, is from the edition cited in the "Works Cited" list at the end of this essay and will be documented by page number and sometimes by scene number.

10. See McDonough, who puts it this way: "Evidently, the construction of his [Edmond's] has relied on sex with a women . . . Edmond accepts that the traffic in woman is crucial to his identity as a man" (198–99). Also see Bigsby's comment, made in a discussion of *Sexual Perversity in Chicago* (which he interestingly calls "a kind of disco *Dance of Death*"), but which applies easily to *Edmond* and to nearly all of Mamet's plays: "Commodity value alone seems to survive—sexual voyeurism, sexual fantasies and sexual possession being offered as correlatives of a vapid materialism. . . ." (*A Critical Introduction to Twentieth Century Drama*, 3: 257).

11. The psychosocial implications of this event are very important. In the murder of the Pimp we see not just the debasement of the female that is the compulsive hallmark of demonic male self-drive, but also the intrinsic violence of authoring, across gender and race that are the attendant features of that drive. In Edmond's scabrous and scatological abuse of the Pimp as he kills him, white misogyny competes with violent racial bigotry to de-sexualize the black pimp. This is a subject that requires serious critical attention in Mamet studies, and of the sort that Deborah Geis has attempted in her recent essay, "You're Exploiting My Space: Ethnicity, Spectatorship and the (Post)colonial Condition in Mukherjee's 'A Wife's Story' and Mamet's *Glengarry Glen Ross*," but that I feel is somewhat outside the scope of my essay. I do, however, somewhat engage with this topic later in this essay, in my discussion of the play's end.

12. McDonough makes a similar point about the significance of Glenna being the only named woman in the play (199).

13. A comment of Bigsby's is worth invoking here: "The power of naturalistic language lies in what it reveals; the force of the language that Mamet's characters speak lies in what it attempts to conceal" (*A Critical Introduction to Twentieth Century American Drama* 3: 266). This has particular resonance for the unspoken directions of Glenna's words in this scene that I am pointing to here.

14. I want to emphasize here, with utmost clarity, that I *do not* mean that Glenna is the cause of Edmond's deadly violence to her, that is, that she goads Edmond to kill her. To say that would be to make the kind of nefarious argument that misogynistic apologists of male chauvinism have traditionally made about how the women who are the victims of domestic/sexual violence are somehow responsible for it themselves. What I am talking about above is the overspill of the powerful energy of discursive engagement into physical violence that Glenna is both swamped by and modulates. She is the facilitator and re- director of such energy, not its source.

WORKS CITED

Bigsby, Christopher. *A Critical Introduction to Twentieth Century Drama*. 3 vols. New York: Cambridge UP, 1985. 3: 251–90.

————. *David Mamet*. New York: Methuen, 1985.

Carroll, Dennis. *David Mamet*. New York: St. Martin's Press, 1987.

Cohn, Ruby. "How Are Things Made Round?" In *David Mamet: A Casebook*. Ed. Leslie Kane. New York: Garland Publishing, 1992, 109–22.

Dellamora, Richard. "Textual Politics/Sexual Politics." *The Uses of Literary History*. Ed. Marshall Brown. Durham: Duke UP, 1995, 144–57.

Foucault, Michel. *The History of Sexuality*. Trans. Robert Hurley. New York: Vintage, 1980. vol. 1. *An Introduction*.

Fraser, Gerald. "Mamet's Plays Shed Masculinity Myth." Interview. *The New York Times* July 5, 1976: 1:7.

Geis, Deborah R. "You're Exploiting My Space: Ethnicity, Spectatorship and the (Post)colonial Condition in Mukherjee's 'A Wife's Story' and Mamet's *Glengarry Glen Ross*." In *David Mamet's Glengarry Glen Ross: Texts and Performance*. Ed. Leslie Kane. New York: Garland Publishing, 1996, 123–30.

Hall, Ann C. "Playing to Win: Sexual Politics in Mamet's *House of Games* and *Speed-the-Plow*." *David Mamet: A Casebook*. Ed. Leslie Kane. New York: Garland Publishing, 1992.

Hudgins, Christopher C. "Comedy and Humor in the Plays of David Mamet." *David Mamet: A Casebook*. Ed. Leslie Kane. New York: Garland Publishing, 1992, 191- 228.

Jacobs, Dorothy H. "Levene's Daughter: Positioning the Female in *Glengarry Glen Ross*." *David Mamet's "Glengarry Glen Ross": Texts and Performance*. Ed. Leslie Kane. New York: Garland Publishing, 1996, 107–21.

Joki, Ilkka. *Mamet, Bakhtin, and the Dramatic: The Demotic as a Variable of Addressivity*. Abo, Finland: Abo Akedemi UP, 1993.

Jones, Nesta, and Steven Dykes. *File on Mamet*. London: Methuen, 1991.

Kane, Leslie. "Stirring Controversy at MLA." *The David Mamet Review* 1.1 (1994): 7.

Lundin, Edward. "Mamet and Mystery." *Publications of the Mississippi Philological Association* n.v. (1988): 106–14.

Mamet, David. "Between Men and Women." *Make-Believe Town: Essays and Remembrances*. New York: Little Brown and Company, 1996, 109–118.

————. *Edmond: A Drama*. New York: Samuel French, Inc., 1983.

————. *Glengarry Glen Ross*. London: Methuen, 1984.

McDonough, Carla J. "Every Fear Hides a Wish: Unstable Masculinity in Mamet's Drama." *Theatre Journal* 44.2 (1992): 195–205.

Mukherjee, Bharati. "A Wife's Story." *The Middleman and Other Stories*. New York: Grove Press, 1988.

Radavich, David. "Man Among Men: David Mamet's Homosocial Order." *Fictions of Masculinity: Crossing Cultures, Crossing Sexualities*. Ed. Peter F. Murphy. New York: New York UP, 1994, 127–39.

Roudané, Matthew. "Mamet's Mimetics." *David Mamet: A Casebook*. Ed. Leslie Kane. New York: Garland Publishing, 1992, 3–32.

Savran, David. *In Their Own Words*. New York: Theatre Communications Group, 1988.

OLEANNA, OR,
THE PLAY OF PEDAGOGY

ROBERT SKLOOT

"Teaching is a performative act."

—*bell hooks*

"That is how they educate us. By osmosis!"

—*Augusto Boal*

When David Mamet's *Oleanna* premiered in 1992 in Boston and New York, under the direction of its author, critics were quick to point out that the two-character play presented a devastating vision of the tense relationships between men and women in contemporary American society. They pointed to the recurrence of a frequent Mamet theme: the inability of language to elucidate meaning and its use as a weapon of humiliation or concealment. Many provided a cultural context for the play in referring to its relationship in time to the Hill/Thomas political brouhaha and to the "P.C. controversy" in American higher education. And some critics made much of the gaps in the play's narrative, which created characters who were both memorable and opaque, particularly the character of Carol, who undergoes a transformation during the play that many saw as unbelievable, politically repugnant, or both. Many critics acknowledged the rage released by men of the audience, whose antipathy toward Carol exploded in extraordinary and immediate vituperative verbal responses. Indeed, their dislike of her was mirrored in the near-final moments when John, reduced in language to a wrathful and graphic expletive, stands over Carol in a posture of savage retribution for her successful effort to destroy his career.[1]

The play's three scenes chart the course of John's downfall, and they also describe the trajectory of Carol's rise to strength despite the final image of her cowering abjectly beneath his threatening (and finally released) aggression. Contradicting her spatial vulnerability, the play projects for her a viable future, whereas it asserts John's as one of utter failure, leaving him, as shown in his last activity on stage, a mere shuffler of papers (47). Above all, the play involves a struggle to achieve and to maintain certain kinds of privilege: economic, sexual, and academic.

In this essay, I want to discuss how *Oleanna* can be linked to Mamet's preoccupation with the issue of *teaching*, of how facts, customs, and feelings are transmitted among inhabitants of the same social and cultural spaces. One important difference between *Oleanna* and the plays that precede it in Mamet's work lies in its more "cultured" location. The play is set in an unnamed college, and though it is probably not an elite institution, it serves to represent one view of life in the academy that is, in any case, rare in the theater. The level of discourse concerning *Oleanna* needs to be "thickened" so that the academic politics and gender relationships it ostensibly conveys can be situated in the larger context of pedagogy.[2]

Thus, for example, in the character called Teach in *American Buffalo*, in the less experienced salesmen being advised by those more experienced in *Glengarry Glen Ross*, and in the young actor seeking the advice and wisdom of his older colleague in *A Life in the Theatre*, we can glimpse something of Mamet's concern with the manner and method of teaching. In effect, this preoccupation turns many of Mamet's venues into classrooms, in such a way that the action in the plays contains the elucidation of a distinct "pedagogy of the oppressed." To be sure, all the plays are far from Paulo Friere's ideal stage of "libertarian education" (53b), what his colleague and disciple bell hooks calls "education as the practice of freedom" (11, 15).[3] What I would like to suggest, using Friere's paradigm, is that *both* Carol and John suffer oppression, and their oppression is to be found in both their behavior *and* the place they inhabit. Subsequently, we shall see how *spatially* Mamet's play can be staged with visual precision so that the shifting dynamic of power between the teacher and student reveals their antagonistic identities and the gestural essence of their struggle.

Mamet need not be faulted for making the play a provocative and violent struggle for power, one that lacks more coherent thinking about specific practices of pedagogy. For this reason, I believe it is possible to amplify his exciting if limited statement of oppression to a level where we can say more than expletives about its dramaturgy or politics. That is, *Oleanna* can be used to reflect upon a comprehensive philosophy of teaching, thus permitting his provocative dramatization to guide us toward a *vision of pedagogy*. In this kind of analysis, the play becomes more than a shrewd exploitation of a contemporary issue by serving as an investigation of pedagogical principles and techniques. It is because Mamet is provoked by issues of *authority* that he has created a play that revolves around the authority of pedagogy; *Oleanna* is his contribution to raising (but not resolving) questions about the use and abuse of power in the profession of teaching.

What *can* be said of Mamet's image of teaching? In what way does that image reflect the world outside the classroom and inside the faculty office? And how may his play be assessed in the light of the work of Friere and Boal so that we can be brought to a new level of insight about the work we do?

Let us return to bell hooks. Several times in *Teaching to Transgress* she refers to her own experience as a student:

> The vast majority of our professors lacked basic communication skills, they were not self-actualized, and they often used the classroom to enact rituals of control that were about domination and the unjust exercise of power. In these settings I learned a lot about the kind of teacher I did not want to become. (5)

hooks's anecdote provides a good description of what we see in Mamet's play, where John practices his bad "teaching habits" on his students in public and private. In a staged presentation of John's character, his problems with communication and confidence as well as his assertion of domination would be emphasized. As such, he models for us a negative image of the teacher.

With hooks' book as a guide, Mamet's play becomes a meta-educational experience, a play that discusses the work of teaching at the same time that it "performs" it. John, older than the usual nontenured faculty for reasons alluded to in the play, reflects on his own profession a number of times. In the first words of act 2, he confesses,

> I love to teach. And flatter myself that I am *skilled* at it. And I love the, the aspect of performance. . . .
> When I found I loved to teach I swore that I would not become that cold, rigid automaton of an instructor which I had encountered as a child. . . .
> Now: I see I have angered you. I understand your anger at teachers. I was angry with mine. I felt hurt and humiliated by them. Which is one of the reasons that I went into education. (28, 29)

We could, of course, question John's sincerity at this moment, beleaguered by the threat of Carol's accusation and anxious at the possible loss of his promised tenured appointment. But he does show an awareness of a kind of pedagogy consistent with the concern to "open up the classroom." This is the exact sense in which hooks defines teaching as "performative act," in that it "offers a space for change . . . to engage 'audiences,' to consider issues of reciprocity" (15). Nonetheless, John's pedagogical method, at bottom, is a clear contradiction of the Friere/hooks liberational model; in fact, his pedagogy is *doubly* flawed, for he is using performative acts *not* to enlarge space for reflection and engagement but rather to beguile and enthrall his tuition-paying audiences.

I would argue that John's most profound crisis is one of self-understanding and, in fact, Carol's onslaught of accusation in the play's last moments is brutally humiliating in these terms. By interrupting him with a newly found confidence and linguistic clarity that she seems to have gained very quickly (some say too quickly), she reverses their roles of student and teacher and reaffirms the type of educational model *unacceptable* to a spirit of liberation. Clearly, there is a splendid irony in seeing how successfully John has transmitted to Carol the facts, customs and feelings of their "professional" situation. She says,

> YOU FOOL. Who do you think I am? To come here and be taken in by a *smile*. You little yapping fool. You think I want "revenge." I don't want revenge. I WANT UNDERSTANDING. (43)

But, of course, understanding is something that cannot be simply demanded. By the play's conclusion, Carol has seemingly unburdened herself of the characteristics of the oppressed person as Friere has advanced them: fatalism, alienation, self-depreciation. ("I'm bad," she confesses at the end of their first encounter.) But, in (the Sartrean) terms of Friere's "pedagogy of the oppressed," she has failed to perceive the major insight that would allow the creation of the liberated, communal, pedagogically satisfying workplace. Friere writes:

> Although the situation of oppression is a dehumanized and dehumanizing totality affecting both the oppressors and those whom they oppress, it is the latter who must, from their stifled humanity, wage for both the struggle for a fuller humanity; the oppressor, who is himself dehumanized because he dehumanizes others, is unable to lead this struggle.
> . . . The oppressed suffer from the duality which has established itself in their utmost being. They discover that without freedom they cannot exist authentically. Yet, although they desire authentic existence, they fear it. They are at one and the same time themselves and the oppressor whose consciousness they have internalized. (29b, 30b)

With these perspectives, John's *expression* of commonality with Carol in his first interview is not as farfetched as it may appear. "Perhaps we're similar," he allows; the actor's performance determines the degree of sincerity with which this similarity is expressed. In fact, they *are* similar because they are both, in their own ways, teachers, although teachers whose gratification comes from oppression of their students.[4]

Thus Carol, turning the oppressive "banking" system of education back on John, asserts her dominance in act 3: "I came here to instruct you," but she leaves the system intact. John's final attempt to reassert his authoritarian prerogatives finds verbal expression in the twice-articulated self-defense: "I'm a teacher. I'm a teacher. Eh? It's my *name* on the door, and *I* teach the class, and that's what I do" (45). He erupts in violence because he senses that being instructed about what to do creates a situation that only guarantees his failure if there is only one right answer to please the teacher. Carol's pedagogy is as repressive as his own. But, in Friere's terms, both remain ignorant that in the teacher-student/student-teacher relationship, "subjectivity and objectivity [exist] in constant dialectical relationship" (32b).[5] Here is Friere's analysis of oppression, deeply influenced by Marx:

> Submerged in reality, the oppressed cannot perceive clearly the "order" which serves the interests of the oppressors whose image they have internalized. Chafing under the restrictions of this order, they often manifest a type of horizontal violence, striking out at their own comrades for the pettiest reasons. (44b)

What then is the oppression that John suffers? On the level of academic politics, John is oppressed by the Tenure Committee and, beyond it, the entire structure of higher education that works to validate and maintain a regressive and stultifying pedagogical practice. In a production that emphasizes John's patronizing and vain attitude, criticism of the Tenure Committee becomes yet more understandable, for it appears that the Committee has approved John's tenure despite a style of teaching that many would find objectionable if not repugnant.[6] John himself loathes the system, and denigrates it in his interview with Carol early in the play, much to her dismay; at the same time he expresses his own self-depreciation.

> The Tenure Committee. Come to judge me. The Bad Tenure Committee. The "Test." Do you see? They put me to the test. Why, they had people voting on me I wouldn't employ to wax my car. And yet, I go before the Great Tenure Committee and I have an urge, to *vomit*, to, to, to puke

my *badness* on the table, to show them: "I'm no good. Why would you pick *me?*" (18)

Later, after Carol's accusations, the Committee reconsiders John's promotion and rejects him, seemingly without providing an opportunity to hear his side of the case. Still, if John's feelings about the Committee are genuine (*or* he may be merely trying to establish common ground with Carol as a kind of anti-authoritarian middle-class, middle-aged liberal, most of the time stooping to conquer the prize of his promotion), his own complicity in the corrupt practices of higher education create serious psychological problems that do not promise well for his future at the college.

And it is likely that John and Carol are similar in their discomfort with and ignorance of their bodies which, in "traditional education," remain outside the pedagogical space. hooks writes of how the erasure of the body from the classroom has negative consequences for the achievement of the liberatory classroom:

> Entering the classroom determined to erase the body and give ourselves over more fully to the mind, we show by our beings how deeply we have accepted the assumption that passion has no place in the classroom. Repression and denial make it possible for us to forget and then desperately seek to recover ourselves, our feelings, our passions in some private place— after class. (192)

In John's private office, both endure a kind of oppression that pronounces *understanding* as the goal of education, i.e., Friere's "banking" model, which is called "prolonged and systematic hazing" by John. Carol spends the first half of *Oleanna* taking notes, a defining academic/psychological gesture. Later in the narrative, these notes will be used as evidence to "convict" John of unethical behavior. John is decisive in his claim to Carol that "I *understand* you." Carol, panicked by her sense of inferiority (or feigning it, as some productions might decide) and by John's authority, shouts (pleads? whines?): "I DON'T UNDERSTAND. DO YOU SEE??? I DON'T *UNDERSTAND.*" As noted earlier, Carol's triumph over John includes her demand that he understand her, a demand that would seem to enlarge the dimensions of John's other *mis*understandings: about his chances for tenure, about the slippages in language's meaning, about his offstage involvements with family and home-buying. (Two *un*written scenes in *Oleanna* are noteworthy for their absence: John's unknown defense before the suspect Tenure Committee and Carol's "instruction/indoctrination" by her "Group." Mamet, like Molière who spared us the encounter of the misanthrope Alceste defending his sonnet at court, appears to believe that showing us less is really providing more.)

When, in the last scene, Carol reveals that she has accused him of attempting to rape her, pointing to evidence in the two physical gestures we have witnessed between them thus far, i.e., his attempt to put his arm around her in the first scene and his "restraining her from leaving" in the second, it comes as a surprise because the text seems to indicate a lack of physical desire in John and may also hint at more than a neutral supplicative entreaty from Carol. Here again, a production would have to build these meanings into its intentions. Nonetheless, the sense of the accusation has several aspects, i.e., that John has "raped" ("forcibly disabused") Carol of her academic expectations in addition to denying her the agency and healthy growth that comes from true liberation. At the same time, Mamet provides opportunity for criticism of the *type* of women who "cry rape" when they feel aggrieved by men and/or powerless in their presence.

Although both John and Carol are portrayed on stage as having a sense of how they present their public images, they nonetheless seem bodiless, which is surprising in a play whose plot involves the accusation of sexual assault. Much attention has been drawn by reviewers to Carol's clothing—how she presents herself to John and to the audience—which begins as dowdy/bulky/dour/shapeless in act 1 and changes to neat and authoritatively "masculine" later in the play. (Several critics declared this image "Maoist.") John's "costume" on the other hand, progressively di sheveled, shows his "decline." Mamet's negative message about one type of feminist ascendancy is clearly asserted and, at the same time, John's messy savagery in the defense of his own textbook provides some sort of psychological justification for his behavior, perhaps less for hers. The Eros that hooks advocates returning to the classroom, presumably so that it won't have retrogressive, harmful effects in the privacy of our offices, looks a lot like Thanatos in persons whose love requires subjugation rather than mutuality.[7]

Although the motivations of the two characters may remain opaque and open to variant interpretations, there is no doubt that Carol is the winner in the struggle. The final visual image Mamet specifies—Carol submissive and cowering on the floor, John arranging papers at his desk—presents a kind of pause in the action, an image of disengagement and, in liberational/pedagogical terms, failure. The play's last words, spoken by Carol, have a multiplicity of voicings available to the actor, and appear to prevent closure in the traditional sense. "Yes. That's right. . . . yes. That's right," she says, leaving ambiguous exactly what she believes is right.

One additional matter of staging *Oleanna* finds a correspondence in the work of Paulo Friere. His idea of the constant dialectic of subjectivity and objectivity finds a precise theatrical expression in the playing of the script. In the London production of *Oleanna*, directed by Harold Pinter, "Carol's battle for psychic 'territory' was reflected in Pinter's gradually allowing her to claim more and more *physical* space."[8] Early on, the stage (John's office, the academic world, the psychological advantage) belongs entirely to John, but in scene 3,

> it was Carol who now felt free to pace the stage, to measure the "patriarchal kingdom," to perch proprietarily on the edge of John's desk—her physical mobility the outward sign of a much more significant inner movement. (Zeifman, 2–3)

Visually speaking, the objects *and* the subjects of domination and submission have reversed places, all the while leaving the principle of a bankrupt pedagogy undiminished, the issue of multiple oppressions unchallenged, and the basic stage picture unchanged.

As noted earlier, Mamet has no thoughts beyond this moment, at least none he chooses to share with us in his play. He is entirely content to present the confrontation of John and Carol, and has been quoted as saying, "I have no political responsibility. I am an artist. I write plays not political propaganda. If you want easy solutions, turn on the boob tube." (Holmberg, 94–95). At the least, Mamet is declaring the self-sufficiency of his play and the autonomy of its narrative, which is why *Oleanna* must conclude (as other Mamet plays do) when the *action* of the script is exhausted whether or not the story has reached reconciling closure ("the boob tube").

But the point of this essay is to ask more of the play than the play asks of itself, specifically, "What kind of pedagogy leads out of the office and into the fresh air of liberated learning?" The metaphor in this inquiry is taken from the *other* epigraph to the published text of *Oleanna*, not the verse of the folk song that gives the play its name but the paragraph taken from Samuel Butler's highly sardonic novel *The Way of All Flesh* (1903). It is worth quoting in its entirety.

> The want of fresh air does not seem much to affect the happiness of children in a London alley: The greater part of them sing and play as though they were on a moor in Scotland. So the absence of a genial mental atmosphere is not commonly recognized by children who have never known it. Young people have a marvelous faculty of either dying or adapting themselves to circumstances. Even if they are unhappy—very unhappy—it is as-

tonishing how easily they can be prevented from finding it out, or at any rate from attributing it to any other cause than their own sinfulness. (4)

Excerpting and displacing Butler's words furthers our speculations about Mamet's perspective on how intellectual and environmental deprivation influences the life and imagination of young people. Placing Butler next to *Oleanna* (song lyric as well as play) obliges us to interpret Mamet's text in pedagogical terms, although it isn't certain that we would understand Butler's satirical excerpt and Mamet's satirical use of it before we see the play, after seeing it, or even at all. I would argue that both epigraphs be included in the program to any production.

The quotation provokes a number of relevant questions. What is the relationship between Butler's words and the academic world of today, a century after they were written? Should we see Carol as one of the London young people: stunted and unhappy and full of self-loathing? Could we see Mamet as intending the excerpt not as satire in itself (how many in the audience would have read the original source or even heard of it?) but as a pedagogical truth in late-twentieth-century ideologies of liberational education, i.e., students are screwed over by their authoritarian professors and made to think their ignorance is their own fault? Or is the epigraph just Mamet being clever, ambiguous, mocking, as well as postpolitical and pointedly postmodern, deferring meaning and endorsing the inevitable futility of promulgating any life-enhancing, truth-discerning, paradise-creating (a reference to hooks here) ideology. *Oleanna*, to be sure, is not only a play but a folk song as well.

I don't believe Mamet wants to think through the implications of his vision of education, and that is both his privilege and his strength. In terms of his playwrighting, he eschews any obligation other than to reveal and entertain. He resists confirming that John's linguistic insight concerning the impossibility of imposing and maintaining meaning on experience through language interests him except insofar as it provides material for his plays. Certainly, John's office (and likely his classroom) fits comfortably alongside the pool halls, movie studios, pawnshops and real estate offices we have seen before in Mamet's work; they are arenas for struggle and domination. And that, in itself, is a harsh evaluation about the pretensions and illusions of our academic world, even if the details of his picture in *Oleanna* may not reflect our particular professional or personal situation.[9] Which brings us back to Paulo Friere and his colleague Augusto Boal.

In Mamet's world, people *lose*. But should they? Is there any usefulness in bringing fresh air to the alleys of the young? Mamet is also a teacher by profession (he runs an acting school) and many of his plays are about teaching, in one way or another. Despite the opacity of meaning in his plays and contradictoriness in his public image, it is clear to me that part of what he "understands" is that teaching is, and is about, love. ("Education is an act of love," Friere has written, "and thus an act of courage" [38a]). And that is why it is worthwhile to speculate on Mamet's thinking about pedagogy, because set beside a theoretical model (Friere) and specific program (hooks), Mamet's writing can serve the interests of all teachers who seek additional insight into the continuing tensions and changes in their professional lives.

In the same way that we can see Tony Kushner's *Angels in America* as a play about the gay experience but larger than that, so *Oleanna* is about political correctness, sexual harassment, radical feminism, etc., but it is more than that, too.[10] We recall John's self-enhancing and smug explanation to Carol in the second scene of *Oleanna* when his philosophy of education is articulated, though as yet untested. His ideas are as vulnerable to criticism as John himself is, and Carol will soon seek and gain the advantage in her own struggle to understand herself and her academic world:

> You said you came in the class because you wanted to learn about *education*. I don't know that I can teach you about education. But I know that I can tell you what I *think* about education, and then *you* decide. And you don't have to fight with me. *I'm* not the subject. . . . I would like to tell you what I *think*, because that *is* my job, conventional as it is, and flawed as I might be. And then, if you can show me some better *form*, then we can proceed from there. (34)

The rules of academe, John says, require him to instruct her, impersonally and authoritatively. Only after Carol understands this will she be permitted to make a suggestion that will open a space for involvement in her own education.

I am convinced that this scene raises issues of great importance that are worthy of consideration, and that they surface whenever we examine our own place in the pedagogy of the oppressed. For these reasons, I believe that Mamet's play can contribute importantly to what has been written about how we teach and how we can teach and learn better.

Notes

This essay was enriched by the suggestions of my colleagues Vicki Patraka, Stuart Greene, and Beth Amsbury, and I thank them here for their assistance.

1. An overview of the critics' responses is provided by Daniel Mufson's "Critical Eye" column in *Theater Magazine* 24, 1 (1993): 111–13.
2. See Lynne Joyrich's "Give Me a Girl at an Impressionable Age and She is Mine for Life: Jean Brodie as Pedagogical Primer," in *Pedagogy: The Question of Impersonation*, ed. Jane Gallop (Bloomington: Indiana UP, 1995), 46–62. My intention is the reverse of Joyrich's, who investigates the film *The Prime of Miss Jean Brodie* as "not simply a film about education." But we both agree that "the ongoing debates around cultural literacy, the curriculum, and the politics of education" may be engaged in "mass-mediated texts [that] are rarely valued for their pedagogical potential . . ." (48).
   The title for this essay is used by Madeline R. Grumet in her essay "*Scholae Personae:* Masks for Meaning," in *Pedagogy*, p. 37. She writes that she has chosen to see " . . . the personal is a performance, an appearance contrived for the public, and to argue that these masks enable us to perform the play of pedagogy."
3. hooks devotes a chapter to Friere, pp. 45–58; the epigraph used for this essay appears on p. 11. Boal's epigraph is taken from *The Theatre of the Oppressed*, tr. Charles A. and Maria-Odilia Leal McBride (New York: TCG, 1985), 115.
4. In her essay "Brechtian Shamanism," Mady Schutzman writes: "The concept of multiple protagonists in the same forum has become more and more common; what had become evident is that there are, in fact, several protagonists in any one scene, each experiencing mutual oppression within a co-dependent power relation." In *Playing Boal: Theatre, Therapy, Activism*, ed. Mady Schutzman and Jan Cohen-Cruz (New York: Routledge, 1994), 149.
5. Chris Amirault finds Friere's ideology to contain two detrimental aspects: it reinforces the institutional structure and it rewards people whose practice conforms to that structure by "reproducing" the very structure it attempts to dismantle. His critique of Friere is based on *Reproduction in Education, Society and Culture* by Bordieu and Passeron (1970), and reinforced by his own experience as a "student teacher":

Friere's terms 'teacher-student' and 'student-teachers' can serve to signal the complex identifications between teacher and student, not the erasure of those positions. . . . Ironically, Friere's *Pedagogy of the Oppressed* has always been oppressive for this reader, primarily because it refuses to give up the banking model in its own textual pedagogy; the text deposits Friere's experience in a reader presumed to be empty. Yet, however oppressive it might have felt, Friere's book has managed to teach a lot of people, myself included.

Chris Amirault, "The Good Teacher, the Good Student: Identifications of a Student Teacher," in *Pedagogy*, p. 76.

6. Richard Hornby makes this point in an otherwise condescending review in *The Hudson Review*, Spring 1993, 193–94.
7. See Jeanne Silverthorne, "PC Playhouse," *Artforum* (March, 1993), 10–11.
8. At the least, we could think here about our teaching spaces, for example the frustrations of teaching in a room with fixed chairs. Pinter is only showing us what we know from everyday experience, every time we, students *and* teachers, say: "OK, let's move the chairs into a circle."
9. I have omitted from discussion in this essay the additional complexity of relationships that occurs when race is involved in the casting of these roles. In the 1994 Los Angeles production, John was played (at Mamet's specification) by the black actor Lionel Mark Smith.

   In her review of the production, Stephanie Tucker writes about the final moments:

   this scene assumed an even uglier resonance: a black man stood over a white woman who had charged him with rape, a visual reminder of the horror inherent in racial stereotyping. If the academy is emblematic of our society, then this production of *Oleanna* foregrounded a theme hinted at in Mamet's text but made explicit with this casting. Racism, like sexism, cuts both ways. . . . (4)

10. In a speech in Madison, Wisconsin on October 19, 1994, Kushner mentioned his admiration for Mamet's *Glengarry*, presumably for its analysis of economic politics, but his loathing for *Oleanna*, presumably for its analysis of sexual politics.

Works Cited

Boal, Augusto. *The Theatre of the Oppressed.* Tr. Charles A. and Maria-Odilia Leal McBride. New York: TCG, 1985.

Friere, Paulo. *Education for a Critical Consciousness.* Tr. Myra Bergman Ramos. New York: Continuum, 1994.

———. *Pedagogy of the Oppressed.* Tr. Myra Bergman Ramos. New York: Continuum, 1970 (1993 ed.).

Gallop, Jane. ed., *Pedagogy: The Question of Impersonation.* Bloomington: Indiana UP, 1995.

Holmberg, Arthur. "The Language of Misunderstanding." *American Theater* (October 1992): 94–95.

hooks, bell. *Teaching to Transgress: Education as the Practice of Freedom.* New York: Routledge, 1994.

Hornby, Richard. Review of *Oleanna*. *The Hudson Review* Spring, 1993.

Mamet, David. *Oleanna.* Dramatists Play Service, 1993.

Mufson, Daniel. "Sexual Perversity in Viragos." *Theater Magazine* 24 (1993).

Schutzman, Mady and Jan Cruz-Cohen, eds., *Playing Boal: Theatre, Therapy, Activism.* New York: Routledge, 1994.

Silverthorne, Jeanne. "PC Playhouse." *Artforum* March, 1993.

Tucker, Stephanie. Review of *Oleanna, The David Mamet Review* 1 (1994): 3–4.

Zeifman, Hersh. Review of *Oleanna,* the London production. *The David Mamet Review* 1 (1994): 2–3.

A Few Good Men

Collusion and Violence in *Oleanna*

Kellie Bean

Although David Mamet's *Oleanna* (1992) concerns itself with the issue of sexual harassment, criticism of the play has experienced a kind of backlash against interpretations focusing on gender politics. Such arguments tend to favor discussions of power, language, or political correctness gone horribly wrong. The play and its author certainly invite readings grounded in its cultural context, concerned as it is with familiar current events. But if we turn attention away from the Anita Hill–Clarence Thomas hearings and Mamet's reputation for heavy-handed machismo, we are left with a play in which a man and a woman battle for ideological ground on stage.

The main characters in *Oleanna*, John, a university professor, and Carol, his student, occupy gender-specific identity positions whose differences are exacerbated by disparities of education and class. He is a successful father, husband, scholar, breadwinner; she is a young, lower-middle-class, female student. While no indicators of cultural power or material wealth attach to her, he is set to accept tenure and buy a house. The ideological subtext of the opening configuration of characters on stage is telling: a young woman seeks guidance from her older male professor. The male professor represents the institution of the university, a sign of cultural authority to which his gender has always enjoyed access and that women like his student have only very recently entered. This institution, a muscular instrument of the phallocratic order, stands behind him, defines and underwrites his authority over his students.

Emissaries from disparate areas of the culture, these characters speak different languages. Early in the play Carol struggles to make herself understood, as her language seems not to signify clearly to her masculine professor. Likewise, and more problematic for Carol, she finds her professor's rhetoric impenetrable. For example, the following exchange typifies the dialogue of the first act, much of which concerns Carol's difficulty with John's language:

> Carol: The *language*, the "things" that you say . . .
> John: I'm sorry. No. I don't think that that's true.
> Carol: It *is* true.
> John: . . .I . . .
> Carol: Why would I . . . ? (6–7)

The conversation continues in the familiar staccato of two people not hearing one another as Carol attempts to articulate the ideological differences between herself and her teacher, which, she correctly intuits, account for their failure of communication:

> Carol: I it *is* true. I have *problems* . . .
> John: . . . every . . .
> Carol: . . . I come from a different *social* . . .
> John: . . . ev . . .
> Carol: a different economic . . .
> John: . . . Look:
> Carol: No. I: when I *came* to this school:
> John: Yes. Quite . . . (Pause)
> Carol: . . . does that mean nothing . . . ? (7–8)

This exchange enacts the ideological and semantic differences Carol tries to describe to John. But his constant interruptions demonstrate a lack of real interest in this student and ensure that he will not understand what she says.

John rejects Carol's description of her own experience out of hand: "No. I don't think that's true," he says. He barrels forward in the conversation, ignoring what she says, impervious to her needs and finally punctuates the discussion of her performance by reading from her work. Inviting Carol to sit for the first time, John reads: "'I think that the ideas contained in this work express the author's feelings in a way that he intended, based on his results'" (8). Cruelly, he reads her work as if he does not understand it. John's performance demonstrates Carol's failure of language and underlines his own success, for he knows that she has read—

and not understood—his book. John controls language from both sides, then: enough to see how badly Carol uses it and so well that his own rhetoric is codified in a published book Carol fails to comprehend. Having established authority over the primary mechanism of communication between them, John invites Carol to explain herself. "What can that mean?" he asks.

One critical response to John's rhetorical aggression against this student has been to claim that "Carol's place [in the drama] . . . could as easily be taken by a male" (MacLeod 204). Such a claim suggests that the relationship on stage between teacher and student is not inflected with gender politics, that in fact we need not consider the gender identity of either character when interrogating this work, and that the play tells the same story with either a male or a female student. I disagree. Male and female characters are not interchangeable on the Western stage; representations of masculine and feminine identity are not ideologically equivalent there. For example, unlike male characters, female characters are held "accountable to male-defined standards for acceptable display" by the "genderized terms of the performance space" (Dolan 62). If we identify theater as a cultural artifact, as a construct deriving from and reflecting the ideological biases of the culture that produces it, then nothing on stage can be read as "value-free," or ideologically neutral, least of all relations between men and women (Austin 76).

Language on stage acquires significance through (among other factors) the gender of the speaker(s) and auditor(s); culturally constructed (and heterosexist) notions of gender roles permeate dialogue on stage. Therefore when John explains his willingness to spend extra time with Carol by telling her "I like you," and cryptically assuring her, "There's no one here but you and me," it seems obvious to note that these lines would necessarily signify differently if they were spoken to a male student (27). The assurance that they are alone might actually comfort a masculine student; indeed, in this case, such an assurance contains the possibility of a kind of conspiratorial relationship between teacher and student, a relationship galvanized by a shared (if unacknowledged) gender prerogative. On the other hand, up to this point in the play John has been at pains to enact for Carol the cultural and ideological prerogatives he enjoys and she does not share. By additionally highlighting their isolation, the masculine professor (even if inadvertently) underscores the female student's vulnerability.

Violence on stage between a man and a woman amplifies gender issues; likewise, gender inflects the language of physical violence. Violence committed by a male character against a female character will invariably expose ideological attitudes toward gender roles. Think, for example, of the visual difference between Stanley's attack on Blanche in Williams' *A Streetcar Named Desire* and Max exchanging blows with Joey and Sam in Pinter's *The Homecoming*. These expressions of character relationships signify quite differently. Blanche finds herself in genuine danger; the biological difference between male and female physical strength and the history of violence against women in patriarchy underwrite her interaction with Stanley, and point to rape as the final outcome. Conversely, the men in *The Homecoming* do not so much threaten one another as perpetuate the hierarchy of the household through physical, though largely impotent, force. The masculinist technology of the theater figures a woman on stage with a man as always already a (potential) victim of masculine aggression. The stage constructs woman as a passive indicator of masculine prerogative and consistently offers her as a potential sacrifice to the men on stage, a sacrifice masculine characters may or may not enact through the physically aggressive behavior patriarchy reserves for men.

Further, because the stage defines woman primarily in terms of her sexual function within a heterosexual coupling (women are identified primarily as wives, mothers, or whores), violence against women always contains the threat of sexual violence. For within the phallocratic system of representation and narrative theater, women "always bear the mark and meaning of their sex, which inscribes them within a cultural hierarchy" as a weaker object vulnerable to a stronger subject (Dolan 63). Moreover, woman functions as the site at which masculine anxieties over power and gender are relieved through physical, and often sexualized, violence. Certainly this is the case in Mamet's *Oleanna*. When in the final moments of the play John says, "*Rape you* . . . ? Are you kidding me . . . ? I wouldn't touch you with a ten-foot pole," he embraces the regressive notion of rape as a sex act based on erotic desire (79). He also seems to believe that by simply denying an erotic investment in his student, he can ignore the possibility of sexual violence between them. In fact, John does not rape Carol, but when he concludes the diatribe with, "You little *cunt* . . . ," John conflates his violent act(s) into a final blow against Carol's sexuality, reducing her to a crass anatomical reference and moving his beating of Carol closer to sexual violence (79).

The stage constructs its own "Woman," a fiction whose meaning derives from a discrete lexicon of signs specific to theatrical representation and virtually without reference to actual biological women. She is, as Jill Dolan puts it, "laden with connotations" deriving largely from external signs, or display. On stage man acts, "woman" means (52). The shift in Carol's costume in the original production of *Oleanna* underscores the stage's requirement for exterior indicators of female identity; in order to signify Carol's transformation between acts 1 and 2, the actress emerges in the second act visually altered, dressed in that conventional and highly recognizable indicator of acquired power: a severe, mannish suit. Mamet's text simultaneously transforms this character through an exaggerated and implausible shift in rhetorical skill. In act 1 she is hesitant, apprehensive, and inarticulate. She speaks in simple sentences: "There are *people* out there. People who came *here.* To know something they didn't *know.* Who *came* here. To be *helped"* (12). In act 2 Carol deploys an aggressive, almost pedantic, vocabulary in service to a suddenly sophisticated wit:

> And you speak of the tenure committee, one of whose members is a woman, as you know. And though you might call it Good Fun, or An Historical Phrase, or An Oversight, or All of the Above, to refer to the committee as Good Men and True, it is a demeaning remark. It is a sexist remark, and to overlook it is to countenance continuation of that method of thought. (51)

Still, the most obvious indicator of Carol's political transformation between acts resides in an unmistakable change in her appearance, suggesting that the transformation of her character is most felicitously communicated as a visual alteration. In this case, the visual marks of her character shift—a movement from demure, deferential good girl to angry woman—signify her behavior as threatening to the masculine authority to which her clothing refers.

Typically, dramatic portrayals of women rely upon a heterosexist notion of gender as a binary construct in which men and women occupy oppositional and mutually exclusive positions. Also mutually defining, these binaries reflect cultural stereotypes of gendered behavior: active male/passive female; strong/weak; subject/object; dominant/submissive. Recent work in feminist film theory interrogates this notion of stable, gendered identity positions in the specular arts, and argues that representations of gender are not so pat, and that audiences do not necessarily experience them as stable. However, Mamet's theater relies on static, oppositional notions of gender for its characterizations of John and Carol. Within the world of the play, the university is defined as an all-male system: male professor, male Tenure Committee. (One woman sits on this committee, a fact John consistently fails to acknowledge.) In fact, every authority figure to which John refers is masculine (the Committee, himself, and Jerry, his lawyer). The marginal, or secondary, characters who seek instruction from John are female (Carol and his wife, Grace). Mamet creates John's image on stage at the expense of the female characters around him. The play contains three clearly recognizable stereotypes of female behavior: an emotionally needy wife who depends upon her husband to conduct the "business" of the relationship; a hysterical student; and a castrating feminist. The women serve as weaker, less educated, less successful examples against which the audience is invited to judge John.

Herb Blau describes theater as "an ideological act in its own right," which "involves questions of property, ownership, authority, force," and I would add gender to this list (qtd. in Dolan 41). For "property, ownership, authority, force" describe the issues that dominate gender relations on stage and inform ideological readings of those relations. Blau's list provides much of the germinal vocabulary required to discuss the exchange of women in patriarchal culture and the manner in which dramatic representation repeats and reiterates that exchange. On the conventional stage, women generally function as property owned and exchanged by men, constrained to that role by the authority of the masculinist technology of the theater.

Carol functions not as property per se, but rather as an object at the mercy of the two masculine forces in the work, as the sacrifice central to the power struggle her resistance instigates. Indeed, John's tenure comes into doubt, not when he publishes and teaches a book that openly questions the value of his profession and potentially belittles his colleagues, but when a troublesome female student refuses to be dismissed. The plot situates the Tenure Committee as the enforcer of the patriarchal status quo, as a validating mechanism that will either galvanize John's cultural identity or destroy him. This power derives from the Committee's apparent ability to grant with tenure a host of signifiers of masculine bourgeois success, and to formally inscribe John within the ideological center (where he will enjoy authority, influence, and security) or condemn him to the margins. His efforts to appease Carol after she presents her grievances against him are in fact efforts to reconcile himself with the Tenure Committee, for he recognizes its function as the source of his institutional and cultural authority. Earlier in the play he describes the tenure process like this: " . . . I go before the Great Tenure Committee, and I have an urge, to *vomit*, to, to, to puke my *badness* on the table, to show them: 'I'm no good. Why would you pick me?'" (23). When Carol assumes that he has already been granted tenure, he corrects her, delineating the Committee's power over him: " . . . they announced it, but they haven't *signed*. . . . 'They might not *sign*' . . . I might not . . . the *house* might not go through . . . Eh? Eh?" (23–24).

Despite his own objections to the tenure process, John advocates the ritual as a necessary one, imposed by "Good Men and True," and endorses the convention of tenure itself as sound (50). Indeed, he confesses that he has been "*covetous*" of tenure (43). This desire—grounded in "The Material"—is in no small part a desire for material security, "A home. A Good Home. To raise my family," he explains (44). John acknowledges here the bourgeois middle-class ethic to which he subscribes, and according to which he has "duties *beyond* the school," duties to "home," which are "of an equal weight" to his own career aspirations (44). Here he explicitly conflates his professional success with his role in the patriarchal family structure, suggesting that the reach and force of the Tenure Committee extend beyond the walls of the university and into the larger culture. Receiving the endorsement of the Tenure Committee would blend John's social and professional ambitions by defining him paradigmatically as both a worthwhile university colleague and a "fundamentally decent man. Loyal to wife and family" (MacLeod 199).

The play positions Carol between the masculine Tenure Committee, then (defined as the keepers of the greater good), and a masculine professor (who would please those men only because they have the power to grant and deny tenure), as a subordinate character who will sustain the negative effects of the convoluted codes of the masculine world around her. Carol will finally be made to stand onstage as the marginalized character (female student in a university defined as a male professor and an all-male committee) whose stereotypical outrage shields the men in the play from the unattractive implications of their own behavior. For example, through Carol the play renders the harassing male professor a victim of an angry female student misguided by an unnamed, but clearly unreasonable, feminist group. And the play effectively screens our view of the Committee; for while these men remain safely offstage, Carol suffers the violence their decision inspires in John.

In its obsessive focus on the potentially corrosive influence of feminism upon the university tradition and the patriarchal family, *Oleanna* aligns itself with the recent backlash against the ostensible rise of liberal politics in the university. Despite the fact that the play is written during a time when women occupy only about ten percent of all full-time faculty positions in American universities, *Oleanna* typifies works exhibiting anxieties regarding the so-called political correctness movement. These anxieties most often manifest themselves in claims of a feminist onslaught against the academy and allegations that a movement toward political correctness offers misguided feminists (like Carol) the opportunity to capriciously derail the careers of male academics (like John), to undermine the traditional values of higher education itself, and to potentially destroy the patriarchal family.

In telling a backlash story, Mamet's play embraces a conservative generic paradigm: American realism. In its "relentless plotting toward the white, middle-class, male privilege," American realism, like *Oleanna*, mystifies its ideological preoccupations through apparently transparent works that tell reassuring and conciliatory stories of the benign wonders of patriarchy (Dolan 85). In the tradition of realistic drama, *Oleanna* portrays a patriarchal family struggling to survive—and relieves anxieties over the family and cultural hegemony by circumscribing troublesome female characters squarely within the patriarchal borders of the stage.

Mamet introduces John's family through a series of one-sided phone calls. The play opens on one of these conversations already in progress. As his student waits quietly in his office, John conducts a tense telephone conversation with his wife, Grace, in which he is consistently impatient and condescending:

> WHY NOW? Is what I'm say. . . . well, that's why I say "call Jerry." Well, I can't right now, be . . . no, I *didn't* schedule any . . . Grace:
> I *didn't* . . . I'm well aware . . . Look: Look. Did you call Jerry? Will you call Jerry . . . ? Because I can't now. (1–2)

Staging the conversation from John's point of view, Mamet conveys the image of a harried husband whose wife must be chaperoned through (protected from?) the complexities of a real estate transaction. John's broken sentences suggest that his wife speaks quickly and nervously on the other end of the phone; John can barely finish a sentence, cannot seem to keep her attention. He interrupts her as if she were a child who cannot be made to listen: "Grace: I didn't," he insists and then must stop her again (because she has apparently not stopped talking) with "Look: Look." John's dependent and demanding wife refuses even to simply "call Jerry" (1).

If we can believe what we hear, John and his wife are in genuine danger of losing the house they hope to buy, she has phoned for help, and he plays the role of rescuing patriarch. John assumes that he can attend to his troubled student in "ten or fifteen" minutes, then arrive in time to rescue the house for his wife and their son. Evoking the infantilizing stereotype of the housebound wife incapable of understanding the world beyond the borders of her domestic space, Mamet characterizes Grace without placing her on stage or giving her a voice. John tells her what to do: have the realtor show her the basement again (an inconsequential activity meant to delay the realtor until he, the brains of the family, arrives), and call Jerry (a man who can stand in for her husband in the meantime). Grace does not determine on her own what to do and is apparently unqualified in John's (or her own) eyes of doing anything meaningful. During these conversations John inhabits an anachronistic caricature of the professional husband who must attend—unassisted—to the family's material comforts and whose wife demands from him emotional security he himself does not need or even comprehend, but which, like the weekly paycheck, he delivers: "I love you, too," he says, "I love you, too" (2).

We learn later that the real estate emergency has been fabricated by John's wife and friends in order to lure him to a surprise party celebrating his promotion. Significantly, these circumstances do not alter Mamet's characterization of Grace as a clinging, passive wife. For later in act 3, when she apparently has no reason to plan a surprise party, Grace continues to interrupt John demanding reassurance. Still reeling from the news that Carol has brought charges of rape against him, John answers the phone and begins the now familiar litany of assurances: "No, no, it's going to be all right," he promises (79). Throughout the play John reveals himself to be utterly the product of a bourgeois world of gendered hierarchies. With John, his wife, and "the boy," Mamet creates a stereotypical nuclear family in which the father dominates the mother and child. The role of the father in this case is to provide material comfort; in exchange he enjoys validation from the community and control of the home. Rounding out this fantasy is John's son, "the boy." John plans to purchase a nice house for his son, send him to private school and, most importantly, hand down to this child his influence, success and name.

Hence, John's outrage when confronted with the possibility that his book may be "removed from inclusion as a representative example of the university"—in exchange for which Carol will drop her complaint against him (75). John finds Carol's demand that his book be banned particularly disturbing, and considers it a violation not just of his academic freedom, but also of his responsibilities to his profession and his son. His "name" appears on that book, John explains with emotion, and his "son will *see* that *book* someday" (76). As a text that formally inscribes his name in a longstanding tradition of academic writing, John's book serves as a kind of intellectual progeny. This assault on his rights as a father cannot be tolerated, and at this point in the play John begins moving toward violence. He decides that Carol is "dangerous" and that it is his job "to say no" to her, to stop her and her undefined "Group" (72).

When Carol first arrives unannounced on this day in John's life she functions as a blocking figure standing between John and his goals. As the play progresses her threat to John escalates; at first only tenure seems to be at risk, then the house, then John's career, then, with the accusation of rape, his freedom. When Carol's power to threaten him can no longer be denied in act 3, John is speechless with surprise. He could not have imagined such a complete reversal of roles. Initially, John behaves with unshakable arrogance and responds to Carol with contemptuous condescension. He initiates their dialogue by belittling her. When, after overhearing him use the phrase on the phone, she asks, "What is a 'term of art?'" he snaps in response, "Is that what you want to talk about?" (2–3). She is confused (it is an innocuous question), and he continues bitterly, asking her a question she cannot answer, "Let's take the mysticism out of it, shall we?" (3). Deliberately exacerbating her feelings of isolation and embarrassment, John punctuates his attack with a direct address— "Carol?"—and makes very clear who controls the space they share; it is his office, and he speaks a language she does not fully understand.

John does not resist the temptation presented by this unscheduled meeting to test (and flex) the boundaries of his authority. Inhabiting his space comfortably, John suggests a dimwitted, although ostensibly radical, reorganization of his course: if Carol agrees to return to his office for private lessons, he will give her an "A" for the class. He explains his motivation by disingenuously taking the blame for Carol's confusion: "I'm going to say it was not you, it was I who was not paying attention" (25). Rather than throwing off the hierarchical confines of the teacher-student relationship, or liberating himself and Carol from the power dynamic inherent in any relationship like it, John reinscribes himself squarely within a new configuration of precisely the same power hierarchy. John might as well say to Carol, "I'll create new rules, and they will reinvent the same relationship (based on class and gender) that ensures my dominance and your submission." Couched in the language of "certain privileged forms of discourse" specific to academe (MacLeod 203), John's plan reveals that his true desires are in fact pedestrian and self-serving: to keep the student in her place and to escape an unpleasant meeting quickly.

John's glib and ill-conceived offer to throw off the "Artificial *Stricture*" of student and teacher, then, belies his own confidence in those very labels to protect his position (21). (Earlier John exposes the lie of his ostensible efforts to dissolve the hierarchical boundaries of the traditional classroom when he thanks Carol for her "obeisance" in coming to his office.) Having made his offer to modify the class, John immediately launches a dissertation on the politics of education and his own psychosocial experience not only with public education but also with Western epistemology—a discussion Carol cannot be expected to understand and which in its insistence on the gap between their personal and professional experiences reiterates the power structure implicit in the "Artificial Stricture[s]" of student and teacher.

In a gesture toward balancing the distribution of power between them, John offers Carol this personal anecdote:

> I used to speak of "real people," and wonder what the *real* people did. The *real* people. Who were they? *They* were the people other than my-

self. The *good* people. The *capable* people. The people who could do the
things, I could not do: learn, study, retain . . . all that *garbage* . . . (16)

In other words, John experienced his own intellectual failure, managed to
become a college professor and now privately shares his conviction that
the very thing he demands of Carol and his other students—that they
"learn, study, retain"—is garbage. Can this be the lesson he hopes to teach
this student? John's unhip and avuncular attempts at iconoclasm merely
highlight how unlike his student he really is: his days of raging against the
machine are far behind him. He now aspires to a kind of triumph of convention as he works to please the established powers that be in exchange
for tenure. Indeed, if Carol and his other students actually embraced the
notions of higher education espoused by John here, he would have no
chance at the hyperconventional life in the suburbs with his wife and son
that tenure will facilitate.

Nevertheless, John speaks of his obligation as an educator in the voice
of a dedicated maverick: "What's important," he tells Carol, "is that I
awake your interest, if I can, and that I answer your questions" (26). But
John poses no genuine challenge to the rules of the university or the gender codes of the culture; even as he appears to jettison the rules of the university, John claims absolute authority over the class:

Carol: But we can't start over.
John: *I say* we can. (Pause) *I say* we can.
Carol: But I don't believe it.
John: Yes, I know that. But it's true. (26, my emphasis)

John essentially ignores Carol's anxieties over the material, her grades, and
the university and instead secures control over the content, terms, and
form of the course. He determines where and when instruction will take
place and even selects the outcome (an "A"). His breezy response to Carol's
very reasonable objections testifies to a brand of arrogance symptomatic of
a secure identification with culturally sanctioned identity positions.

As a member of the marginal community of female, lower-class students (she includes herself in a group of "hard-working students" who
"slave" to attend the university), Carol is bound by rules that no longer
control John and that he carelessly suggests they ignore. As a student pursuing a degree, Carol must pass John's course. As her professor, John apparently need not even make sense. He instructs Carol as follows:

If I do not want to think of myself as a failure, perhaps I should begin by
succeeding now and again. Look. The tests, you see, which you encounter,

in school, in college, in life, were designed, in the most part, for idiots. *By idiots. There is no need to fail at them.* (22–23)

The lesson: if she wants to stop failing, she should try succeeding instead. Teaching seems to annoy John, even as being a teacher empowers and defines him. He has accepted the inconvenient responsibility of instruction long enough to practice rhetorical aggression against his students and to receive the material reward and social validation represented by tenure, promotion, and the house in which he intends to raise his family. But having come this far, John cannot conceive of any further obligation to his student: " . . . what can I do . . . ?" he asks Carol; "*Teach* me. *Teach* me," she begs him (11). He never does.

Instead, John retreats into what Marc Silverstein calls "the ideological rhetoric of the 'human'" both in the first act, when he redefines the terms of their relationship, and later, when he struggles to control Carol and to defend himself (110). For example, in act 2 John explains the value of "convention" as "the essence of all human communication" (53). He argues that conventions allow the two of them, despite their differences, to "agree that we are both human," and in this human sameness he hopes to discover the means to resolve their conflict—namely, persuading her to drop the complaint against him (53). John ignores the obvious political questions of how social conventions are established and who they serve; certainly the conventions of the language have not served Carol, for she understands little of what he says or writes. As I have indicated, the "conventions" of "human communication" to which John has access, and that he deploys in service to his own ideological ends, alienate Carol. Further, John persists in ignoring the discrepancies of power inherent in relationships between masculine professors and female students and prefers to argue blandly that he and Carol simply have "positions" and "desires" that are in conflict (53).

But when Carol forces him into an explicitly political argument, John's disingenuously nonideological rhetoric fails him, and he resorts to physical force (as he will again later in the play): "*He restrains her from leaving*" his office (57). As this and the final violent moments of the play demonstrate, the stage serves masculine dominance. Although the plot punishes John for his treatment of Carol, the visual argument of the play celebrates John's power over Carol. *Oleanna* ends with a stark image of female submission to masculine dominance. Mamet's stage instructions emphasize that, as she "*starts to leave the room,*" John "*grabs her and begins to beat her,*" and the curtain falls as Carol cowers below John, vulnerable to his next violent act (79).

Disguised as a discourse questioning the power structure of the university, Mamet's play in fact indulges in the mystifying rhetoric of patriarchy that, rather than questioning cultural norms, consolidates power around masculine identity and the ideological center. Even John (or Mamet?) cannot sustain the fiction of equality between himself and his female student for more than a line or two, for just as he argues, "we're both human," he also explains that while he and Carol "are two people," they have "subscribed to . . . certain *arbitrary* . . . Certain *institutional*" notions of the university (10, my emphasis). John acknowledges here, inadvertently but unmistakably, that he and Carol occupy arbitrarily constructed identity positions: teacher and student. Moreover, he acknowledges that these positions have been constructed by the institution of the university, the institution that supports him and his family and grants him authority over students.

Like individual men in patriarchal culture, John stands as a kind of symptom of the masculinist ideology guiding his identity and behavior. His connection to an unnamed, unseen force—the Tenure Committee—that confers power based on one's relationship to it imitates the role of patriarchal authority in Western culture. That is to say that by occupying the appropriate identity position, both within the university and without, John enjoys security and privilege that Carol does not. We see this discrepancy very clearly in the opening of the play. On the phone John displays arrogant confidence that what he believes he deserves as a member of the masculine bourgeois world will be his (the house), and Carol does not even understand what he is talking about.

Always present but invisible to Carol, the Tenure Committee stands behind John as the mechanism that reifies his identity as the natural provider of grades and class credit and underwrites her role as the submissive facilitator of his identity. Like dominant ideology, the Tenure Committee, through its tacit power over the members of the faculty it polices, influences the behavior of the group's individual members, and inspires (if not determines) their ideological standards. In order to receive material and professional advancement, John enacts the Committee's approved notions of academic identity. This ideological imposition masquerades in John's career as academic freedom and disguises a collusive relationship as the diverse reality of university life. He writes, for example, an apparently iconoclastic book, but even as he criticizes the institution, he subscribes to the established conventions for acquiring increased status within that institution: he publishes a scholarly book.

An important component of academic identity in *Oleanna* includes the appearance of autonomy and independent thinking, which John's ostensible radicalism is meant to imply. Imported from the world of masculine violence, this academic bravado finally takes the form of arrogant intellectual aggression enacted against a female student. But John remains emphatically within the parameters of acceptable behavior sanctioned by the dominant university culture; hence, his comfort with standard conventions and his approval for tenure and promotion. John merely stages a resistance to the status quo, feigns an attempt to undermine the paternal powers that be, while in fact seeking out the security of that position for himself. For example, he claims a disdain for the revered Tenure Committee, members of which he "wouldn't employ to wax [his] car" (23), and in his book accuses the institution they represent of not educating, but of the "Virtual warehousing [of] . . . the young," and of being "something-other-than-useful" (11, 28). Still, laying even problematic or ambivalent claim to an association with the central authority of the university perpetuates that association, and John continues to enjoy a comfortable identity position by siphoning off ideological power from the center.

Mirroring the totalizing mechanism of power relations in patriarchy, John's vexed relations with the Tenure Committee are repaired through the oppression of a member of a marginalized group. In this case, his female student. This oppression reinforces John's cultural authority and, as it is implicitly sanctioned by the Committee, reinvigorates his relations to the powerful center. Creating a circuit of exchange in which power constantly returns to those who already have it, John, the Tenure Committee, and the university all affect a general offer of access that is false, and that has treacherous effects on the female character who takes the bait.

Believing she enjoys equal access to the rhetoric and instruments of the university, Carol dares to challenge her professor's authority by rightly objecting to his treatment of her—and essentially leads herself to the slaughter. Aligning herself with his colleagues, she prematurely claims victory over John:

> Your superiors, who've been "polled," do you see? To whom *evidence* has been presented, who have *ruled*, do you see? Who have weighed the testimony and the evidence, and have *ruled*, do you see? That you are *negligent . . . guilty . . . wanting*, and in *error* . . . (63–64)

What she fails to realize during these moments late in the play is that the vast misogynist tradition of patriarchy stands behind her masculine professor and ensures his dominant place not only as a professor with a student, but, more important, as a man in a closed room (his office) with a woman. That tradition allows him to treat her disrespectfully, to "be personal" with her, to touch her, to offer her a better grade in exchange for more frequent visits, and, finally, to beat her.

Behind this female character, who the playwright seems at pains to render unsympathetic, John and the Tenure Committee hide their convoluted power struggle. And David Mamet disguises a vicious misogynist fantasy in a weak argument against political correctness, that meaningless phrase popularly used as code to disguise, among other things, misogyny. The final moments of the play emphatically reiterate masculine authority on stage. No matter what havoc Carol has visited upon John, he finally dominates her unequivocally, and in a paradigmatically masculine style— through violence against her. He forces her to the ground, where she acknowledges her final defeat, head bowed and "*To herself*": " . . . yes. That's right" (80).

Yes. That's right. In this play the relationship between a masculine professor and his feminine student imitates gender roles in patriarchy, in fact, reiterates the power discrepancy inherent in those roles. Yes. That's right. As a woman on stage, Carol sutures relations between powerful men and is punished for attempting to step outside that role. Yes. That's right. On Mamet's stage, like on many others, woman suffers the violence inspired by the power struggles between men.

WORKS CITED

Austin, Gayle. *Feminist Theories for Dramatic Criticism.* Ann Arbor: U of Michigan P, 1990.

Dolan, Jill. *The Feminist Spectator as Critic.* Ann Arbor: UMI Research Press, 1988.

MacLeod, Christine. "The Politics of Gender, Language and Hierarchy in Mamet's *Oleanna.*" *Journal of American Studies* 29 (1995): 199–213.

Mamet, David. *Oleanna.* New York: Vintage Books, 1992.

Silverstein, Marc. "'We're Just Human': *Oleanna* and Cultural Crisis." *South Atlantic Review* 60 (1995): 103–19.

WOMEN ON THE VERGE, UNITE!

KAREN C. BLANSFIELD

David Mamet is, by all accounts, a man's playwright. Actresses long-ing to sink their teeth into visceral roles like Lady Macbeth, Blanche DuBois, and Hedda Gabler do not generally turn for inspiration to America's foremost macho playwright, whose milieu runs the gamut of pool halls, porn theaters, cheap bars, Hollywood offices, and other tradi-tionally male arenas, and whose characters do "guy" things: curse, gamble, cheat, wheel and deal. By and large, women in Mamet's plays have been peripheral at best and absent at worst, with their occasional presence rel-egated to inherently subordinate relationships such as father/daughter or teacher/student.

Clearly, Mamet's is a man's world. Simon Trussler notes that at a time when "many male dramatists are concerned to recognize the insights of feminism, Mamet is unusual in his complementary rather than contra-dictory concern with the significance of male bonding," and he acknowl-edges that the playwright is "very much his own man, for whom *being* a man in the late twentieth century presents special challenges and prob-lems" (6). This proclivity has escaped neither notice nor criticism, rang-ing from those who accuse Mamet of being a misogynist, to those who acknowledge his limitations—Esther Harriott, for instance, notes simply that the playwright's "acute ear has not been tuned in to women" (67)—to those who deplore Mamet's inability to portray women accurately. Betty Caplan charges that "Mamet's notion of gender is so rigid [that] . . . he is prevented from seeing the wider issues"; still, she ac-knowledges that "in the end, it has to be said that Mamet pays women an appalling, underhand compliment. He finds the Gorgon too daunting to contemplate" (35).

Mamet readily admits that he doesn't "*know* anything about women"; he says that when he realized "*they* are people too . . . ," he also recognized they must "have thoughts and feelings too." And, he adds wryly, he spent "the last twenty-five years trying to figure out what those thoughts and feelings *are*" (*A Whore's Profession* 240). With his professed affiliation between gender and content, Mamet could be the darling of the politically correct faction. "Well, I happen to be a man," he says. "Claire Booth Luce wrote a wonderful play about women, which *I* couldn't write, not being a woman" (qtd. in Harriott 84). In some respects, Mamet is merely a pragmatist; as he said in a *New York Times* interview, "I'm more around men; I listen to more men being candid than women being candid" (qtd. in Radavich 123). In short, Mamet writes about what he knows. Certainly the absence of women from Mamet's world is conspicuous, and certainly this absence helps to define that world. And whether present or not, women do tend to be ill-regarded, generally cast into such deplorable roles as "cunts" and "whores."

Yet for all their marginality, women wield a strange and startling power in Mamet's plays, for they are central to the men's images of themselves, to their sense of power—or lack of it. Women are feared and mistrusted; they can disrupt the male bonding that is the lifeblood of Mamet's characters. Their absence, as Christopher Bigsby points out, "underscores the emptiness" of the frontier myth of masculine self-sufficiency and also helps account for the sterility and hardness of Mamet's world (15). In their rare appearances, women are able, with little or no effort, to undercut the male's shaky or self-inflated ego. This power is evident from early Mamet plays, such as *Sexual Perversity in Chicago* (1974) and *American Buffalo* (1975), through the later *Edmond* (1982).[1] In subsequent plays, women gain increasingly central and more powerful positions in Mamet's tough world, elbowing in on power plays and business deals. In both *House of Games* (1985) and *Speed-the-Plow* (1988), women penetrate "two of the most macho sanctuaries in American culture" (Hall 137) to become "players," and even if they lose in the end, they nevertheless disrupt the balance of the men's world to some degree, though not without cost: they become disillusioned, like Karen, or acquire the man's ruthless tactics, like Margaret Ford. In fact, the cool ending of *House of Games* recalls that of Robert Altman's *The Player*, in that both murderers go free.

I

Sexual Perversity in Chicago is virtually a testimonial to the power of the female in Mamet. The blowhard Bernie Lithko apparently has little more to do in life than prognosticate about his imaginary and outlandish sexual exploits to his friend Danny, who may or may not believe him. Indeed, these macho fantasies, in which of course Bernie always triumphs, seem to be his sole raison d'être in an otherwise pathetically empty life, and when he encounters any real relationship with the opposite sex, he's exposed to his own vulnerabilities. In fact, when his suave pick-up lines to a woman in a bar are rejected, he erupts:

> So just who the fuck do you think you are, God's gift to Women? I mean where do you fucking get off with this shit. You don't want to get come on to, go enroll in a convent. You think I don't have better things to do? I don't have better ways to spend my off hours than to listen to some nowhere cunt try out cute bits on me? I mean why don't you just clean your fucking act up, Missy. You're living in a city in 1976. (56)

As Bigsby observes, Bernie's "derisive metonym is his attempt to contain the threat posed by women who can so easily destroy his self-image" (46–47). Moreover, for Danny to establish a serious relationship with a woman is also threatening, as it disrupts Bernie's own hold over his friend. Deborah's power to come between Danny and Bernie, though not intentional, is evident when Bernie asks Dan, "So what are we doing tomorrow, we going to the beach?" and Dan replies, "I'm seeing Deborah." While Bernie won't admit his own jealousy and resentment, he subtly attempts to undermine the developing relationship with seemingly innocuous comments such as, "You're seeing a lot of this broad. You getting serious? But what the fuck, that's your business. Right?" (63).

A similar power play exists between the women, as Joan's insidious influence upon Deborah suggests. Like Bernie, she resents her friend's budding romance, and she poisons Deb's optimism with tales of her own failed relationships, her curt treatment of Dan, and her snide remarks, such as, when Deb leaves to move in with Dan, "I give you two months" (67). In fact, this whole quartet seems to be caught in a vicious circle: Deborah has the power to disrupt and probably destroy Bernie's bond with Dan; Bernie subtly molds Dan into his cynical image—to the point where Dan appropriates Bernie's language ("cunt," "Missy," etc.)—and thus infects this blooming relationship; Joan exerts a similar power over Deb, poisoning the waters for Deb and Dan, while Dan seems to get the wrong end of the stick all around. The result is a disruption of any real intimacy or potential familial bond. In the end, Bernie and Dan are back at the beach, gawking at babes and shoring up their own pathetic egos with brawny, crude comments. Stephen Gale cites the theme of *Sexual Perversity* as the "fear of trusting the opposite sex," a fear that of course cuts both ways in this play. Gale notes that Bernie's desire for a relationship with a woman is curtailed by his fear of rejection and his experience "that he cannot trust them" (210–11); Bernie projects this sensibility onto Dan, and Joan projects the same onto Deb. Although Deborah acts as a kind of "force of virtue," representing "Danny's one true hope for a non-perverse relationship," this short-lived salvation is destroyed by the fear of both their "friends"—who are oblivious to the destruction they have wrought (Skeele 516).

The woman's power to provoke profound change in male self-perception and behavior, as seen in Bernie's reaction to Joan, is also evident in *American Buffalo*, although no women actually appear on stage. As Teach first enters the junk shop in act 1, he's muttering, "Fuckin' Ruthie, fuckin' Ruthie, fuckin' Ruthie, fuckin' Ruthie, fuckin' Ruthie," like some primal chant (9). When Don asks what is wrong, Teach rants about an episode that had just occurred in a coffee shop: sitting down next to Ruthie and her friend Grace, Teach had picked up a piece of her toast, prompting Ruthie's sarcastic remark, "Help yourself." Or at least Teach interprets the remark as sarcasm:

Help myself.

I should help myself to half a piece of toast it's four slices for a quarter. I should have a nickel every time we're over at the game, I pop for coffee . . . cigarettes . . . a *sweet roll*, never say word. (10)

Teach continues to vent his wrath, calling Ruthie "a Southern bulldyke asshole ingrate of a vicious nowhere cunt," blowing the issue hugely out of proportion and accusing her of deliberately hurting him (11). "There is not one loyal bone in that bitch's body," he growls (14). Yet when Don sends Bob over to the coffee shop for breakfast, Teach says to "tell him he shouldn't say anything to Ruthie," as though he's fearful that her finding out about his reaction will only lower him further in her estimation, or maybe spark a confrontation he fears he will only lose (13). The big talker who's boastful in front of his buddies can only stifle his rage in the face of "that bitch."

Perhaps Teach is prone to overreaction: certainly, as Dennis Carroll points out, Teach regards everybody as an adversary, a paranoia illustrated by his exchange with Ruthie (35); and no doubt, as Gale argues, Teach's anger "really masks his feelings about Bob" and his jealousy over the "newly emerging relationship between Bob and Don" (213). Nevertheless, it's revealing that in a play so indisputably male-dominated, the person who acts as the catalyst for Teach's suppressed rage should be female. Teach's outbreak, like Bernie's tirade when Joan coolly rejects his advances, suggests how threatened he is by a woman getting "one up" on him. For both Bernie and Teach, denigrating women offers a means of asserting their own significance and power, of reinforcing their own sadly sagging egos. The fact that women elicit such reactions with no effort indicates just how powerful they are—or are perceived to be—and how insecure the men are. More than misogyny is at work here, and the issue of the woman's real power remains unresolved as long as that power is linked to her perceiver's insecurity, which, at its deepest level, is self-loathing. If the male were secure in his sense of identity, would the female's apparent power then dissolve?

Edmond, in the play of the same title, offers another illustration of this responsive mode, though perhaps in a more complex way.[2] In scene 13 (of the play's 23 scenes), Edmond comments to a woman on the subway that her hat is similar to one his mother had. Understandably, given the threatening nature of urban environments, the woman walks away. But Edmond's reaction to this seeming rejection is as unbalanced and frightening as Bernie's and Teach's: he explodes, resorting to foul, insulting language and even physically accosting her:

> . . . who the fuck do you think you *are?* . . . I'm *talking* to you . . . What am I? A *stone?* . . . Did I say, "I want to lick your pussy? . . ." I said, "My mother had that same hat . . ." You *cunt* . . . What am I? A *dog?* I'd like to slash your fucking *face* . . . I'd like to slash your motherfucking *face* apart. . . . (58)

What warrants such a tinder-box response, such an obsessive need to dominate or at least not be dismissed? Again, as with Teach, it is a woman responding normally who inadvertently provokes a rage long suppressed, revealing a man desiring power but feeling powerless and victimized, an anger only exacerbated by an association with his mother that adds a Freudian dimension.

This scene is a pivotal moment in the play, coming approximately halfway through and foreshadowing the actual knifing of Glenna. The scene marks a dramatic shift from Edmond's naïve passivity to his reckless attempts at gaining control of his life. Consider the events that lead up to this scene. Edmond leaves his wife, prompted at least partly by the machinations of a female fortune-teller who says, "You are not where you belong"; he is befriended in a bar by a fellow who listens to him and pays for his drink; when Edmond tries to do the same for a B-girl in the Allegro bar, she rejects him because he doesn't have enough money; he is subsequently cheated at the peep show, where he is trying to make some kind of human contact, at the three-card monte street game, at the whorehouse that he learns of through the pamphlet distributed by a hawker, and at the hotel, where he can't even make a phone call and where

his signs of disintegration are becoming more evident. "Do you want to
live in this kind of world?" he challenges the clerk. "Do you want to live
in a *world* like that? I've been *hurt?* Are you *blind?* Would you appreciate
it if I acted this way to *you?* (*Pause.*) I *asked* you one simple thing. Do they
need a *dime?*" (51).

In the scene following this encounter, Edmond pawns his wedding
ring, a symbolic as well as economically desperate gesture, and—on the
spur of the moment—buys a World War II "survival" knife. Certainly Edmond has found himself in a war zone, the hellish underworld of the city,
and now, armed with a knife, he displays the confidence of the aggressor,
first testing his newfound power and control on the woman in the subway and then on the onlookers, screaming, "Is everybody in this town *insane?* . . . Fuck you . . . fuck the *lot* of you . . . fuck you all . . . I don't need
you . . ." (59). Perhaps his outburst is meant to force some kind of connection with others, though its effect clearly signals his complete isolation. From this point on, Edmond equates control with violent
aggression. When a pimp attempts to mug him, Edmond viciously assaults him, both verbally and physically, probably killing him; in the coffeehouse, he boldly propositions the waitress Glenna, saying, "I want to
fuck you" (67); and finally, in the play's climactic event, he murders her
with his knife in an outbreak of madness, presumably sparked by her refusal to join him in his experience of self-discovery:

> Edmond: Now: I want you to change your life with me. *Right* now, for what-
> *ever* that we can be. *I* don't know what that is, *you* don't know. Speak with
> me. Right now. Say it.
> Glenna: I don't know what you're talking about.
> Edmond: Oh, by the Lord, yes, you do. Say it with me. (76)

Like the woman in the subway, Glenna is naturally terrified at this raving
madman, and her spiraling fear and yelling incurs his panicked retaliation
as she tries to telephone for help. Yet in the end, he blames her for his actions: "You stupid fucking . . . *now* look what you've done. (*Pause*) Now
look what you've bloody fucking done" (78).

Ironically, women have determined Edmond's fate throughout his pathetic quest for self-identity. Although he leaves his wife, a seemingly as-
sertive action, because he doesn't "want to live this kind of life" and she
doesn't interest him "spiritually or sexually" (18, 20), the female fortune
teller also plays a role, telling him, "you are unsure what your place is"
(16). His journey through the urban jungle is charted by satanic females:
the call girl in the Allegro, to whom he says, "I'm putting myself at your
mercy . . . I don't want to be taken advantage of" (27); the spangled leo-

tard-clad girl in the peep show; the whore, to whom Edmond again admits, "I've never done this before," only to be rejected because he can't produce the necessary cash; and finally Glenna, whom he tries to subjugate in order to force some kind of spiritual connection free of crass commercialization, but who paradoxically proves the catalyst for Edmond's imprisonment.

The women in *Edmond* are in the unenviable position of both dominating and being dominated by men, of being the presumed source, according to Edmond, of his unhappiness, yet also the means by which he seeks contentment and understanding. In the end, jailed with a domineering cellmate and subjected to the harsh treatment and name-calling he himself once inflicted, Edmond does discover the peace that he had sought, by becoming his black cellmate's "bitch." Here Edmond finds himself at the other end of the knife, feminized by virtue of his submission, circling back to a parody of the home situation he had left. He finds freedom behind bars, and as the "feminine" partner in this relationship, Edmond has ironically if unknowingly yielded to the ultimate power of the female.

II

In Mamet's later works, women assume more central and powerful roles, although still not as artistically well wrought as his male characters. Margaret Ford, the psychiatrist in *House of Games*, and Karen, the temporary secretary in *Speed-the-Plow*, mark a definitive shift toward front and center for Mamet's females, and one that he will continue in such works as *Oleanna* and *The Cryptogram*.

House of Games, a screenplay based on a story devised by Mamet and his friend Jonathan Katz, traverses the usual Mamet territory of con games and casual deceit, but this time features a woman, Dr. Margaret Ford, as the main character. Though not particularly endearing (but then, what Mamet character is?), Ford is tough, strong, and complex; "much darker," observed critic Jack Kroll, "than the traditional 'Hitchcock victim'" (87). Author of a newly published best-seller, titled *Driven: Compulsion and Obsession in Everyday Life*, Ford is just that: an ambitious, chain-smoking workaholic who deals with a myriad of troubled patients, including a murderess, and whose professional status lends her an authority heretofore not seen in Mamet's females.

Ford does not evoke the sort of emotional outbursts that male characters in other Mamet plays display; rather, she is more on a par with the men in *House of Games* and is, in many respects, made of the same stuff as they are. These men seem more cocky and self-assured; they don't depend on the woman's perception for affirmation of their identity—at least not to the degree or in the manner of Bernie, Teach, and Edmond. However, they do use Ford as a way of flexing their con men muscles and proving their brawny aptitude. In fact, toward the end of the story, they joke about having pulled some of the oldest tricks in the book over on her:

> Businessman: Well, we showed her some con men.
> Mike: We showed her some *Old* style . . .
> Mr. Dean: Yessir . . .
> Mike: Some *Dinosaur* con men. Years from now, they'll have to go to a *museum*, see a frame like this. (62)[3]

In a sense, the tables are turned in *House of Games:* the woman is under the illusion that she wields some kind of power over the men—a consciousness not evident in other plays—and the men do not suffer from insecurities as they do in plays such as *American Buffalo* and *Sexual Perversity.* Yes, they do bond as a bunch of males, and their circle does exclude women, and Ford is still referred to as a "whore" and a "bitch." But it is Ford who pushes them into the arena of violence they claim to have avoided ("*I* never shot anybody," says Mike), and proud as they are of their exploits, Ford does, in the end, have the last word (69).

Ford initially approaches the hangout known as the House of Games to get one of her "friends"—actually one of her clients, Billy Hahn—off the hook for a gambling debt of $25,000. Ford has diagnosed Hahn as a compulsive who "succeeds in establishing a situation where he is out of control" (11); what she *doesn't* know is that Billy's claim is part of the whole setup in which she is about to become enmeshed. What she also doesn't realize at the time is that she is seeking some kind of excitement and change in her own life. Her friend, Dr. Maria Littauer, recognizes this need and encourages her to slow down and "Give *yourself* all those rewards you would like to have" (8). More important, Ford's nemesis, Mike, sizes her up at the outset. As he says at the end of the play, "This is what you always wanted. I knew it the first time you came in. . . . You sought it out" (70). Joe Mantegna, who plays Mike in the film, says in an interview that his character knows Ford "needs something, is searching for something." He says of Mike and Ford, "They are the same person, really. But he tells the truth, she doesn't" (87).

In the initial scene at the House of Games, Ford demonstrates her sense of self-confidence and control in her clothing (she's wearing "jeans and a leather bomber jacket"), in her persistence to see the guy named Mike, and in her tough-talking demands (calling Mike a "bully" and demanding to "talk turkey" with him) (11).[4] "I want you to *listen* to this, 'cause you threatened to kill a *friend* of mine," she says. "And I'm putting you on notice, 'Mike,' that that behavior doesn't go. . . . You aren't going to *do* that because if you do you're going away for Life" (13). Mike informs her that the debt is in fact only $800, not $25,000, and agrees to wipe it out if Ford will help him win a hand by ascertaining whether a fellow player is bluffing. Thus the control has shifted: Ford is now aiding Mike, not realizing this "assistance" is yet another stage in the setup, and she furthermore offers to back up his bet of $6,000. When Mike loses the hand, Ford is writing the check when she abruptly regains control of the situation:

> Ford: You know what? I don't think I'm going to pay you.
> Joey: *Don't* get the guy mad . . . for *heaven's* sake: *don't* get the guy *mad* . . .
> Mike: *Pay* the man.
> Vegas Man: You crazy bitch. Pay me what you *owe* . . .
> *He picks up the revolver. The other men retreat.*
> Ford: No. I don't think I will (*she folds up the check and drops it in her purse*), and I will *tell* you why not: is that *you cannot threaten someone with a Squirtgun!* (24)

This comic touch seems to make fools of these tough guys, but it's obviously a deliberate ploy on their part to gain her trust for yet a bigger heist. Mike is gambling on his instinct that Ford will be back for more; he knows her better than she knows herself. As he says later, when one of the con men asks how he knew Ford would take the bait, "Go for it, the broad's an addict," and he further complains that "The bitch is a born thief" in reporting the loss of his lucky pocket knife (61–62). But at this point in the course of events, Ford still seems in control; before leaving, she demands from Mike the I.O.U. that assures her client is "square" on the bargain, and when Mike asks her who she is, she simply replies, "Thank you for a lovely evening" (27).

If the "game" ended here, there would be no consequences on either side; the script would end mildly, both sides would get something out of the "transaction," and everyone could go home early. But of course there would be no story or insights. It is Ford's deliberate choice to return to the House of Games, ostensibly to write a book about the confidence racket, that catapults the plot forward and ironically ensures her own commitment to and entrapment in the setup. That choice, an uncommon assertion for one of Mamet's females, reveals her own need to be drawn into a different, more sinister world, a need not unlike Edmond's, and with similarly dire consequences. Like Edmond, Ford has begun to question her own life—seeing it as "a sham, a con game," and herself as impotent when it comes to helping her patients (30). Furthermore, the implication through her Freudian slips around Maria ("pressures" instead of "pleasures," "my father" instead of "her father") is that Ford subconsciously regards herself as a whore thanks to her father, so she sets out to fulfill that role and thus conquer it (8, 30).

Having already prostituted herself by unwittingly conspiring with Mike in his con game, Ford symbolically consummates this illicit relationship that same night. At her apartment, "*dressed in a chaste flannel nightgown*" and having just finished a cup of tea, Ford gets into bed, then picks up the House of Games chip that Mike had given her as "A souvenir of your close escape from con men" (25–28). She "*gives a big belly laugh . . .* [and] *snuggles down into the bed*" (28). Later, of course, Ford literally consummates the relationship, responding to Mike's blunt inquiry, "Do you want to make love to me?" by blushing—a clear indication of her desires. "*That's* a tell," says Mike. "The things we want, we can do them or not do them, but we can't hide them" (38). But she has hidden them from herself, until Mike forces her to confront them. He asserts that she wants "someone to come along, to take you into a new thing. Do you want that? Would you like that?" Ford replies, softly, "Yes" (38).

But whether acknowledging her desires or not, Ford has already acted on them. She alone makes the decision to return to the House of Games, rejecting a respectable dinner invitation to do so, and she initiates the involvement with Mike when she says, "I've got a *proposition* for you" (33). Although her scholarly pose is noble, her explicit sexual terminology betrays her true desires, and Mike is not fooled. Even though she deludes herself into believing she is keeping an objective, authoritative distance, she has in fact sold herself for a sordid pleasure she refuses to acknowledge. When she realizes that she has been taken, she literally recoils, and then, like a snake, lashes out with a fatal blow. In the film version, this moment of recognition occurs behind a "frame" of decorative pillars at the tavern, through which Ford is peering down at her betrayers.

As in other Mamet plays, the woman's power in *House of Games* is ambiguous. In one sense, Ford does disrupt the tight male bond with her intrusion, bringing violence with her. But this intrusion is temporary as the men continually regroup, like a horde of flies hovering over some clump of filth. In another sense, Ford permanently breaks up the group and retains the upper hand by killing Mike, a final and unquestionable assertion of control. She also commandeers the male's perception of the female as whore by living up to it—which of course is also capitulating to it—and ultimately taking revenge for it.

Yet by the end, Ford has become one of the con men, inadvertently slipping into the jargon, and in so doing, unwittingly betraying herself to Mike when she admits she took *his* pocket knife (66). At the airport, where Ford stages a coincidental reunion with Mike, she initially has the upper hand: Mike doesn't know she's on to the con; he doesn't know that her fear of being followed is false; and he thinks he has the usual ability to take charge and run the show.[5] Ford's con status works for a short while, as she plays the helpless female, scared of this mob involvement, and clinches Mike's help by telling him she brought all her savings and stashed it in a locker. She "confesses" to him about taking the knife, saying, "I *knew.* That I was being *punished.* . . . That I was bad" (65–66).[6] But it is in confessing that Ford slips up by "cracking-out-of-turn," thus clueing Mike to the con. "Oh, you're a bad pony," Mike says. "You see, in my trade this is called, what you did, you 'cracked out-of-turn.' . . . You crumbed the play" (66–67). Having been found out, Ford threatens Mike with the ultimate authority, ordering him to beg for his life; when he refuses, thinking she is bluffing, she shoots him. Before he dies, he calls her a whore, bringing her back to the identity she had sought to both escape and confirm (70).

Yet Ford accomplishes all this by becoming a man. She already has the prototypical tough self-confidence; as Mantegna says, she and Mike really are the same person. But Ford also acts as a typical Mamet guy by retaliating against what she perceives as a betrayal of trust. The irony, of course, is that she gives her trust to a con man, knowing full well who and what he is, and the further irony is that she is a renowned specialist in the kind of behavior to which she herself succumbs. Then there is the sexual element. "You raped me," Ford tells Mike. "You took me under false pretenses." To which Mike responds, "Golly. Margaret. Well, that's just what 'happened,' then, *isn't* it? . . . It wasn't *personal.* Okay?" (68). Ford does take it personally, though, and her method of retaliation is a macho one, to kill Mike with the gun she'd taken from Billy Hahn. But although she triumphs in this physical sense, she carries on Mike's legacy as a con artist (con woman?), for in the final scene, acting on Mike's advice to always "take something, . . . to assert yourself, take something from life," Ford steals a gold lighter from a woman in a restaurant, and "smiles" (41, 72).[7]

Like Margaret Ford, Karen in *Speed-the-Plow* is the catalyst that disrupts the male bond, and though her damage is not final like Ford's, she does wreak considerable havoc and provoke a male character into uncharacteristic introspection. A temporary secretary working for Hollywood mogul Bobby Gould, Karen seems to be both manipulative and helpless, worldly yet naïve, an ambiguity that shapes the men's reactions to her. The cynical view of Karen, notes critic Jack Kroll, is that she is "a girl on the make," but the sympathetic one is that she is an idealist, someone with values and principles (67). Director Gregory Mosher played on this ambivalence as pivotal to the play, saying that the audience is meant to go out asking, "Is she an angel? Is she a whore?" (Henry 98–99).

The men in *Speed-the-Plow* are movie hustlers in the classic Mamet tradition of "the penny-ante thieves of *American Buffalo* . . . and the poker–playing conmen of *House of Games*" (Rich 65). Gould, newly appointed head of production, and his protégé, Charlie Fox, are planning a "buddy film" with a major star, who has agreed to sign on, provided the deal is sealed within 24 hours. The loyalty between Bobby and Charlie is emphasized through the fact that Charlie has brought this deal to his pal rather than to the star's rival company. "You could have Gone Across the Street," Bobby says to Charlie. "And that's the point, Charl. That you absolutely *could*. And it was 'loyalty' kept you with us . . ." To which Charlie replies that The Home Store "is where I work, Bob, it's what I *do*" (14–15). They are buddies in a world where the buck counts the most, even as they insist that Hollywood is really a "people business." As Bobby says, "I'm a whore and I'm proud of it. But I'm a *secure* whore" (26).

The men's attitude toward Karen is typical of Mamet's male characters. To Bobby, she seems to be an airhead, as he must constantly explain to her simple tasks such as getting coffee and making lunch reservations. Charlie tries to size her up through the typical Mamet categories of virgin or whore, though he has some difficulty. "I just thought, I just thought she falls between two stools," says Charlie. "That she is not, just some, you know, a 'floozy' . . . on the other hand, I think I'd have to say, I don't think she is so *ambitious* she would schtup you just to get ahead. *(Pause)* That's all" (35). At any rate, Karen becomes a pawn in the boys' game when Charlie, who simply assumes Bobby is planning to seduce her, bets him five hundred dollars that he won't succeed. Bobby, of course, considers the challenge a shoe-in.

Bobby's approach to Karen resembles the maneuvers between Mike and Margaret in *House of Games*, with the male offering to open a door into a hidden world. Bobby entices Karen to seek out something new and different in life:

> Karen: I'm sure that much of a job like this, a job like this . . . is learning to think in a business fashion.
> Gould: That's what makes the life exciting, *addictive, you* know what I'm talking about, you want a *thrill* in your life?
> Karen: . . . a thrill . . .

Gould: To *make* something, to *do* something, to be a *part* of something. Money, art, a chance to Play at the Big Table . . . Hey, you're here, and you want to participate in it.

Karen: Yes.

Gould: That's what the job is. It's a job, all the bullshit aside, deals with *people*. (40–42)

Bobby offers Karen the chance to do a "courtesy read" of a novel he has received from "An Eastern Sissy Writer," a tract titled *The Bridge: or, Radiation and the Half-Life of Society: A Study of Decay* (23). He tells her to bring him a report that evening, at his house. Bobby, of course, has no intention of using the script nor of weighing Karen's evaluation of it, but what he doesn't realize is that Karen deduced his motives from the outset. She knows what he wants and, as it turns out, what she wants as well. Bobby does win the bet, but not because he manages to seduce Karen; as Karen admits in the end, she sleeps with Bobby because he "green-lighted" the radiation project.

Much to Bobby's surprise—he is, after all, head of production and as macho as they come—Karen persuades him with her idealistic response to the book as well as with her attentions to him. He is stymied when she "forgives" him for lying to her and says she would have come to see him anyway. "I looked in your heart," Karen tells him. "I saw you. And people can need each other. That's what the book says. You understand? We needn't be afraid" (59). By the end of the night, Bobby has decided to abandon the buddy film and go with the radiation project. Joe Mantegna, who starred as Bobby in the original production of *Speed-the-Plow*, remarks that Karen "momentarily prompts his conscience, forces him to go back to the ideals of a five-year old, of being true to yourself, true to your ideals" (68). For a woman to exert this kind of influence over a hard-knuckled Hollywood shark is remarkable indeed. And it is clear that only a woman could, or would, attempt this kind of conversion. As Bobby says to Charlie later, "She *does* understand me. . . . She *does* understand me. . . . she knows what I suffer" (71).

The result of this one-night stand is the disruption of the buddy relationship between Bobby and Charlie and of their buddy film, as well as a change in Bobby's attitude toward Karen. He tells Charlie to "be careful what you say about her," (70) and when Charlie asks him about the bet, Bobby is puzzled:

Gould: Five c?

Fox: The broad come to your house?

Gould: The broad.

> Fox: You fuck the temporary girl? You fuck her?
> Gould: I'm going to go to see Ross myself. (63)

Going to see Ross alone, of course, symbolizes the breakdown of their collaboration, and Charlie feels betrayed because he could have "[g]one across the street" with the project. Bobby recognizes that he has re-neged but considers his own epiphany more significant. "I was up all night thinking," he tells Charlie. "The notion, yes the notion that our life is *short* . . . that, in some way . . . I believe in the ideas that are contained in the book. " Charlie retorts, "Hey, I believe in the Yellow Pages, Bob, but I don't want to *film* it" (67). Bobby, however, is convinced that he has wasted his life but that he has now found something. "I think . . . that we have few chances . . . To do something which is right," he says (68–69). Charlie tries to convince him that this is all an illusion, that he has been had, and that Karen is only after power:

> How do I *know?* . . . she's here in movieland, Bob, and she trades the one thing that she's got, her *looks*, get into a position of authority—through you. . . . She lured *you* in . . . Bob: that's why she's here. . . . Why did she come to you? . . . She *wants* something from you. You're nothing to her but what you can *do* for her. (71–72)

Bobby is slow to come around, though, believing that Karen has shown him to be a good man. Only when Charlie demands to ask Karen one question before being booted out is Bobby finally convinced that his friend is right:

> Fox: My *question:* you answer me frankly, as I know you will: you come to his
>   house with the preconception, you wanted him to greenlight the book.
>   (*Pause*)
> Karen: Yes.
> Fox: If he had said "No," would you have gone to bed with him?
> Karen: (*Pause*) I don't think that I'll answer you . . .
> . . . .
> Gold: *I* would like to know the answer.
> Karen: You would . . .
> . . . .
> Gould: Without the bullshit. Just tell me. You're living in a World of Truth.
>   Would you of gone to bed with me, I didn't do your book. (*Pause*)
> Karen: No. (*Pause*) No.
> Gould: Oh, God, now I'm lost. . . . Oh, God. I don't know what to do. (77–78)

Karen's influence over Bobby has been nearly fatal in terms of "the business," although in the end Bobby and Charlie are together again—in the nick of time to rescue their buddy movie. But that Karen could have wrought such a radical change in Gould is remarkable, and as one critic notes, "In *Speed-the-Plow,* the perception of women as sexual 'weakeners' or 'corrupters' of men receives its most direct expression" (Radavich 132).

III

Matthew Roudané writes that in Mamet's world, "Women are marginalized because they aren't brokers, players, in a world where spirituality and emotion is devalued, and everything is negotiable" (5). In Mamet's world, power and virility reflect masculinity, money equals potency, and business deals prevail over emotions and feelings. When women like Margaret Ford and Karen become players, they become dangerous and threatening. Yet even from the sidelines, even from their marginalized positions, women wield a subtle if vital power and influence. In *Glengarry Glen Ross,* when Ricky Roma has finally clinched the deal with James Lingk and gotten him to sign a contract, Lingk's wife makes him back off. "My wife said I have to cancel the deal," says Lingk, as Roma deftly aims his verbal lassoes. "She called the consumer . . . the attorney, I don't know. The attorney gen . . . they said we have three days . . . She told me not to talk to you" (82, 84, 93). In *A Life in the Theatre,* the older actor Robert blames his female costar for making him look "brittle" in the eyes of his young protégé John. "When we're on stage she isn't there for me," Robert complains (129). And of course in later Mamet plays, as women like Margaret Ford and Karen become more central, they also become more powerful, a trend that culminates (to date) in *Boston Marriage.*

Whether on the verge or in the forefront, Mamet's women are more potent than initially seems apparent. That power is generated by the man's fear of them, by the male's vulnerability, and by his insecurity. For Mamet's men, rejection by the female is so devastating because of their pathetic dependence on women for their identity. Having created a macho culture from which women are excluded, and that is at least partially defined by their absence, Mamet's men have ironically bestowed power upon women by virtue of their own fear—the fear of rejection that will deny their masculinity. Though Mamet's women remain largely on the verge in his work, they nevertheless are present throughout, exerting an influence that renders them potent and that empowers them to shape and influence the male arena of Mamet's world.

Notes

1. In reviewing a New York revival of *Edmond,* critic Ben Brantley comments on the play's contemporary relevance and compares the lead character to Robert Bly, Bernhard Goetz, and Timothy McVeigh. "Like them," notes Brantley, "he's running scared." In Brantley's view, Mamet catalogs "the desperate measures taken by American white men who have felt their sexual and racial dominance threatened, implicitly evoking everything from tree hugging to the Militia Men."

2. It's irresistible to speculate on the irony in this character's name, Edmond Burke. The coarse, limited speech of Mamet's Edmond contrasts sharply with the eloquence and oratorical repute of the eighteenth-century philosopher and political theorist Edmund Burke. Their philosophical aptitudes are equally disparate: unlike the philosopher famed for such insightful and influential tracts as *Vindication of Natural Society* and *Reflections on the French Revolution,* Mamet's Edmond is, in the words of critic Ben Brantley, "all too ready to embrace whatever world view he's exposed to in his downward trek." Though rhetorically inept, Edmond is, in Mamet's view, quite articulate because "He was capable of using words to express exactly what he wanted to say" (qtd. in Harriott 81).

3. Unless otherwise noted, references to *House of Games* are taken from Mamet's screenplay and cited by page numbers. References to the film itself will be indicated in the text.

4. The softness of the leather jacket can be seen to reflect Ford's femininity even in her masculine garb. In the film version of *House of Games,* Ford's character is dressed in a smart business suit when she makes her first visit to the bar, and she carries a stylish black briefcase. While illustrating her femininity, this outfit also asserts her professional status and success, in contrast to the sleazy con men.

5. Again, Ford's clothing in the film version reflects her assuredness and authority. As in her first visit to the House of Games, Ford is professionally clad: she wears a white business suit and white blouse, adding a feminine touch that also implies her innocence of the sordid affair and her cleansing herself from the whole experience.

6. Ford's confessional status is reflected in the film by her sitting beside Mike, her head against his shoulder, his arm around her, a pose also suitable to the confident, take-charge male comforting the distraught female. In the subsequent confrontation, the two characters both stand, equal to each other, until Ford demands that Mike sit, which he does, ending up crouched and dying in the corner.

7. In the film version of this final scene, this new identity is underscored by Ford's highly uncharacteristic clothing: she is wearing a long flowered dress and large white earrings, standing beneath palm trees in a posh hotel (reminiscent perhaps of the Las Vegas environment to which Mike was headed).

WORKS CITED

Bigsby, C. W. E. *David Mamet. Contemporary Writers.* London: Methuen, 1985.

Brantley, Ben. "In Mamet's 'Edmond,' an Empty Man's Odyssey." *New York Times* Oct. 2, 1996: C 13.

Caplan, Betty. "The gender benders." *New Statesman & Society* July 2, 1993: 34–35.

Carroll, Dennis. *David Mamet. Macmillan Modern Dramatists.* London: Macmillan, 1987.

Gale, Stephen H. "David Mamet: The Plays, 1972–1980." *Essays on Contemporary American Drama.* Ed. Hedwig Bock and Albert Wertheim. Munich: Max Hueber, 1981. 207–23.

Hall, Ann C. "Playing to Win: Sexual Politics in David Mamet's *House of Games* and *Speed-the-Plow. David Mamet: A Casebook.* Ed. Leslie Kane. New York: Garland Publishing, Inc., 1992. 137–60.

Harriott, Esther. *American Voices: Five Contemporary Playwrights in Essays and Interviews.* Jefferson, NC: McFarland & Co., Inc., 1988.

Henry, William A. III. "Madonna Comes to Broadway." *Time* May 16, 1988: 98–99.

Jones, Nesta, and Steven Dykes, comps. *File on Mamet. Writer-Files.* London: Methuen, 1991.

Kane, Leslie, ed. *David Mamet: A Casebook.* New York: Garland Publishing, Inc., 1992.

Kroll, Jack. *File on Mamet.* Comp. Nesta Jones and Steven Dykes. London: Methuen, 1991.

Mamet, David. *American Buffalo, Sexual Perversity in Chicago,* and *Duck Variations.* London: Eyre Methuen, 1978.

———. *Edmond.* New York: Grove Press, 1983.

———. *Glengarry Glen Ross.* New York: Grove Press, 1982.

———. *House of Games.* New York: Grove Press, 1983.

———, Director. *House of Games.* Screenplay by David Mamet. Perf.: Lindsay Crouse, Joe Mantegna, Mike Nussbaum. Orion, 1987.

———. "In The Company of Men." *Playboy* April 1990: 173.

———. "Sexual Perversity in Chicago." In David Mamet. *American Buffalo, Sexual Perversity in Chicago,* and *Duck Variations.* London: Eyre Methuen, 1978, 51–75.

———. *Speed-the-Plow.* New York: Grove Press, 1985.

———. *A Whore's Profession.* London: Faber and Faber, 1994.

Mantegna, Joe. Interview. *File on Mamet.* Comp. Nesta Jones and Steven Dykes. London: Methuen, 1991.

Radavich, David. "Man among Men: David Mamet's Homosocial Order." *Fictions of Masculinity: Crossing Cultures, Crossing Sexualities.* Ed. Peter F. Murphy. New York UP, 1994. 123–36.

Rich, Frank. *File on Mamet.* Comp. Nesta Jones and Steven Dykes. London: Methuen, 1991.

Roudané, Matthew. "Mamet's Mimetics." *David Mamet: A Casebook.* Ed. Leslie Kane. New York: Garland Publishing, Inc., 1992, 3–32.

Skeele, David. "The Devil and David Mamet: *Sexual Perversity in Chicago* as Homiletic Tragedy." *Modern Drama* 36 (1993): 512–18.

Trussler, Simon. "General Editor's Introduction." *File on Mamet.* Comp. Nesta Jones and Steven Dykes. London: Methuen, 1991, 5–6.

"It's the way that you are with your children"

The Matriarchal Figure in Mamet's Late Work

Leslie Kane

"It is not a carved animal
It is a story:
Things by their name"

—*David Mamet, "Zaa"*

"*Love* is the mucilage that sticks the tattered ribbons of experience—
the stiff construction-paper Indians and pumpkins of experience—to
the scrapbook of our lives."

—*David Mamet,* A Sermon

"It has been said," writes David Mamet, "that the difference between a fairy tale and a war story is the one begins 'Once upon a time,' and the other, 'This is no shit'" ("Make-Believe Town" 185). Two recent Mamet tales, "The Room" (1995) and "Soul Murder" (1996), begin with neither, but clearly these are "war stories" from the front. Both are no more than a few pages, but despite—or possibly because of—their brevity, the poignant portraits, like most of Mamet's shorter works, acquire a piercing depth. "The Room" recovers a personal memory of youthful daring and threatened punishment sparked by a man's chance association while awaiting an appointment; "Soul Murder" narrates the story of a boy in a state of distress from the perspective of a man awaiting a train who helplessly observes a child's inhumane treatment.

Recalling his childhood in the "Fifties," the man in "The Room" remembers how as a boy he imagined himself magically "stepping through the little mirror" mounted, if memory served, above "A mirrored vanity-table top" in the bathroom of his home, into "the better room" (163–64), a safe haven whose access was predicated upon his precise alignment of mirrors, bravery in locking the door, and skill and luck in replacing the objects perfectly, which would thus "avoid calling down his mother's wrath" and "camouflage[d] his path of retreat" (165) from pirates who doubled as pursuers and playmates. The pirates, he remembers "never wished me ill" (166), but implicit in this wonderful tale of childhood ingenuity and the power of magic is the threat that lurks beyond the door: the wrathful mother whom Mamet typically leaves unexamined, a powerful force whose motives were either not understood or understood all too well.

Conversely, in "Soul Murder," a bone-chilling tale from the opening beat, the only voice we do hear is that of the mother. Beginning in medias res, the action takes place in a transit lounge, a site reminiscent of the marginal, not-home spaces favored by Mamet in many longer dramatic works,[1] between some place undefined and a home toward which a family is traveling. The family consists of a mother and her three children, "two good children" favored by the mother and a young boy who sits with "his head in his hands" and "his hands . . . pressed over his ears" (75), rocking as emotionally disturbed or autistic children do, to block out the sound, an incessant stream of carping commentaries, belligerent commands, and menacing threats directed toward the boy whom she judges ungrateful, unworthy, and unwanted. Promising punishment seemingly out of all proportion to the crime, his rejection of an item purchased but no longer wanted, the mother threatens, "I'm going to *rake* your toys and *box* them. And I'm going to ship them away" (75), but her actions speak louder than words when she hurries to catch her train, two children in tow and rage reserved for the distraught, figuratively abandoned boy. Helpless to intervene, his brother and sister look "guiltily" (76) at the victim of their mother's wrath, relieved to be out of it for the moment.

Until several years ago, we might not have even recognized these remarkable tales as Mamet's. Along with their clipped sentences, lack of back story, trope of magic, portent of devastation, and implied betrayal, the stories share two distinguishing domestic elements—being at home or homeward bound and the terrible wrath of a maternal figure[2]—topics presumably of little interest to Mamet who had heretofore (with the exception of *Reunion*) eschewed the domestic scene overtly configured as a familiar, familial home. In fact, in David Mamet's canon, Mothers, as figures of beneficence or betrayal, have been missing in action. Yet, from the

first, Mamet's characters have been homeward bound: homecoming in
Red Pony, homemaking in *Reunion*, thinking about home in *The Woods*,
home buying in *Oleanna*. It was the playwright who wanted to be anyplace but home. "A nice Jewish Boy," he told Terry Gross, "I wanted to be
anything but a nice Jewish boy. I wanted to be Jack Kerouac. Or Jack
London. Or someone named Jack. So the one thing I didn't want to write
about was that day-to-day bourgeois existence . . ." (1994). Enamored of
the picaresque, the playwright believed that "the domestic scene was best
left to anyone else but me . . ." (Interview, Bragg 1994).[3]

Even when the subject of home has been pivotal in numerous Mamet
works, a matriarchal figure has been marginalized out of sight. Thus, although Ruthie in *American Buffalo* and Ruth in *The Woods* exhibit maternal behavior—the former implicitly correcting Teach for his bad table
manners, worrying about Bob's welfare, and reminding Don of his familial obligation to visit Fletch in the hospital and the latter refusing to tol-
erate Nick's abusive behavior, cradling the terrified man in her protective
arms, and rocking him to sleep with a bedtime story—recognizable domestic space or conventional maternal relationships are absent from innumerable works. (For example, nothing is said of Levene's daughter's
mother in *Glengarry;* little is known about Carol's mother in *Reunion*,
other than that she is, presumably, an abused woman who has remarried;
and little is heard directly from Grace in *Oleanna*.) That absence has sup-
ported the supposition of some that Mamet knew little about women, as
he has himself quipped ("Women" 21) or, was a misogynist, as his critics
have argued.[4] Hence, while wives, daughters, secretaries, and prostitutes
exert a strong pull of affection, obligation, or intimidation in such works
as *Edmond, Glengarry Glen Ross, Speed-the-Plow*, and *Oleanna*, women as
a gender, and mothers in particular, have been "ghosts" hovering along the
margins or vilified on stage, as Hersh Zeifman aptly affirms.

A reconsideration of Mamet's canon in the last decade, however, reveals that mothers and grandmothers are everywhere in the plays, films,
and fiction, demanding, I would argue, a reconsideration of the figure of
the matriarch and the place of home in his work. For example, *Homicide*
and *Passover* offer a veritable plethora of mothers and grandmothers of
every stripe—those defending home and those betraying it. Mamet's
mastery of his subject is especially notable in his depiction of mothers as
teachers, disciplinarians, family historians, and raconteurs for whom reminiscence, recollection, and history constitute the fabric of their lives. Yet,
surely the mothers in *The Cryptogram* and *Jolly*, both the quick and the
dead, are among Mamet's most riveting portraits of the matriarchal figure principally because these woman, capable of loving and hurting
deeply, are profoundly human—tender, fallible, destructive. Therein lie

their complexity, ambivalence, appeal. Moreover, in Donny and Jolly, the mothers in *The Cryptogram* and *Jolly*, respectively, the playwright illumes the correlation between one's accessibility to reminiscence and recollection and an individual's propensity for record-keeping. Selfless and self-serving, creative and corrupt, loving and heartless, devoted and destructive, and protective and disloyal, Mamet's mothers profit from ambivalent, unsentimental portraits. Yet, inasmuch as their legacy is largely fear and wrath, Mamet's mothers abundantly illustrate that "The things which one is drawn to write about don't stem from intellectual prejudice or even affection, but rather from something much deeper" (Interview Harriott 78). Thus, when Mamet comes home—literally and aesthetically—in *The Cryptogram* and *Jolly*, two works in which the maternal figure is central, whether the domestic space is the living room or the kitchen, the setting is a temporal one opposing past and present, belonging and exile, as it is in the best of his work.

I

In her seminal work, *Staging Place: The Geography of Modern Drama*, Una Chaudhuri posits that "modern drama at first employs, as one of its foundational discourses, a vague culturally determined symbology of home, replete with all those powerful and empowering associations to space as are organized by the notion of belonging." However, among the many "departures from the discourse of home as originally established," she contends, is the emergence of "an increasingly precise and unsentimental recognition of home *as* a discourse. . . . laid out in such a way as to guarantee its inhabitants a certain psychological homelessness" (xii-xiii, 11). Setting *The Cryptogram* in the family home, at once recognizable and dissolving, a place as marginalized in Mamet's canon as the three marginalized Others who take center stage—a mother, a child, and a gay man, none of whom have previously made an appearance in a Mamet dramatic work—the playwright, in effect, "codes the familiar as the familial, . . . the nearly extinct" (Chaudhuri 165).[5] The site of border crossings and confidence games as fierce as we have ever seen in a Mamet play, the interaction among these marginalized Others in the family home brings the "picture" of the present into sharp focus and locates the action not in an observable place but rather in the cryptic space of memory, a technique that "belie[s] the 'narrowness' of the domestic play space" (Haedicke 9). Juxtaposing the old idea of belonging, affiliation, and "all those qualities of rootedness" (Chaudhuri 252) with images of displacement, Mamet progressively discloses the defamiliarization of the secure haven of home space by intimations of rupture, sounded early in the shattered tea kettle, and uprooting, literally depicted in packing boxes at play's end. Long eschewed by the playwright, the domestic space is delineated as "Donny's living room in 1959" and the time as three evenings, the last separated by a month's interval, yet "Mamet is here tapping a new vein of direct emotion," as Michael Billington noted in his review of the London production, "both in the anguished wife who yearns to know why all the men of her life betray her and even more in the boy who is simultaneously the play's moral touchstone and tragic victim" (792).

The Cryptogram is dominated by a child with an agile mind, fertile imagination, inquisitive nature, and developing independence. A preadolescent boy approximately ten years old, John is an animated, articulate, astute child, whose fiercely intelligent mind is revealed by his precise questions and keen responses in the opening moments of the play. There John and family friend Del are engaged in a lively lesson while his mother Donny is offstage preparing a cup of tea for Del and herself on the presumption that her insomniac son has finally gone upstairs to bed. Given that the matriarchal figure "assumes a complex significance, sometimes real, and sometimes symbolic" (Wandor 69), and that "Donny is off-stage when the play opens and [is] perceived as a 'disembodied voice'" (Haedicke 9), much as this technique is employed in *Hamlet*, Donny both draws our attention to her and bolsters John's memory of her as the sound of forbearance or rage. Thus her reassurance, " . . . I'm alright . . ." (7), coupled with a shattered kettle, announce from the outset the interplay of chaos and order, foretell dwindling sources of comfort, and augur rupture in the obligations and covenants of marriage, friendship, and parenthood, none as disastrous as that between Donny and her son. Indeed, as John Lahr observes, "Mamet works his way back to childhood—specifically, to that irrevocable, buried moment in a child's life when the safety net of parental embrace collapses, and the world . . . is suddenly full of danger" ("Betrayals" 70).

Hence, when Donny enters the living room, her first words to John— "What are you *doing* down here" (10)—set the accusatory tone for much of their interaction. Escalating in intensity throughout the play, Donny's frustration with John and her impatience with him ultimately shatter his (and our) presumptions of parental love and loyalty, specifically, but not exclusively, that of the maternal figure in a play Mamet has characterized as a "rollicking, frolicking tragedy about a dysfunctional household" (Interview Stamberg 1995). John's presence in the family living room long after his bedtime is the first of several acts that defy her authority. From the first, John's premonitions and misgivings, reflected in his desire to remain in the family living room rather than ascend the stairs to the feared second floor and in pointed, reiterated questions that rarely receive direct responses, are indices that something is awry. In fact, they reveal that "the child's consciousness serves as a congenial instrument for capturing instabilities of meaning" (Sokoloff 39), and that this troubled child repeatedly fails to engage the attention of his distracted mother. As the playwright told Lahr:

> ... I had all this stuff about the kid not going to sleep, and it finally occurred to me, about the billionth draft, well, it's about why can't the kid sleep? It's not *that* the kid can't sleep. ... the kid can't sleep because he knows, subconsciously, that something's unbalanced in the household. But then why is nobody paying attention to him? I thought, Aha! Well, this is perhaps the question of the play. (Interview 66)

Insistently inquiring about the delayed arrival of his father—"Why isn't he home?" (5); "Will he be home soon" (11); "When is Dad coming home?" (38)—John not only underscores the excitement with which he eagerly anticipates his planned excursion to the woods on the following day with his father (a man with whom he spends little time); he also prophesies the absence of his father as an enduring condition, the only constant in his faithless, fading world.

Conversely, "consumed with guilt" (40) about a weekend alone, Donny's "fantasy of rest . . ." (24) belies a mother on the brink of physical and mental exhaustion only partially explained by the boy's anxiety and insomnia. Rather, by implication, Robert's lack of involvement with his son and his late return from the office are as paradigmatic as John's insomnia, a fact that is authentic to the 1950s in which the play is set, specific to Robert's philosophy of parenting (which from John's infancy tended to be harsh), and sufficient cause to worry Donny, though she does not verbalize her fears as John does. Learning that theirs is a nightly "minuet" (15) whereby John seeks to postpone bedtime, presumably to catch a glimpse of his father, we ascertain that Donny's and John's relationship is both typical of the parental/child dynamic and unique, notably in the nature and subject of their discourse. For example, when Donny tells John events that occurred when his father was a pilot nearly two decades earlier, John wonders aloud whether Donny worried about Robert and whether she told him of her fears, queries that speak volumes about her disquietude occasioned by John's sleeplessness, Robert's late arrival from the office, and John's maturity. In fact, Mamet complicates his unsentimental portrait of the matriarchal figure by depicting Donny as distracted and well-intentioned, protective and disloyal, comforting and crushed by pain, rendering her his most complex woman, a mother betrayed into betraying her own son. Inspired by "an amalgam of something that either happened . . . or something that one can imagine happened, or some mish-mosh of the above . . ." (qtd. in Stamberg), *The Cryptogram*'s maternal figure, who bears a resemblance to the mother in Mamet's autobiographical essay, "The Rake," is similarly modeled in part on the playwright's mother, Lenore Mamet, a woman with a penchant for narrative, rhetorical accusation, and choleric temperament.[6]

Thus, when Del intercedes between Donny and her distressed son, successfully winning John's reprieve from bedtime by convincing her that "he's not *going* to sleep . . ." on the night prior to "a Trip to the Woods . . ."(12, 15), Donny permits the boy to go up to the attic on the pretext that he can "Neaten it up" (13) and gather items for his forthcoming trip in the hope that he will tire and finally fall asleep. At this juncture her reprimands are replaced by pleasantries and warm words of appreciation, amply illustrating that "Love expresses itself, so it doesn't need a lot of words," whereas "aggression has an unlimited vocabulary" (Mamet qtd. in Lahr, "Child's Play" 33). In his absence Donny confesses her need for a rest, musing on the passage of time in which John has grown into such a warm, engaging, intelligent, and taxing young man. Appearing on the landing of the stairs with a new line of interrogatories inspired by his rummaging in the attic—"Which coat?"; "How cold was it last week? Del?"; "And, the fishing stuff. Is it there?" (17–19)—and wearing an old coverlet that he fears he has torn, John is even more agitated than before. "Misfortunes come in threes" (29), he tells his mother, whose command to "Calm down, John" (37) fails to adequately address the gravity of his verbalized and unspoken concerns and an uneasiness that has deepened into apprehension. Donny reenacts that paradigm in subsequent acts when she minimizes his report of hearing voices and thoughts of suicide. Here, physically tired and distracted by Robert's failure to appear, Donny finds herself unable to decipher John's allusion to his waiting for "The Third Misfortune" (28). Aware that his mother has forgotten the child's book about which he speaks, a fact that provides further evidence of Donny's inattention, John both cues the lines and reminds his mother of the significance of a favorite story, one that provides the boy with a context for voicing his premonitions and that conveys an implicit "assurance hidden in the story," which Mamet, after Bettelheim, views as fundamental to a child's "spiritual need" (Interview Schiff).

Whereas John is the family's clairvoyant, Donny serves as its historian. Hence, when the boy discovers the blanket in the attic, his mother recounts the story of its purchase in England while his father was stationed there during World War II. Used to camouflage Donny and Robert as they made love and as a "coverlet" (45) for John when he was a baby, the blanket, she assures her son, was "torn so long ago" (25). "You can absolve yourself" (30), she tells him, employing a phrase intended to put his mind at ease but one that will prove ironic coming from this woman. For during the course of three dramatized evenings we spy little to absolve Donny, whose discourse is an amalgam of comforting words, confusing remarks, and coercive threats, and whose rage is easily sparked by the smallest infraction—"what Lynn [Mamet] calls 'hoops of fire'" (Lahr, "Fortress" 73). Thus, Donny routinely perceives John's need for assurance as disobedience and confuses his distress with the crimes of his elders.

In fact, from the opening beat, John's skills of observation are tested. Although his matter-of-fact "I couldn't find 'em"(1) pertains to a pair of slippers he has packed for the camping trip, "what John really can't find in the environment of subterfuge and coded speech which engulfs him is the reality of his parents and of his own emotional life" (Lahr, "Betrayals" 71). Hence, when Del offers him his father's pilot's knife to open the fishing box in the attic, John repeatedly insists upon clarification: "Where did you get the knife, though?" (28). The telling line, asked by John and again by his mother in scene 2, is a case in point. For Mamet the line, and its subsequent variants that keep the knife prominently in view, like those that keep the absent father "alive" in the play, functionally focuses attention on "the real story." "In my beloved novels," writes the playwright, "there is no question of waiting till the final act to see the knife used— the knife is used in every scene" ("Northern" 90). Similarly in *The Cryptogram*, "the dramatist . . . seizes upon the knife as both embodying and witnessing the interchange, subtly changing its purpose through the course of the drama." In short, "The appearance of the knife," writes Mamet, "is the attempt of the orderly, affronted mind to confront the awesome" (*Knife* 67).

On the following night an agitated John is still more disoriented, literally and physically evincing an altered state prompted by his father's nonappearance and his overhearing a conversation between Donny and Del regarding Robert's intent to leave his wife. Exhibiting evidence of trauma anxiety and the futile search for the familiar in the defamiliarized, the Otherness of the child, then, serves a performative role, one that linguistically reveals a child no longer "at-home" in speech or setting, an outsider locating himself in an alien world. As the child was formerly shown to be Other in the discourse of adults, then, as now, that conversation "stubbornly refuses to yield up its secrets" (Zeifman, "Cipherspace" 1). Answering John's questions in diverse ways she hopes will reassure her feverish child, Donny finds logic ineffective in soothing the troubled boy, whose distress is reflected dramatically in disjunctive discourse. Yet, when a distraught John asks, "You know my globe? You know my globe. . . ."

Maybe there's nothing on the thing that it is of . . . ," Donny endeavors to dispel fear with fact. "I've been there. To many of them" (53), she tells the boy, for whom the past now holds little weight. As he continues to ramble, his jumbled thoughts revealing the impact of the trauma of his father's abandonment, Donny for the first time addresses him as "Johnnie," the affectionate name a sharp reminder of the youthfulness of the boy and of her game attempt to calm him even as she steers him upstairs. John's bid to win a reprieve, however, competes with the arrival of Del, who diverts Donny completely with a story of his not finding Robert in all the locales to which she has dispatched him. Hence, as Del administers medicine to the feverish boy, obviously physically ill and mentally bewildered, Donny, vexed at Del's failure to accomplish his mission, directs her annoyance at the hapless boy, at whom she snaps, "You're going to take it and you're going to *sleep*" (56). When John protests, she not only insists, she intimidates him by threatening to take him "to the Hospital," her reiterated "Johnnie" (56, 57) now reflecting more pique than tenderness. "In a happy family, the denotations and connotations of words are fairly close to the surface," the playwright told Lahr. "But in an unhappy family relationship/political situation/trial, you are dealing with an adversary. . . . You listen with a much more attenuated decimal point of meaning to gauge the other's intent" ("Child's Play" 34).

Yet, when John is less fearful of her wrath and the threat of hospitalization than he is of going upstairs, Donny takes a less abrasive tack in response to his insistence that she is insensitive to his terror, adopting instead a mode of expression that validates his concerns and accomplishes the goal of getting him to bed. "I . . . I . . . I know it *frightens* you . . ." (57), she concedes. But in leaving unnamed that which frightens him *and* her, her words do little to quell his anxiety, though importantly she offers the inferred protection of her bed. Despite her "Shhhh" (59), intended to soothe him, John has correctly foretold his father's abandonment and the implied divorce of his parents as renting the fabric of his life. Indeed, the Third Misfortune, which John feared on the previous evening, has proved the third in the logical continuum of shattered kettle and torn blanket. "What's happening to me . . . ?" (59), he asks Donny, and indeed as Mamet told Charlie Rose, "It was a very traumatic time. You know it was the—they got divorced in the 50s, and I didn't know anybody who'd been divorced, let alone have it happen to my family . . ." (PBS Interview, 1994).

Cradling her fearful child, Donny attempts again to soothe his troubled heart by promising what she, and the medicine, clearly cannot deliver. "Alright, alright, I'm going to *promise* you," she tells him, "I'm going to *promise* you if you take this and . . . you take this and go upstairs, then you won't be afraid" (57), but her quartet of "promises" (the latter two punctuated by pauses) assures neither John nor us that she is capable of keeping them any more than his father is. Endeavoring to offer solace and succor in the face of the enormity of his loss, his mother offers assurance—"Hush. . . . Shh. You've only got a fever. . . ." (59)—misguided in the belief that mendacity serves the best interests of the child. From the playwright's perspective, however, Donny's act is an abuse of power. "In the family, as in the theater," he writes, "the urge to control only benefits the controller. Blind obedience saves him the onerous duty of examining his preconceptions, his *own* wisdom, and, finally, *his own worth*" ("Unhappy" 32). Hence, Donny's "good intentions" (21) to protect the boy by deception from the truth of his father's abandonment inevitably miscarry. "It's a fierce and ironic moment: an act of violence couched in the language of love," observes Lahr ("Betrayals" 72), that reveals how much more harm, however unintentional, is done by her concealing what the boy has already intuited.

Subsequently, an exhausted John is sent upstairs where he sleeps fitfully, or not at all, overhearing the conversation in which Del apologizes to Donny for failing to find Robert and endeavors to divert her with drinks, stories, and games. Permitting herself a single expression of despair, Donny's armor slips as she laments, " . . . what am I going to do? You tell me . . ." (66), yet in a marvelous Chekhovian moment Del does not hear her anguish. As he weaves a contrived tale of a bogus camping trip and of how he came into possession of Robert's knife, she becomes increasingly attentive to the clues by which he betrays himself. Ascertaining the facts of the elaborate deception perpetrated on her and her boy, Donny reacts to the shock of the double-barreled betrayal of her husband and friend of 20 years by unceremoniously and unhesitatingly throwing Del out of her home. Only when she is alone at last does she finally yield to sorrow and pain, her cries "Bobby. Bobby. Bobby . . ." (75), a wrenching release for this grieving wife and mother. Ironically her cries are overheard by John, awakened by a nightmare, who answers for the man who has abandoned them both. Worriedly, he asks her repeatedly, "Are you dead?" (75), and, as Michael Feingold correctly conjectures, "In a sense, he is not wrong. The house is full of dead things: love, marriage, friendship, affection between mother and son" ("Unsaying" 97). If Donny had "A fantasy of rest"(24) about which she speaks in act 1, we can only imagine that since John spied the letter intended for his mother on the stairs of the family home (presumably planted by the complicitious Del), she has had little or no sleep; coveting a brief respite from her exhausting maternal responsibilities, Donny has surely realized her worst nightmare.

In act 3, the play's briefest, Mamet brings the mother-son relationship into sharp relief. A month has elapsed during which Donny's home has been transformed from an unsettling place to a barren space with packing boxes. As she efficiently attends to the final details of their move set for the following morning, Donny, nonetheless, thoughtfully considers John's needs. Gathering several items that would give their new place some semblance of familiarity long before it resembles a home, her gesture of maternal concern, typical of Mamet's minimalism, is nearly overlooked by the audience. That which is impossible to overlook is John's shattered world and the troubled boy who "yearn[s] for both a father, who has yet to appear, and for the putative stability of the family" as he has known it (Haedicke 18–19). Yet a bone-tired Donny, despite her good intentions, lacks even a credible cover story to protect her son from the harsh reality of their physical and emotional exile from their home. Offering to soothe John's broken heart and troubled mind, evinced by his disturbing talk of death, Donny addresses the fear that a month ago she was reticent to acknowledge; the task enormous, she fails to provide both the protection and reassurance that John needs:

> Donny: What do you want me to do? John? I am not God. I don't control the World. If you could think what it is I could do for you . . . If I could help you. . . . (80)

Now, as the ubiquitous kettle boiling offstage draws her back to the kitchen to brew a comforting cup of tea, she leaves with a parting acknowledgment that she is cognizant of John's fear, but that, in truth, " . . . everyone has a story. Did you know that? In their lives. This is yours . . ." (80), she adds, her remark the culmination, I believe, of her earlier reassuring remark that although "Things occur. In our lives," given the mysterious nature of life, we are often unable to decipher their meaning as they occur despite age and experience. "[W]e assume they have a meaning. We must" (79), she tells him, her observation, recalling one made by Ruth to Nick in *The Woods*, intended to encourage them both.[7] Though Donny's life lessons are less clear to the boy than Robert's, that the "green" fishing line is strongest, or Del's, that anxiety engendered by upheaval is common to adults and children alike, her precepts may, in retrospect, be infinitely more important. And, though she is far better at commanding than comforting, it is clear that when the men of her (and his) life betray and desert them, she stays, attempting to bring order out of chaos.

Although Donny specifically acknowledges that she is speaking to John as if he were "an adult" (80), adult discourse has largely characterized their communication from the first, when Donny admitted to John that she worried about his father during the war or ceded responsibility to him for packing necessities for the trip to the woods that she may have overlooked. Yet here her honesty, in stark contrast to the cover story that Donny fed John along with the medicine for his fever, would be more welcome if John had not deteriorated to a point of utter dependency and despondency. In admitting that she is "not God" (80), all-knowing and all-powerful, Donny acknowledges both that she "cannot re-sanctify the Family with its stable hierarchies and identities" (Haedicke 19) and is not possessed of superhuman power to read the future or face the task before her without faltering. Hence her words spoken to John—"At some point, we have to learn to face ourselves" (80)—seem woefully inadequate and retrospectively intended for herself.

Paralleling act 2, when Del's intrusion upon an intimate moment between mother and son disturbed the delicate balance of their communication, in act 3 he once again impinges between the distraught boy and his mother, urgent issues of suicide and survival having displaced "Issues of sleep" (3) that were the subject of former nights and erstwhile security. Although Del proposes to speak with him, John's only concern is deciphering his mother's request, her voice emanating from the kitchen where she has gone to make tea. But her question is barely understood by the boy who anxiously ascends the stairs to avoid speaking with Del, whom he holds accountable for the debacle of his life, apparently having overheard the adults' conversation in act 2. Although Del quickly turns his attention to petitioning Donny's forgiveness, given the fragile, fatigued state in which we find her, attenuated by the needs of her severely depressed son and the innumerable demands of the imminent move, she has little time, patience, or energy for another heartbroken individual.

Familiar with Del's propensity to prolixity and pained by his appearance, which calls to mind his perfidious deed, she seizes control of the moment. "What do you need to say? . . ." (82), she asks, a remark that augurs John's subsequent petition for the blanket, an iconic emblem similarly bespeaking the security that Del also seeks. Donny's exhaustion and shattered nerves are reflected immediately in her discourse, but what remains unspoken is the impact of literally breaking up her home. Thus, at his first slip, mistaking Robert's survival knife for "a Combat Trophy" (84), Donny goes on the offensive, picking up from their last argument with such vehemence that we imagine only a moment and not a month had expired between them. Apologizing for her unintended harm to him, Donny inadvertently opens up a space in which Del proceeds with his apology. Hence, when John appears, asking for the blanket, now packed with items to be moved, she is impatient and deaf to *his* appeal that he is "cold" (90), bringing to mind all the previous allusions to warmth throughout the play—slippers, coat, hat, blanket, tea—that now fail to warm the child. John correctly perceives the protective coverlet of maternal affection gradually withdrawn, one which reflects the magnitude of her devastation and of his need. Illuminating the gap between his expectations of her and her ability, or desire, to meet those expectations, Donny's rhetorical questions—"What can I *do* about it, John? . . . What do you expect me to do?" (89)—cloak her helplessness in accusation and seemingly excuse her failure to adequately shelter and protect her son or empower him to cope with loss. Indeed, Donny's reiterated comment in response to his repeated request for the blanket is emblematic of her failure to address the larger question of their altered familial situation. Undeterred, John's persistent litany emphasizes his desperate need for the blanket, which he hopes will give him some measure of warmth in an increasingly cold world. Thus, in retrospect, we understand that the rip in the iconic security blanket in which she had long ago wrapped her child, and which he thought he had torn, betokens an irrevocable severing of their relationship.

Since Del has come to Donny's home with his own agenda, now interrupted by John's intrusion, his endeavoring to defuse this latest escalation of conflict between Donny and her son thus serves his own purposes. Running interference between them as he has on numerous occasions—namely, in act 1 convincing the weary mother dealing irritably with John's chronic insomnia to permit the boy to stay awake until such time as he would naturally fall asleep or proffering Robert's knife to open a sealed box, and in act 2 giving medicine to the feverish boy—here he offers to settle the boy in bed for the night. Applying a similar method of negotiation now, Del stands in for Robert, much as he has assumed numerous responsibilities of John's absent father, such as teaching life lessons, fetching medicine, interpreting John's coded references to "The Third Misfortune." Donny cedes to his intervention, her respite from John's incessant demands and mind-numbing depression a microcosmic "fantasy of rest" realized at last. In the deal successfully brokered by Del, John promises his mother—the word's quadrupled repetitions rendering ironic the breech in promises between the child and his caretakers in this play—that he will finally go to sleep. However, given the "upheaval" (8) implicit in "what they're [he's] *leaving*. . . . And what they're [he's] going *toward*" (6), it seems doubtful that the hard-won blanket will offer either security or slumber. With John safely dispatched upstairs, Del proceeds with his apology for betraying Donny, but she will have none of it, scars having barely formed on her wounds: "No, look here: don't tell me I'm going to make a sacrifice for you and it's for my own good. . . . Don't you dare to come in my house and do that. You faggot" (94).

The climax of *The Cryptogram* occurs when Donny, a "tender but ground-down, maternal but patience-frayed mother" is, as Paul Taylor observed of the London production of the play, "incited to sudden and swinging verbal violence against her son," in effect "betrayed into betrayal" (796). When John appears once again, the ire intended for Del, and by extension Robert, who has betrayed her and her son, is directed at John whose "crime" is negligible in comparison to the adult males, both straight and gay, who have deceived Donny. Nonetheless, he is made to bear responsibility for their deeds, much as he bears the brunt of her anger at them. Unable to open the box containing the blanket without the iconic knife, John has failed in the literal sense of the word to keep his promise to his mother. Punishment is swift and terrible, her wrath of biblical proportion:

> I DON'T CARE. Do You Know What It Means To Give. . . . to give your word? I DON'T CARE. . . . I don't care. Do you hear. I don't care. . . . Go away. You lied. . . . I love you, but I can't like you. (96–97)[8]

Though John "hears" her loud and clear and feels every stab of her lacerating speech—for "in Mamet's plays it's not just how people speak but how they listen that betrays the influence of the emotional abuse" (Lahr, "Child's Play" 33)—he is undeterred in his mission to accomplish access to the blanket. Having only recently been reminded by his mother that "*Each* of us. . . . Is alone" (90), John withstands her rage, holding his ground against her as she rebuffs his challenge much as she does Del's: "I'm *speaking* to you, John. . . . Do you want me to go mad? Is that what you want? Is that what you want?" (99). "All rhetorical questions," observes Mamet, are "sneaky accusations because they masquerade as a request for information" (qtd. in Lahr, "Art" 54), and Donny's mastery of the form, as Zeifman has also noted in "Cipherspace," proves her most lethally aggressive tactic directed against the vulnerable boy. Confusing him with the men of her life, Donny both displaces her anger and frustration on the boy and exploits her power position.

Capturing the paralyzing pain of a child and a parent in the face of irreparable rupture, *The Cryptogram* builds a convincing case that "Donny is the type of woman who is better at demanding than at giving, better at recrimination than at compassion" (Peter 796). But lest we distance ourselves from her horrific behavior under conditions of extraordinary stress in the closing moments of this play, we are reminded that "She is us," as Felicity Huffman, who deservedly won an Obie for her portrayal of Donny in Mamet's production of the play, observed.[9] Turning her wrath on her vulnerable son, an "equally marginalized figure" who hears voices and speaks of suicide, Donny not only punishes the figure who is "the most marginal of all" (Zeifman, "Cipherspace" 8) for the injustices perpetrated on her, she, like Del and Robert, "tragically sacrifice[s]" him (8). Yet, I do not believe that John goes to the top of the stairs with the intent to commit suicide, as numerous critics contend. Rather, I offer an alternative interpretation of the closing moments of the play in which Mamet reveals John, a young man who matures in a crucible of pain, as literally, physically, and ethically distanced from Donny. Armed with a knife and in pursuit of comfort in a cold world, he stands on a "rung of awareness," as Lawrence Kushner would have it (132), a vantage point from which he acquires "a vision of the truth" (116). Virtually and metaphorically empowered to survive, he not only listens to himself, but to a Higher Voice that does not lure him to his death. Instead, driven by terror and faithlessness, the act of listening to voices in his home and in his dreams now enables John to listen for an audible voice—his own. Indeed, posits Kushner, "the Way" is neither book nor scroll, but "living in accordance with . . . the highest expression of right behavior" (124).

A brilliant, heart-rending tragedy revised over the course of nearly 15 years,[10] *The Cryptogram*, informed by recollection, is a play about facing deeds and demons—John's, Donny's, Del's, Mamet's, our own. Indeed, the figures of home and family in *The Cryptogram* become the site for an exceptional homecoming—that of the playwright. Yet, linked inextricably to the matriarchal figure, the familial home, however much coveted by his characters, remains elusive in Mamet's world: a conundrum more in the longing—or loathing—than in the reality. For as the playwright told Stamberg, "the cryptogram of the title is the cryptogram of our memory of our youth—what went on and what did it mean? And a lot of our efforts in later life attempt to decode that—that message" (NPR 1995).

II

Comprised of a trio of plays that resonate with one another—*Disappearance of the Jews, Jolly,* and *Deeny* (1982, 1989, revised 1998)—*The Old Neighborhood* is a companion piece to *The Cryptogram*. This memory play traces the return of Bobby Gould to Chicago after a long absence, during which he endeavors, in the writer's words, "to close out some unfinished business" (Interview Holmberg 8).[11] In a series of intimate reunions with old school chum, Joey, his sister Jolly, and former lover Deeny, Bobby, a laconic figure on the verge of divorce from his non-Jewish wife, proves a passive listener—absorbing and reacting to his more voluble partners. Occasionally, however, his rage breaks through, revealing a man in his thirties alienated from friends, family, community, and religious identity—the quintessential Mametian marginal man. Whereas *The Disappearance of the Jews* dramatizes a conversation between two old friends who chew over old times, lost opportunities, and faded dreams, their longing for connection with their Jewish heritage and feelings of disappointment in themselves and in their marriages revealed or implied in the rich subtext, *Deeny* is an acknowledgment of lost love and a recipe for renewal. *Jolly*, the longer middle play, is the centerpiece of this trilogy, its ruminative questions into the nature of mothering, memory, guilt, atrocity, love, and legacy affecting and unsettling. Significantly, in contrast to *The Cryptogram*, Mamet sidelines Jolly's dead mother—and teenage daughters (both of whom exert a perceptible power enhanced by their absence)—opting instead to configure her as a matriarchal figure tied to the past and responsible to the future.

A tautly woven fabric of pain, rage, regret, bitterness, and joy, *Jolly* is an incisive work whose poignant look at sibling ties, common and conflicting memories, astonishing loyalty, and atonement is an integral, complementary component of the playwright's exploration of maternal love and abuse. In effect the play is a moving dramatization of Mamet's account of childhood abuse recounted in "The Rake," in which he and his sister Lynn (whose recollections inform *Jolly*) grew up in the "bleak and brutal terrain—full of cloaked threat and blighted feeling" (Lahr, "Betrayals" 70) of a dysfunctional family stretching back for generations, living at times in separate homes "appeas[ing] . . . unappeasable adults" (Weber, "Mellower Mamet" 12). *Jolly* also evokes the sights, smells, and sentiment of such nostalgic prose pieces as "71st and Jeffery" and "When I Was Young—Zosia and Willa."

Paralleling a technique perfected by Saul Bellow in which "The fragmentary nature of the flashback[s]" precludes the work from "bogging down in the past" (Alter 108), Mamet's *Old Neighborhood* acquires a sweep—which the playwright characterizes as "epic" (Holmberg 9). Unifying subject and structure through progressively more painful recollection, the interconnected trio of plays paves the way for release and renewal. In fact, Bobby's return to the old neighborhood and to Jolly's home after a long separation, coupled with the brevity of his visit, provide an authentic, accelerated time-frame for the exploration of their past, while her ongoing battle with her stepfather for her rightful portion of her recently deceased mother's estate proves the catalyst for Jolly's expressions of anger and resentment. As sister and brother weave a quilt of remembrances by recalling familial rituals, their divergent memories and current coping mechanisms vis-à-vis the manipulative, malicious stepfather and the death of the mother become the ground on which past and present collide, a pattern already established in *The Disappearance of the Jews*.

Mamet characterizes *The Old Neighborhood* as "an old-fashioned play" typical of the 1950s, "a kitchen play, a reflective, family-oriented play" (qtd. in Weber 12), a point brought home by the kitchen, which serves as the setting for *Jolly*. Reinforcing the disparity between the warmth of her home and the coldness of her childhood abode (the solidity of an oak table in Zigler's production mocks innumerable glass-topped tables shattered in "The Rake"), the sustenance and nurturing that Jolly affords her family are implicit in her proud acknowledgment, "I turned into a fine cook" (66). Jolly's home cooking—from fancy feast to pedestrian pancakes—not only manifests her love for her family, it provides an apt metaphor for her self-actualization as "*home maker*," her accomplishment and pride in herself, a recipe for facing down the demons of her past. Indeed, Jolly's need to keep the larder full is not merely a compensation for or disapprobation of starvation in childhood, it is a heartfelt commitment to keep her girls and her husband physically and mentally healthy. "You ain't seen *nothing* . . ." (66) she tells Bob, though increasingly we perceive that her daily struggle to be supermom and wife is nearly undone by the bitterness and pain that holds her hostage to the past. The kitchen, then, becomes a warm space in which to teach her daughters to be "at home" in the kitchen, a place where she lovingly instructs them in the art of nurturing, thereby carving out a family heritage markedly different from her own.

Through the recitation of stories that recapture their youth and reveal the bedrock of their loyalty to one another, Jolly's and Bobby's deceased mother, a woman identified only by her maternal role and her abysmal performance of it, is kept alive in *Jolly*, much as the absent father Robert is in *The Cryptogram*, by recurrent reference to her. In fact, through Jolly's recounting of her mother's words and actions, the dead matriarch attains a vitality that belies the ghost who haunts Jolly's dreams. Among the issues that the playwright explores in *Jolly* are the bonds that link children to parents, siblings' common and conflicting memories, and the impact upon intimate relations of one's past. However, pivotal in this play is Mamet's portrait of Jolly, a loving mother and caregiver who has survived a destructive, abusive relationship with her own mother and stepfather, and finds herself paralyzed by ambivalent, conflicted emotions—mourning a woman she has long detested. In fact, the familiar Mametic technique of "ghosts" on the margins of the action, as Zeifman would have it, such as Ruthie, Grace, and Fletch in *American Buffalo,* the downtown bosses in *Glengarry Glen Ross,* and John's wife and attorney in *Oleanna,* is central to that portrait. Similarly, utilizing the now ubiquitous Mamet telephone, the playwright brings the offstage stepfather into Jolly's home through her recitation of their telephone conversations, even as her stepfather severs contact with her and rationalizes his virtual abandonment of his granddaughters.

Like numerous Mamet works, among them his two person one-act play, *A Life With No Joy In It* (1991), *Jolly* opens on a familial conversation already in progress, its scrim of civility quickly torn away to expose deep wounds that both sister and brother have sustained, and that have etched themselves on the psyches of the siblings so that, as Jolly, who is anything but, comments wryly, "It's a miracle that we can Wind our Watch" (74). In fact, Jolly appears "almost gnawed away by unappeased anger over her childhood, her mother's death, her stepfather's maneuvers over the estate" (Feingold, "Unsaying" 97). Yet, remarkably in this profoundly moving play, this woman, with every reason to betray others as she has been betrayed, emerges as a caring caretaker with a strong center who is not only capable of balancing her disparate roles of wife, mother, daughter, and sister, she is literally and figuratively invested and involved in the life and future of her family. Engaged in fruitful, pleasurable activities with her daughters, such as making fudge and playing Monopoly (itself an ironic Mamet tell, given that this game presupposes the loss or retention of property at a toss of the dice), Jolly grapples with a personal history of rejection and censure and the recent death of her mother, which threaten to destabilize her.

"Although the act of returning home is an archetypally regressive act . . . it is used in the later modern drama," argues Chaudhuri, "not to recuperate identity but rather to stage the difficulties, even impossibility, of such recuperation" (92). Accordingly, in *Jolly* Mamet simultaneously balances past and present realities as brother Bob travels home to Chicago and the comfort of Jolly's love, and the siblings travel "home" to a horrific past that bears little likeness to the haven that is Jolly's home. Counterpointing the trust and betrayal that score this drama, Jolly bridges the past and present by recounting a recent conversation that establishes a context for the current crisis and chronicles a familial history of patriarchy and maternal disloyalty.

> Jolly: . . . and he said, " I disapprove of you." "Of what?" I said. "Of, well, I don't know if I want to go into it . . ." "Of something I've done . . . ?" I said. "Yes." "To you?" "No." "To *whom?*" I said. He said he would much rather not take it up. "Well, I wish you *would* take it up," I said, "because it's important to me." "It's the way," he said. "It's the way that you are with your children." (43)

Bobby's exhortation to "take an oath never to *talk* to, *meet* with . . ." (44) the aforementioned stepfather speaks to their betrayal and collective pain and her responsibility to protect "the children most especially" (44) from the man who readily admits that therapy has not only afforded him a glimpse into his past, it has freed him to speak his mind in the present. "That's their way," concludes Bobby. "That's their swinish, selfish, *goddam* them. What *treachery* have they not done, in the name of . . . of 'honesty'. . . . Well, *fuck* him. . . . he didn't like the way you raise your kids . . ." (45–46).

Enraged, Bob is unable to complete his thought, but his intent is implicit: the sane, safe course of action for Jolly is to terminate all future communication with their stepfather, with whom the siblings insinuate there is a long history of "emotional terrorism"—manipulation, power games, and violence (L. Mamet qtd. in Weber, "Mellower" 12). However, against the advice of her husband Carl, who fears further contact will only result in additional pain, Jolly is more charitable, endeavoring to attain and sustain communication with her stepfather despite his repeated rejection of her requests for financial assistance, reproach of her method of mothering, and betrayal of his granddaughters. Hence, the omnipresent Mametic telephone, rendered ironic as a means of communication, functions here not merely as means of bringing this offstage personae into the action (as the one-sided conversations in *American Buffalo* and *Oleanna* effect the stage presence of the middleman, wife, and attorney, respectively), but of giving the stepfather voice. Indeed, Jolly's caustic recitation of his remarks is at once a wry and unsettling means of presenting evidence of his ongoing emotional abuse and his ability, even after the death of her mother, to intervene between her and her mother.

Calling attention to the confessional, redemptive nature of the play, Carl repeatedly urges Jolly to relate chapter and verse of her dealings with the stepfather, confirming that Bob is more influential in dissuading her from continuing communication with the former than he. "Tell him about the money. . . . Tell him" (55), he urges, in that marvelously Mametic minimalism by which we come to know Carl as a man of few words and great depth. As Jolly recounts her discussion with her stepfather apropos of the proceeds of her mother's estate and chronicles her being forced to plead her rightful portion and justify exigency occasioned by her husband's unemployment, moving costs, and basic child care, she tells Bob, "And he says 'no.' (*Pause*) Just 'no.' (*Pause*) Just 'no'" (57). Thus, although she has implored the stepfather to "invade the trust [fund] . . ." (57)—an inventive play on the prototypical Mamet theme of "taking and offering of trust" (Brewer 127)—he denies her request. Recalling the conversation from memory, Jolly continues her tale. " . . . Oh. Oh. And it gets better," she adds. "He didn't say 'No.' He said . . . he said, 'I am not convinced I would invade the trust if I *could*' . . ." (57), at once denigrating her cause of action, denying his full responsibility, refusing to acknowledge her appeal for help, and corroborating the wisdom of Bob's previously stated admonition that she cease all further contact with him.

Yet, it is not only the recollection of shared memories, but the recitation of events largely unknown to Bob that confirm Jolly's distinctive talent as a raconteur whose reminiscences are peppered with scatological language previously the purview of Mamet's men. Moreover, her sporadic bursts of rage speak credibly to the harrowing experiences of a woman despised, rejected, and betrayed as a child, a history that threatens to be repeated by the stepfather with her own daughters.[12] This protagonist bears notable similarities to Mamet's sister Lynn, the mother of two daughters whose story of physical and emotional abuse by her mother and stepfather is recounted in "The Rake." However, in *Jolly*, Mamet has made significant changes in his dramatization of an emotionally brutalitized mother of two daughters consistent with his view that "dramatic biography . . . end[s] up reverting to fiction." If the drama is "To be effective," he keenly observes, "the dramatic elements must and finally will take precedence over any 'real' biographical facts" (*Knife* 29–30).

Like Donny in *The Cryptogram*, Jolly serves as the chronicler of the past, but whereas Del has to be reminded by Donny of the places, events, and tokens of the past about which he has forgotten or has no knowledge, Bob and Jolly have both shared and separate memory of the events of their youth. Thus, when Bob attempts to rewrite history or has a faulty recollection of the events that bears out the fact that siblings, even within the same home, do not share identical experience, Jolly typically amends the record or feeds him cues to refresh his memory. Hence, when he protests that he was in residence in their childhood home "part" of the time, Jolly corrects him—"NO. You weren't there, you know. You weren't there. *I* was there . . ." (47)—in effect implying that at the most traumatic moments of her life, the only times that count, she endured alone a brutal stepfather, an ineffectual mother who did not protect her, and rival step-siblings—defenseless, humiliated, and full of self-loathing. In short, he was neither ally nor protector, a paradigm apparently repeated when Jolly, a mother of two, was more recently burdened with the care of their dying mother. "In a good play," Mamet contends, "information . . . important to what happens later in the play . . . is delivered almost as an aside" (Playboy Interview 53). Thus, in relating a single appalling incident of her childhood, Jolly illustrates both the root cause for her rage against her abusive mother and her festering resentment of her brother.

Jolly: . . . Do you know, you don't know, 'cause you weren't there—when they first came. *Mother* told me, I was ten. So she was, what eight; she was going to sleep in my bed. She took up the bed, as she was a "creeper," you know. I'm a rock. You put me in a bed. And unmoving. Morning. She was all over the place. And I went in and told Mom that I couldn't sleep. She said, "She is his daughter, and this is the case. If you can't sleep, sleep on the floor." . . . And she wouldn't let me take the covers. (*Pause*). (48)

Jolly's recollections of rejection—of being kicked out of bed by a stepsister and deprived of her blanket, an iconic sign that signals her exilic, unprotected status within the home—are bound up in this test of a mother's love. And whereas Donny sought erroneously to protect John by lying to him about his father's abandonment, Jolly's mother not only refuses to sugar-coat the truth, she similarly reveals herself to be derelict in her care of her child by refusing to acknowledge both Jolly's pleas and her needs, opening the floodgates for all manner of future emotional abuse. That the support is nonexistent, in fact, that it is accompanied by the withdrawal of maternal protection—the ripping away of the proverbial blanket—results in scarring evident in every memory Jolly recalls. Moreover, like her mother who failed the crucial test of protecting her against the intruder in her bed and in her home, her stepfather similarly fails now to respond to her current emotional and financial needs. His refusal to honor her request for her portion of the estate "Until. . . . I stop asking" (54), despite the fact that monetary assistance and mementos of her dead mother are as vital to the adult's well being as were the emotional needs of the child, illustrates that neither parent deems (or deemed) her expression of need deserving of attention or action. Such behavior Mamet characterizes as corrupt given that the parent considers his or her decree "more worthy than the legitimate interests of the child" ("Corruption" 96). In fact, discussing the division of her mother's estate with her brother, Jolly confirms that like Miss A in Mamet's *The Shawl* she has been deprived of her inheritance—both heritage and heirlooms—those things with long association to her mother such as the armoire in the hall, her mink coat, her antiques. Judged an unworthy recipient now as then, Jolly explodes, her pain palpable: "What do I get? NOTHING. NOTHING. Nothing . . ." (53). Protesting that hers was a proprietary relationship, she laments the injustice of her being deprived of possessions belonging to her mother. "But she was my mother. And I was there while she was dying. *I* was there. *I* was there. He'd drop her off, and I was left, an infirm woman," while Carol, that "sonofabitch that *cunt* that *cunt* that *Carol* . . ." (53), the stepsibling who failed to show her stepmother respect by attending her funeral, is nonetheless rewarded with the armoire. That these two adults dwell on their deprivation "with such virulence after so many years dramatizes its lasting psychological significance," suggests Arthur Holmberg, wisely noticing their seemingly insatiable need to pick the scabs off the scars ("Neighborhood" 9). Hence, when Bob simplifies their miserable history as cruelty toward both children, neither of whom were loved, Jolly cuts to the quick: "They loved *you*, Buub" (61). While Jolly certainly alludes to the favored position of male children in a Jewish family,[13] Bob repeatedly insinuates she was/is singled out for punishment. "What in the hell *possesses* a man. To *treat* you like that . . ." (60) he asks. But in lines cut from an earlier version that more closely mirror "The Rake," Jolly finds the answer in patriarchy: "Well, I don't know. I don't know if *any* of 'em liked women. . . . Look at Mom. And Papa Jake. . . . *He* never loved her one day . . ." (47).[14] However, as their tortured family history is recounted in reminiscences, recriminations, and regrets "firmly anchored in every day, petty details of family relationships" (Christiansen CN1), the play's apparent indirection culminates in Bob's overdue, heartfelt apology to Jolly for his neglectfulness, which the playwright evocatively and astutely leaves ambivalent. Whether he failed to protect his beloved sister, share the burden of his dying mother's care, or visit Jolly after their mother's death, we are deeply moved by his remorse and by her compassionate heart.

In act 2, set in the middle of the night, Jolly and Bob meet in the kitchen. A nightmare (recurrent, we presume) has driven her from bed, and the custom of taking his children to the bathroom late at night has awakened him. As they collaborate in drawing a picture of the past, their small talk yielding to an "exclusive code" (King 14), Jolly's memory proves more reliable than his. "I *remembered.* Way back . . ." (46) she tellingly admits, feeding him cues that stimulate his flawed recollection of "Christmas Day," the "fucking" skis, "The Big Present," and the "Plaid Reversible Raincoat," a great Mamet tale in which Bob recalls how he defied his mother by returning the unwanted raincoat to Marshall Fields. And then, for what seemed like a year, he faced her interrogation—"Where is that raincoat, Bubby . . ."—until the saleswoman "Sent to fucking *Germany* to see, could they replace that raincoat" (65). Recalling mind games played with their mother, particularly at Christmas—an alien tradition for these "Mockeys [Jews] with . . . Mistletoe" (71)—Jolly and her brother became adept at charade. Learning that deception was safer than truth, they survived by subterfuge, mastering the ability to profess pleasure in gifts they did not want in order to avoid their mother's wrath. Nevertheless, they were branded ungrateful children responsible for ruining festive familial "occasions" and banished to their room until they made "A Complete and Contrite Apology" (72, 85). In short, there was "a lot of adaptation. . . . a lot of games that had to be played, a lot of cons, just to survive . . . [their] family."[15] Nearly 30 years later Jolly's reminiscence comes up with bile:

"'fuck her, *though* she's dead.' (*Pause*) 'Fuck *her*, and fuck the *lot* of 'em'" (60). Her rage evinces behavior that the playwright maintains is universal, namely the desire to confront one's opponent from a position of strength: "'If I could go back there again, what I'd say to that son of a gun' . . ." (Mamet qtd. in Lehrer).

Drawing a sharp distinction between her mother's emotional detachment from her children and her involvement in the life and education of her daughters that encompasses everything from teaching them to cook to planning weekend activities they and their friends might enjoy, Jolly reaches a disquieting conclusion that says as much about her (or their) relationship with the deceased mother as it does about her *as* a mother. "If they had *loved* us. Mightn't they have *known* what we might want?" she asks Bob rhetorically. "I know what *my* kids want . . ." (66). Although Jolly couches her question in the conditional tense, the answer is self-evident, given that her intuitive, unequivocal, perspicacious judgment of her daughters' emotional and physical needs betokens a beneficent mother whose actions, both implicit and explicit, stand in stark contrast to the depraved indifference of her cruel mother. Juxtaposing past and present realities and using her own home as object lesson, Jolly draws an invisible line between the two. "You see, Bob? Do you see? This is a *family* . . ." (68). In redefining the term "family" for her sibling, also a survivor of a Broken Home, Jolly, in essence, uses her current familial experience as an exemplar of a supportive family unit recognizable by its elements of respect, love, communication, ceremonies, acceptance, joy, and shared burden. Her minimalist description is tacitly confirmed by Carl's subsequent acknowledgment to Bob that he endures the saga of the siblings' "misfortune" because he loves Jolly, apparently with or without the baggage of her life whose weight changes not a wit. Indeed, parenting has not only afforded Jolly an opportunity to bring forth "'all the love that we [she and her brother] as children weren't allowed to show'" (L. Mamet qtd. in Freedman 46), it has, in light of her recent role reversal—caretaker for her own infirm mother—made Jolly nostalgic, even melancholic, attuned to her daughters' heritage, her need to secure remembrances of the past, and more keenly aware of the impact of her mother's death.

Informed by that mind-set, Jolly confidently believes that her nurturing care and the skills she has taught her girls will forge positive memories. "I'm going to be dead. Some day," she tells Bob, but "*they* are going to be in a kitchen. And they're going to say To their girls . . . '*My* mom used to do it this way'" (68). Her mother, she complains, failed to teach her anything. However, such a statement, ostensibly adding fuel to the fire, is fallacious: her mother taught her self-loathing, infidelity, fear, equivocation, the necessity of survival skills. By contrast, Jolly reveals the

innumerable ways in which she is, or tries to be, a "good mother"—
spending time with her daughters, making a home to which they would
want to bring their friends, knowing what they want, teaching them productive, valuable skills, worrying about them as she does Bob's happiness
and safety. Thus, Jolly "emerges as both loving matriarch and wounded
adolescent, sentimental and devastatingly clear-eyed" (Brantley B3).

When Bob comes into the kitchen in act 3 admitting to having slept
well and feeling "safe" in her home, he is subjected to a paradigmatic
Mamet quiz. "Safer than Other Places . . . Safer than Anyplace in the
World?" (80), Jolly asks playfully, illustrating her previously stated position that hers is a home in which one can feel safe—"A house full of folks
who love you" (82)—even if she suffers from uneasy dreams. And, indeed,
where else would Bob feel safe now? Having distanced himself from his
anti-Semitic wife and resolved never to return to her, Bob is heartsick and
figuratively homeless. Ironically, this exchange sets us up for the play's
final nostalgic reminiscence and shocking conclusion, which reveal that
the impression of warmth, protection, and safe haven from the winds that
buffet their lives and shattered their childhood is, despite Jolly's valiant
effort, illusory, for she suffers from bone-chilling nightmares that invade
sleep even as they render her carefully wrought illusion of refuge yet another deception she has perfected. Hence, although Jolly, like Mamet's
male characters, "talks a good game," we intuit through implication,
avoidance, and indirection that "she really does not have it together as
she'd like us, and Bobby, to think" (Siegel F4).

However, Bob intuitively discerns Jolly's distress when she attempts to
tell the story of a time shortly before her mother's death when her mother
paid her and her family a visit. But no sooner has she begun to speak—
"And she'd come, 'Mom' . . . She'd come to see us . . . 'Mom' . . ."—than
Jolly can no longer speak of her mother. Bob's trice repeated, "It's okay,
Jol" (69–70), convinces neither of them. Yet, if we miss this nuanced, intimate moment in which the ambivalent nexus of loss, love, and rage is
backlit, Jolly's story of going the wrong way on a one-way street, one of
the great Mamet soliloquies punctuated by rapid-fire queries and obscenities directed against the hapless driver, seems irrelevant. In context
Jolly's story confirms that this "haggard, sexless, unattractive *house-wife*,
with her *kids* in her station wagon . . ." (77) is clearly not "okay." It reveals
that the darkness that she keeps at bay, now stirred up by her mother's
death, literally obscures her vision. Indeed, she confirms as much, telling
Bob, "I'm a sick woman . . . how could I not be" (76). Her narrative is significant, moreover, for it brings to light her collision course with death,
both literal and figurative. In confiding in Bob, which ironically extends
Carl's earlier injunction to "Tell him [Bob]," Jolly's narrative exposes a

ravaged emotional terrain borne out by her concluding remembrance and nightmare vision. Additionally, it rivets attention to the fact that story-telling is, as Adam Newton argues, a "participatory act" in which "the bonds between teller, listener, and tale . . . stand as emblems of restoration and return" (123).

Just prior to Bob's departure, Jolly finally reveals the nightmare that shattered the serenity of sleep on the previous evening—and others, we presume—when her safe haven is revealed to be a thing literally of the distant past, an alternative reality. "We could go back," she tempts Bob, *way* back, before the calamitous childhood and anguished adult years, to all the joys of early childhood in the 1950s—"To the Jeffery Theatre. And Saturday kiddie Shows. . . . And the Chocolate Phosphate at J. Leslie Rosenblum's, 'Every Inch a Drugstore'" (82–83) to which their father would take them—memories recounted, as well, by Mamet in "Seventy-first and Jeffery" and "When I Was Young—A Note to Zosia and Willa." However, while the playwright aligns the joys of an urban childhood with sport in the street, as city boys do—"bike chases," hunt-ing for golf balls (presumably for spare change to go to the movies), playing "kick-the-can or capture-the-flag," stickball or a game of tag ("Capture" 4–5)—what Jolly remembers is an idyllic vision that betrays her nostalgic need for stability: a home warmed by love and imbued with tradition, both familial and cultural, an intactness that preceded a family fractured by divorce and de-Semitization, and a childhood sav-aged by cruelty. In that idealized time and place, "Dad would come home every night, and we would light the candles on Friday, and we would do all those things, and all those things would be true and that's how we would grow up" (83). In short, in the ceremonies and rituals, the sights and smells of the "Old Neighborhood," Jolly finds a prescription for happiness and the pain of loss. As the playwright recently told Gross, "I thought that nostalgia was rather a longing for the past; a kind of bittersweet wetzschmerzy, a gooshy [sic] feeling. But I find that that's not true at all. . . . The overwhelming effect, the important effect, was one of loss" (1997).

While the pull of the past, especially cultural memory, may be a source of strength in Mamet's domestic plays, essays, and the novel *The Old Religion*, it may well be that the remembered past is illusory, even untrustworthy, and that Jolly's idealized home precludes her full en-gagement in her present reality. In fact, as Iris Fanger observes, "Mamet is too shrewd an observer and too suspicious of sentiment to suggest any comfort waits back home" (18). Hence, Bob Gould's apparent goal in *The Old Neighborhood* is a search for the solace of family and familiar terrain, what the playwright describes as his "attempting to close out some unfinished business." The recognition that he achieves is "Perhaps . . . on the order of you can't go home again, perhaps not" (Interview Holmberg 8–9). Even more than Bob, Jolly needs such closure or recognition, for her nostalgia is not merely problematic. Apparently benign, it still undermines her healthy mothering of two daughters firmly anchored in the future.

In the wrenching final moments of this work, Jolly finally reveals the nightmare about which she spoke earlier and has deferred telling until the light of day. A frightening glimpse into ritual murder, her dream is a chilling dramatization, delivered in her inimical fashion, of the deception and denial perpetrated by her mother. Appropriately, Jolly mimics her mother's voice, much as earlier she had her stepfather's. In each case this technique lends veracity and underscores her detachment from parents whose cruel interaction with their youthful and adult daughter she narrates. Describing her dream to Bob, Jolly recalls the scene in which her mother and herself as a young child are separated by a door. Jolly has the ability to open the door, and the insight to know that this act would be at her own peril. While her mother sweet-talks the young girl into trusting her, Jolly intuits imminent danger. In the "sweetest voice," Jolly hears, "'Julia, Let Me In.' 'I will not let them hurt you. . . . You are my *child*. . . . I won't let them hurt you, darling. . . . you are my *child*. . . .' I open the door, this sweetest voice, and there is *Mom* with this *expression* on her face . . . (*Pause*) And she wants to kill me" (84). No "cautionary tale," Jolly's dream is "a straight out horror," what Freud terms "the *latent* dream" and the playwright "the dream we would rather forget" (Mamet, "Noach" 60; 59). Yet, as a war story straight from the front, *Jolly* is, in truth, as much a story of a maternal love as that of an adult child grappling with the ghosts of the past.

Bridging past, present, and future and weighing the burden and blessing of memory and motherhood, *The Cryptogram* and *Jolly* present harrowing and humane dramatizations of the complexity that colors the relationships of mothers and children, reflecting with searing intensity upon the lessons that betrayal teaches. "It's the way that you are with your children," implies Mamet, that speaks tellingly about the performance of this formative role, one that turns on the ability to protect, defend, love, and teach one's children well. In Mamet's world, then, mothering literally melds philosophy with methodology: it invests in or cripples futures. Thus although the voice from beyond the door or beyond the grave challenges and brutalizes children and adults alike, if individuals "undergo the pain of . . . giving birth" to themselves (*Neighborhood* 97), suggests the playwright, they possess the potential to relinquish pain, to conserve heritage, and to choose life.

Notes

1. Matthew C. Roudané's "Mamet Mimetics" incisively addresses this paradigmatic technique. See especially his section, "Scenography."
2. Notably in "Kryptonite: A Psychological Appreciation," Mamet writes that "Superman . . . presents to the world two false fronts: one of *impotence*, and the other of *benevolence*, both disguises created to protect him from Woman's fury . . ." (179).
3. In his well-known interview with Melvyn Bragg, the playwright acknowledges that although he thought that he was writing in the picaresque mode, in retrospect, *American Buffalo* is admittedly a family play.
4. Although Dorothy Jacobs acknowledges that Mamet "tends to reserve some possibility for gendered communication and reconciliation between fathers and daughters" in such works as *Dark Pony* and *Reunion* and affection between sister and brother in *The Water Engine*, she concludes that whether sidelined to the margins or engaged in the dramatic action, when female characters appear in Mamet's works in roles as varied as Carol in *Oleanna*, Miss A in *The Shawl*, and Karen in *Speed-the-Plow*, they are portrayed as engendering distrust and disparagement, confirming, as it were, the predominant "sexist attitudes" held by the men. Yet, she argues cogently, not only is something substantive lost, "Something revelatory is gained" (117–120), a position clearly at odds with Guido Almansi's view that Mamet's "best plays are immune from any female contamination" (191).
5. On Othering in *The Cryptogram*, see my further discussion in "Coming Home," in *Weasels and Wisemen*; Zeifman and Haedicke also take up this issue in conference papers delivered at "Mamet at 50: An International Conference and Celebration" (1997), and ATHE (1997), respectively.
6. Mamet quotes Lenore Mamet in Lahr's "Fortress," a profile of the author on the occasion of his 50th birthday; similarly in Lahr's recent interview with the playwright, "The Art of the Theater: IX," Mamet recalls his mother's preference for the rhetorical mode. And, in my interview with the playwright, he recollected her talent as a storyteller.
7. In *The Woods* Ruth expresses the position that real things and events "exist all independent of our efforts to explain them" (40), a premise that runs through much of Mamet's work.
8. Donny's words echo exactly Lenore Mamet's phrase cited in "Fortress" (73).
9. Huffman discussed *The Cryptogram* at the "Actors' Panel Session," which also featured William H. Macy, Lionel Smith, and Natalyia Nogulich, at "Mamet at 50," November 1, 1997. See also Mamet's discussion of tragedy in *Three Uses of the Knife* (esp. 65–71), and his interview with Lahr in which he states, "we understand the tragic hero to be ourselves" ("Art" 69).
10. Gregory Mosher informed me that an early version of this work was "a ready-to-go play" of three scenes written after *A Life in the Theatre* and

prior to *Glengarry Glen Ross*. During the course of the next 13 years, Mamet revised the play on numerous occasions. *The Cryptogram* premiered under the direction of Mosher at the Ambassadors Theatre, London in 1994, undergoing several other revisions prior to Mamet's production which premiered at the C. Walsh Theatre, Boston, February 2, 1995, moving to New York, April 13, with its cast intact.

11. *The Old Neighborhood* was written concurrently with Mamet's filming of *Homicide*. Originally intended for production at the Mark Taper Forum in the early 1990s, the play, revised prior to its premiere performance in 1997, opened under the direction of Scott Zigler at the American Repertory Theatre, Cambridge, MA, April 11, 1997. With a change of cast it moved in November to New York's Booth Theatre, where it enjoyed a long run. Notably, the creative team, all of whom had previously worked on productions of Mamet's plays—director Scott Zigler, set designer Kevin Rigdon, and lighting artist John Ambrose—support the play's evocation of memory in lighting and blocking of actors in opposite corners of the stage, as if separated by time.

The play underwent the typical Mamet revision process both prior and during its premiere run. Key changes between the 1989 version and that revised in 1998 include deletion of overt references to patriarchy and autobiography (specifically events detailed in "The Rake)," and the use of Yiddish phrases (i.e., "the little *Tchatchkes* [14]; Nana Rivka [45]). The following speech is a longer version of the minimalist one that appears in the revision:

Jolly: Well, I don't know. I don't know if *any* of 'em. . . . if any of them liked women. Yes. That is what I mean. The Europeans. The whole thing. Do you Know. Separate galleries in the shul. Do the *Worsch*, lie down, shut up. . . . Look at Mom. And papa Jake. . . . and he never loved her. Never loved her one day. And she knew it. Spent her whole life. Looking for. That love she never got. . . . With *Dad* . . . with that *swine* "Mistreat me . . ." her whole life. And at the end. Who was there? Who was there for her?"(47)

12. Mamet addresses this issue again in *Almost Done,* a monologue written for a woman who contemplates the "remorse" she believes her father, never having known his great-granddaughters, "will feel" (9).

13. As heirs to the family name, Jewish sons, especially in earlier decades in the twentieth century, were given religious instruction, afforded access to higher education, permitted to partake in religious ceremonies, and inherited family businesses, opportunities not afforded their sisters; their place in the family structure was an elevated one. In her discussion with me, Lynn Mamet remarked that her brother held this place in his grandmother Clara's heart.

14. This quotation is found in the manuscript of *The Old Neighborhood* (1989).

15. Describing her family to me, Lynn Mamet touched on a key Mamet structure, casting light, as well, on the methodologies adapted by Jolly to survive as a child and as an adult. Mamet's sister has fond memories of the warmth and sanctity of her mother's parents' home, hallowed by love and the ritual of Jewish traditions. For example, she recounted that the mirrors in her grandparents' home were covered on Yom Kippur (evidence of an observant Jewish home), that she was expected to fast on Yom Kippur even when she was a small child (rather than the customary 13 years of age), and that family Friday night dinners were followed by attendance at synagogue. Ashkenazi Jews, her maternal grandparents and her paternal grandmother spoke Yiddish (Interview 1991).

WORKS CITED

Almansi, Guido. "David Mamet, a Virtuoso of Invective." In *Critical Approaches: European Views of Contemporary American Literature*. Ed. Marc Chénetier. Carbondale: Southern Illinois U P, 1986, 191–207.

Alter, Robert. *After the Tradition: Essays on Modern Jewish Writing*. New York: E. P. Dutton, 1969.

Billington, Michael. Review of *The Cryptogram* by David Mamet. *Guardian* [Manchester] June 24, 1994, sec. 2: 13. Rpt. in *Theatre Record* June 18–July 1, 1994: 792.

Brantley, Ben. "A Middle-Aged Mamet Goes Home, to Mametville." *New York Times* November 20, 1997: B1+.

Brewer, Gay. *David Mamet and Film: Illusion/Disillusion in a Wounded Land*. Jefferson, NC: McFarland, 1993.

Chaudhuri, Una. *Staging Place: The Geography of Modern Drama*. Ann Arbor: U of Michigan P, 1995.

Christiansen, Richard. "Mamet Returns to His Old Stomping Ground." *Chicago Tribune* April 30, 1997: CN1.

Fanger, Iris. "Mamet's *Old Neighborhood* Rouses Yearnings of a Trip Home." Review of *Old Neighborhood* by David Mamet. *Christian Science Monitor* April 28, 1997: 18.

Feingold, Michael. "Codehearted." *Village Voice* April 25, 1995: 97.

———. "Unsaying Substance." *Village Voice* December 2, 1997: 97.

Freedman, Samuel G. "The Gritty Eloquence of David Mamet." *New York Times Magazine* April 21, 1985: F32+.

Jacobs, Dorothy H. "Levene's Daughter: Positioning the Female in *Glengarry Glen Ross*." In Kane, *Glengarry Glen Ross*, 107–122.

Haedicke, Janet. V. "Decoding (M)other's Cipher Space: *The Cryptogram* and America's Dramatic Legacy." ATHE, Chicago. August 1997.

Holmberg, Arthur. "The Old Neighborhood." *American Repertory Theatre News* 18. 3 (1997): 7–9.

Kane, Leslie. *Weasels and Wisemen: Ethics and Ethnicity in the Work of David Mamet.* New York: St. Martin's, 1999.

———, ed. *David Mamet: A Casebook.* New York: Garland, 1992.

———, ed. *David Mamet's "Glengarry Glen Ross": Text and Performance.* New York: Garland, 1996.

King, Robert L. Review of *The Old Neighborhood* by David Mamet. *North American Review* 282. 5 (Sep.-Oct. 1997): 14.

Kushner, Lawrence. *The Book of Words: Talking, Spiritual Life, Living Spiritual Talk.* Woodstock, VT: Jewish Lights Publishing, 1993.

Lahr, John. "Betrayals." *New Yorker* August 1, 1994: 70–73.

———. "David Mamet's Child's Play." *New Yorker* April 10, 1995: 33–34.

———. "Fortress Mamet." *New Yorker* November 17, 1997: 70+.

Mamet, David. *A Life With No Joy In It. Antaeus* 66 (Spring 1991): 281–86.

———. "Capture-the-Flag, Monotheism, and the Techniques of Arbitration." *Writing in Restaurants.* New York: Penguin, 1987, 3–7.

———. "Corruption." *Some Freaks.* New York: Viking Penguin, 1989, 92–98.

———. *The Cryptogram.* New York: Vintage, 1995.

———. Interview with Melvyn Bragg. *South Bank Show.* London Television, Oct. 1994.

———. Interview with Terry Gross. *Fresh Air.* National Public Radio. WHYY Philadelphia, October 17, 1994.

———. Interview with Terry Gross. *Fresh Air.* National Public Radio. WHYY, Philadelphia, October 29, 1997.

———. Interview with Esther Harriott. *American Voices: Five Contemporary Playwrights in Essays and Interviews.* Jefferson, NC: McFarland, 1988, 76–97.

———. Interview with Arthur Holmberg. "It's Never Easy to Go Back." *American Repertory Theatre News* 18.3 (March 1997): 8+.

———. Interview with John Lahr. "David Mamet: The Art of the Theater XI." *Paris Review* 142 (Spring 1997): 50–76.

———. Interview with Jim Lehrer. *The MacNeil/Lehrer Hour,* PBS, October 12, 1987.

———. Interview with Leslie Kane. Boston, MA., March 12, 1992. Unpublished.

———. Interview with Geoffrey Norman and John Rezek. *Playboy,* April (1995): 51+.

———. Interview with Charlie Rose. *Charlie Rose Show.* PBS, November 11, 1994.

———. Interview with Susan Stamberg [and Felicity Huffman, Ed Begley, Jr., and Shelton Dane]. *All Things Considered.* National Public Radio. WBUR, Boston. February 6, 1995.

———. Interview with Stephen Schiff. *West 57th Street.* CBS News. January 7, 1989.

———. "Kryptonite: A Psychological Appreciation." *Freaks,* 175–80.

———. "Make-Believe Town." *Make-Believe Town: Essays and Remembrances.* Boston: Little, Brown, 1996, 181–89.

————. "The Northern Novel." *Make-Believe Town*, 85–91.

————. *The Old Neighborhood.* Unpublished manuscript. 1982, 1989. Revised April 1997.

————. *The Old Neighborhood.* New York: Vintage, 1998.

————. "The Rake." In *The Cabin: Reminiscences and Diversions.* New York: Turtle Bay, 1992, 3–11.

————. "The Room." *Grand Street* 13.4 (1995): 163–66.

————. "Seventy-first and Jeffery." *Cabin*, 125–28.

————. *The Shawl and Prairie du Chien.* New York: Grove, 1985.

————. *Some Freaks.* New York: Viking Penguin, 1989.

————. "Soul Murder." *Granta* 55 (1996): 73–76.

————. "The Story of Noach." In *Genesis: As It Is Written, Contemporary Writers on First Stories.* Ed. David Rosenberg. San Francisco: Harper San Francisco, 1996.

————. *Three Uses of the Knife: On the Nature and Uses of Drama.* Columbia Lectures on American Culture. New York: Columbia UP, 1998.

————. "An Unhappy Family." *Writing*, 31–33.

————. "When I Was Young—A Note to Zosia and Willa." *Freaks*, 154–57.

————. "Women." *Freaks*, 21–26.

————. *The Woods.* In *Three Plays: The Woods, Lakeboat, Edmond.* New York: Grove, 1987.

Mamet, Lynn. Interview with Leslie Kane. Cambridge, MA, September 20, 1991. Unpublished.

Newton, Adam Zachary. *Narrative Ethics.* Cambridge, MA and London: Harvard UP, 1995.

Siegel, Ed. "The Talk is Rich in Mamet's *Old Neighborhood.*" Review of *The Old Neighborhood* by David Mamet. American Repertory Theatre, Cambridge, MA. *Boston Globe* April 18, 1997: F1+.

Sokoloff, Naomi B. *Imaging the Child in Modern Jewish Fiction.* Baltimore: Johns Hopkins UP, 1992.

Taylor, Paul. "Brute Strength." Review of *The Cryptogram* by David Mamet. Ambassadors Theatre, London. *Independent* July 1, 1994. Rpt. in *Theatre Record* June 18–July 1, 1994: 796.

Wandor, Michelene. *Look Back in Gender: Sexuality and The Family in Post-War British Drama.* London: Methuen, 1987.

Weber, Bruce. "Thoughts From a Man's Man." *New York Times* November 17, 1994: C1+.

————. "At 50, a Mellower David Mamet May Be Ready to Tell his Story." *New York Times* November 16, 1997, sec. 2: 7+.

Zeifman, Hersh. "Cipherspace: David Mamet's *The Cryptogram.*" Mamet at 50: A Conference and Celebration." Tropicana Hotel, Las Vegas. October 31, 1997.

————. "Phallus in Wonderland: Machismo and Business in David Mamet's *American Buffalo* and *Glengarry Glen Ross.*" In Kane, *Casebook*, 123–35.

Reinscribing the "Fairy"

The Knife and the Mystification of Male Mythology in *The Cryptogram*

Linda Dorff

> You take a knife, you use it to cut the bread, so you'll have strength
> to work; you use it to shave, so you'll look nice for your lover; on
> discovering her with another, you use it to cut out her lying heart.
> —*Huddie Ledbetter, quoted in David Mamet,* Three Uses of the Knife

Although *The Cryptogram* (1994) appears to make a departure from the male-centered worlds of David Mamet's earlier plays, representing his first domestic drama in which the defining figure of patriarchy—the father—is notably absent, the play nevertheless engages in an obsessively enigmatic examination of the myths that construct Mamet's worlds of men. In an interview on *The South Bank Show*, Mamet remarked that until recently, he had felt that "the domestic scene was best left to anyone else but me, that it wasn't the fit subject for drama" (*South Bank Show*), until he realized that *American Buffalo* (1975) was "really just a family play—it is a play about a father and a mother and a little kid" (*SBS*). If *American Buffalo* is to be understood as a family play, then it would seem more precise to say that it is a metadramatic attempt to define the family in terms of male mythology, to the exclusion of women. *The Cryptogram* engages in a similar attempt, which is far subtler, for it is disguised as the inverse of *American Buffalo*: in the manner of Mamet's con-game drama and cinema, it pretends to be a family play, set—not in a place of business—but in a family home. By subtracting the (heterosexual) patriarch, it masquerades as a drama of Others, focusing on a woman, a gay man, and a child. But rather than exploring marginalized identities as alternative subjects of drama, the characters negotiate their relationships to each other through a system of mythical objects that refer to the absent father, positioning him as the (present) subject of the play. The play's minimalist action is driven by the characters' attempts to decode the mythologies attached to these objects, but this hermeneutic activity is blocked at every turn. Legends about the father encoded in one of these objects—the knife—are revealed to be false, exposing his respective betrayals of his son, his wife, and his friend. But the heterosexual male mythology for which he stands is reinscribed at the play's end with invective that is all too reminiscent of Ricky Roma's indictment of Williamson at the end of *Glengarry Glen Ross* (1983) as he calls him "you stupid fucking *cunt*. . . . You *fairy*. . . . You fucking *child* . . ." (96–97). It is as if Mamet has made visible these male-to-male terms of abuse in the physical form of the characters of *The Cryptogram*, who aim similar invectives at each other.[1] This reinscription of misogynist, homophobic verbal abuse is, at best, disturbing, precisely because it is mystified through insoluble cryptograms that ultimately serve to affirm and, therefore, to recirculate the fictions of male mythology.

Until recently, most scholars and audiences have tended to take quite a different view of Mamet's plays, praising them as critiques and exposés of the "world of men" (*Glengarry* 105). In this vein, Hersh Zeifman claims that in *American Buffalo* and *Glengarry Glen Ross*, "Mamet makes use of this exploration of 'the gendered perspective' for specific thematic ends: a dramatic world in which women are marginalized to the point of literal exclusion provides *in itself* the most scathing indictment imaginable of the venality and corruption of American business" (124). A few critics, however, have taken issue with such interpretations in response to Mamet's plays of the 1990s. While Mamet claims to have represented an "even-handed" (McDonough 101) view of sexual harassment in *Oleanna* (1992), for example, Carla J. McDonough disagrees, arguing that "Mamet's play stacks the deck, perhaps unconsciously on Mamet's part, in favor of his male character, effectively shutting down the possibility of real exposé by its lack of character development in regard to the female character" (95). Indeed, it would seem that plays such as *Oleanna* and *The Cryptogram* are moving away from the critique-exposé direction of his earlier "world of men" drama and shifting instead toward attempted defenses of the belief systems with which Mamet's men identify.

The ideological systems that I identify as male mythology are fictional systems by which males in a social order construct the gender "male" as a subject identified with the phallus. According to Lacan's "mirror stage" (2), in which gendered identity is formed, the biological penis is equated in the symbolic order with the phallus, which (Lacan claims) organizes all cultural information, especially language (66). As Jill Dolan has observed, when the phallus is seen as the structural determinant for meaning in language, women are relegated to a position outside discourse, for "the phallus is exchanged [only] between men" (12). This phallic (symbolic) exchange is highly visible in Mamet's earlier drama, in which male-to-male conversation is privileged and women are relegated, in *Sexual Perversity in Chicago* (1974), to the status of "inanimate objects" (53). Inasmuch as Mamet is a master manipulator of the symbolic order at the linguistic (aural) level, producing litanies of phallic obscenity, his plays also activate a chain of visual signification that obsessively presents objects/props as symbols of the phallus. These include the knives in *Edmond* (1982), *The Shawl* (1985), and *The Cryptogram*. In these plays, the knife is used as a phallus that literally and figuratively penetrates feminized Others—women, children, and gay men—in order to establish gendered difference and, thereby, power over them.

As a symbolic system, the function of male mythology extends beyond structuring gender identification to shaping the ontological constructions of a culture. In her work on male subjectivity, Kaja Silverman locates a "dominant fiction," which "not only offers the representational system by means of which the subject typically assumes a sexual identity, and takes on desires commensurate with that identity, but forms the stable core around which a nation's and a period's 'reality' coheres" (41). Silverman points out that the dominant fiction of sexual difference based upon the equation of the penis with the phallus is largely unconscious, emphasizing the degree to which a society's collective belief in what is real depends upon repression of the fact that the penis (or male gender) does not always equal the phallus (a position of authority). In noting that "classic male subjectivity [identity formation] rests upon the denial of castration" (44), Silverman could be describing the unconscious anxiety that motivates so many of Mamet's male characters. Certainly, when one of his male characters loses power, he immediately unleashes a string of misogynist or homophobic invective at another character—as if to accuse the Other of being castrated and, thereby, to deny his own castration, or lack of authority.

In order to reinforce this denial of castration, Mamet shrouds his *allegiance to* and *belief in* male mythology in mysticism, disguised in the forms of dramatic con games and linguistic conundrums. In linking

Mamet's writings with those of the leaders of men's movements such as
Robert Bly, David Savran notes that the writings of both evidence a
strong sense of "'mystery' in male bonding" (186). While mysticism of
this type would seem to be grounded in a desire to refer to an authoritative male subject, thereby (theoretically, at least) producing a stable image
of a male self, Savran notes a seeming inability in the writings of Bly to
enact such a mystical conjunction. In Bly's *Iron John* (1990), Savran locates "a failure, despite its repeated attempts, to produce anything resembling a stable, integral and full male subject, one based on presence (as
opposed to absence), on hardness (as opposed to flaccidity). Rather, masculinity is continually figured as a *lack,* and the phallus as an elusive and
mysterious commodity"(174). This emphasis upon failure and absence
(two of the fundamental schema for denoting the father in *The Cryptogram*) are cloaked by Mamet in mysticism, in order to maintain belief
in the fictional equation between the penis and phallus.

This mysticism is manifest in the generalized concern with cryptography (a method of concealing information), which lies at the core of much
of Mamet's drama. In Mamet's earlier plays, male mythology is concealed
and finally revealed through metaphors of con games, poker, and business
deals. In *The Cryptogram,* however, as in his other plays of the 1990s, the
method of concealment becomes increasingly mystical in form and context, frustrating both characters' and audiences' attempts to decode the
cryptograms. Unlike Poe's story "The Gold Bug" (1843), which employs
a cryptogram with the purpose of demystifying popular myths,[2] these
cryptograms defy solution, as the play's characters repeatedly complain,
"It's all such a mystery" (21). Clues to Mamet's mystification of male
mythology in *The Cryptogram* appear in an essay published five years
prior to its 1994 production, in *Some Freaks,* "Kryptonite: A Psychological Approach," which examines the Superman myth. Mamet figures
Kryptonite as Superman's secret, which, if revealed, will bring about his
destruction. It is not an accident, I would like to suggest, that Kryptonite
and Cryptogram are phonetically similar. If Kryptonite is Superman's secret—which, if revealed or decoded, can destroy the myth of his super-
masculine powers—then the cryptograms in the play also carry the power
to deconstruct male myths. Mamet writes, "Only Kryptonite cuts through
the disguises of wimp and hero, and affects the man below the disguises.
And what is Kryptonite? Kryptonite is all that remains of his childhood
home. It is the remnants of that destroyed childhood home, and the fear
of those remnants, which rule Superman's life"(178).

In Mamet's language, Kryptonite becomes an imaginary knife that
"cuts" not only the "wimp" disguise but also that of a "hero," suggesting the castrating force that destroys the patriarchal family home

staged in *The Cryptogram*. In his admission that "Superman comics are a fable, not of strength, but of disintegration" ("Kryptonite" 178), Mamet would seem to suggest that male myths are constructed—not to celebrate strength, which is an illusion—but to protect the weakling (at least on the symbolic level) from association with castration. The attempt to protect the weakling extends, in Mamet's all-male-cast plays, to the banishment of women, who, as McDonough has noted, are marginalized in "offstage space" due to a male "fear of femininity" (72), a fear that, as David Radavich has observed, is frequently manifested in homophobia (46–47).

Male mythology in Mamet's plays is deeply conflicted, for while his characters will go to any lengths to avoid intimacy—coded as femininity/castration—with each other, yet they long for it. In his essay, "In the Company of Men," Mamet writes that:

> Men . . . get together to bitch. We say, "What does she *want?*" And we piss and moan, and take comfort in the fact that our fellows will, at some point, reveal that, yes, *they* are weaklings, too, and there's no shame in it. This is the *true* masculine equivalent of "being sensitive." No, we are *not* sensitive to women, but we are sensitive to our own pain, and we can recognize it in our fellows. What a world. (87)

The revelation that "*they* are weaklings, too,"—that is, the breaking of the mythic code of Machismo, which Zeifman identifies as superior male strength and cunning (125)—may take place only in the company of men, as if it were a secret that straight white men alone know. Robert Vorlicky theorizes that the "virile myth" (*Act Like a Man* 17) of masculinity restricts individualization and demands avoidance of such self-disclosing dialogue (*ALM* 16), as if to attempt to produce a hegemonic "real" behavior that corresponds seamlessly with the mythology.

Although *The Cryptogram* would appear to deconstruct the seams between the "real" and the mythic through its revelation of the father's various betrayals, the mystification of male mythology is so romantically and so nostalgically embedded in the play's *logos* that it becomes a sort of hymn to the phallic (symbolic) order. This mysticism is encoded in two dramaturgic systems of the play: it first appears through linguistic coding in which characters seem to communicate with each other about the absent father in a shorthand lingo that is loaded with oblique allusions to a metaphysical plane that is impossible for them, or the audience, to decode. On a second level, the action of the play seems to be driven by the characters' vain attempts to decode a collection of objects connected with the father. On the first, linguistic level, the conversations between Donny,

Bobby's wife, John, her son, and Del, their gay male friend, center obsessively on Bobby's absence. John's repeated question, "When is Dad coming home?" (38), constructs the father's absence as the central cryptogram of the play. As Del, who functions as the surrogate father/husband—a stand-in for "Dad" in the first part of the play—attempts to allay John's anxiety, he only seems to fuel it, for he cannot offer him any solutions to the puzzle:

> Del: What does it mean "I could not sleep"?
> John: . . . what does it mean?
> Del: Yes. It means nothing other than the meaning you choose to assign to it. (4)

Lines like these early in the play function as a warning that linguistic signification is random, subject to an infinite multiplicity, problematizing both the characters' and audiences' ability to extract definite (symbolic) meanings from the dramatic situation. Yet in the text for the play, which is not seen by the audience, Mamet emphasizes certain words and phrases with capitalization, quotation marks, and italics, as if to indicate that they bear significant meanings. When Del refers to John and his father's camping trip to the woods that John is looking forward to the next day, for example, the "T" in the word "Trip" (4) is capitalized, as is the "W" in "woods" (4), signaling the importance to John of this father-and-son outing. To the reader, these capitalized words appear to be a code referring to a male myth, which John confirms when he acknowledges that "it's something. To go out there" (5). This "something," however, is not able to be explicated by John, Del, or Donny.

While Mamet frequently places such emphasis on words in his writing, this linguistic coding is particularly significant when it refers to such male myths, for it points to big ideas that men cannot articulate when together, for it would be considered to be a femininized activity. In his essay "In the Company of Men," Mamet derides the notion of "male bonding [as] an odious phrase meant to describe an odious activity" (87). In its place, he celebrates "hanging out" and "spending time with the boys" in places and activities like "The Lodge, Hunting, Fishing, Sports" (88), capitalizing the first letters as if to fill The Lodge with mystical male meaning. Indeed, such big ideas would suffer from verbal definition, interfering with what Mamet identifies as the ideal way for men to be together, having "That Fun Which Dare Not Speak Its Name" (87). This obvious allusion to Lord Alfred Douglas's description of male homosexuality substitutes "fun" for the all-too-vulnerable word "love," which is verboten in the lexicon of male mythology. In fact, as Eve Kosofsky Sedgwick points out, Douglas's description[3] comments upon the societal investiture in maintaining ignorance and secrecy in "public speech" when referring to nearly *any* type of male-to-male form of intimacy (74). The appropriation of Douglas's 1894 phrase, restated in Mamet's 1990s capitalization-code, expresses a flip dismissal of homosexual implications about male bonding. Radavich has documented the ways in which homophobic dismissals in Mamet's male-cast plays, such as *American Buffalo* and *Glengarry Glen Ross*, begin with "homosexual slander" (50) (homophobic name-calling) and escalate into "'homosexual panic'" (54) as men try to protect themselves from the "threat of emasculation" (51) by absent women and other men. Within the all-male universe of these earlier plays, homophobic dismissals may be contextualized as logical extensions of a heterosexual male mythology, and, therefore, may be construed as critiques of such.

The Cryptogram, however, with its openly gay man, a woman, and a child, stages a different world—one in which the audience might reasonably expect discourse patterns to shift away from heterosexist male mythology. But as verbal cryptograms are exchanged it becomes clear that they nearly all refer back to the absent patriarch, establishing an off-stage straight man and his mythology as the present and controlling subject of the play. Del, Donny, and John are cast as—to borrow *Sexual Perversity's* reference to women—"inanimate objects" (53). As an extension of their objectified status, the three are preoccupied by a collection of objects in the attic, all of which symbolize the father. These objects are essentially family mementos—a photograph, a stadium blanket, and a knife. They are, effectively, antiques, for they no longer have any functional use. In *The System of Objects*, Jean Baudrillard[4] observes that, while functional objects fulfill a utilitarian purpose in the present time, "antiques refer to the past giv[ing] them an *exclusively* mythological character. The antique object no longer has any practical application, its role being merely to *signify*" (74).

Baudrillard theorizes that antiques may signify mythology on two levels, both in terms of a "nostalgia for origins" (76) and as an "obsession with authenticity" (76). He notes that "authenticity always stems from the Father: the Father is the source of value here. And it is this sublime link that antiques evoke in the imagination, along with the return journey to the mother's breast" (77). Certainly, the motivation behind the fascination with objects in *The Cryptogram* lies in the nostalgia for origins embodied by stories about the father. But this nostalgia and the accompanying desire for authenticity—that is, *proof of the truth* of these stories—is continually frustrated.

While the play's aborted dialogue attempts to interpret the narrative meaning of the family's past, it focuses obsessively upon the "mass of things" (42) in the unseen attic, gesturing at Harold Pinter's play *The Collection* (1962). As Mamet's most obvious linguistic influence, Pinter's language continually frustrates the desire of the spectator or characters to understand an authentic story, or myth. Perversely, Pinter's play refers only once to the objects named in its title:

> James: Hawkins was an opera fan too. So's whatsisname. I'm a bit of an opera fan myself. Always kept it a dead secret. I might go along with your bloke to the opera one night. He says he can always get free seats. He knows quite a few of that crowd. Maybe I can track old Hawkins down and take him along too. He's a very cultivated bloke, your bloke, quite a considerable intelligence at work there, I thought. He's got a collection of Chinese pots stuck up on the wall, must have cost at least 1500 a piece. Well, you can't help noticing that sort of thing. (67)

The Chinese pots themselves bear very little significance to the play's meaning, other than the connotation of orientalism that they place upon the object—"the bloke"—to whom James refers. Rather, it is the *idea* of the collection of useless objects that function as antiques to which James responds. They function *only* on the symbolic level and to James they signify the quantitative wealth of the "bloke." James also reads their qualitative signs, but does so by implying that the "bloke" is homosexual, or at least a feminized (castrated) man through code words such as "opera fan" (which James must maintain as a "secret" identity) and "that crowd" (i.e., "knowledge" of the queer opera crowd). When James says "You couldn't say he wasn't a man of taste" (67), Pinter employs a double negative to confuse the audience's ear, while allowing James to give a dubious compliment. Ironically, he tells his wife that by sleeping with the "bloke," "by accident," she has "opened up a whole new world" (67) for him, implying that he has some homoerotic interest in the "bloke." This "accident," like Pinter's play itself, experiments with the randomness of plot, character construction, and symbology. Mamet, to a large degree, adopts Pinter's project in *The Cryptogram*, indicated when Del says that things mean "nothing other than the meaning you choose to assign to [them]" (4).

As if to search for the father, or the family's authenticity, Donny sends John up the prominent staircase to "see if you find any things up there" (13). The staircase, which is the only part of the set that gestures at the attic, would seem to be a ladder up to the higher allegorical meanings one might assume are attached to the attic's store of antiques. Donny has found a photograph in the attic that she shows to Del, saying, "Isn't it funny? Though? The things you find?" (17). Rather than prompting memory, however, as an authentic antique might, the photograph of

Bobby, Donny, and Del before the child's birth causes Del to repeatedly claim that "I don't remember" (31), severing his connection with the family's past, as well as fracturing his present identity within it. Although Del recognizes that he is wearing Bobby's shirt in the photo—a sign that could point either to his male bonding with Bobby or to his role as a surrogate husband to Donny—he distrusts it, remarking that "photography is . . . very seductive" (23).

Like the photograph, the blanket is also an antique that refers to the family's past, confusing the bond between mother and child, who argue about when it was torn, or when its ability to signify the unity of the family was broken. Speaking from offstage, Donny calls out:

> Donny: It was torn long ago. You can absolve yourself.
> John: . . . I *thought* that I tore it.
> Del: But you see, in reality, things unfold . . . independent of our fears of them.
> John: I don't know what you mean.
> Del: Because we *think* a thing is one way does not mean that this is the way this thing must be. (30–31)

When Del explains that "in reality, things unfold," he echoes Mamet's ontological idea, which recurs in several plays and films, that "things change" at random, independent of human narratives or attempts at myth-making.[5] In *The Cryptogram*, the "things" that change are expressed on two metadramatic levels: first, circumstances change in the father's absence, altering the structure of the family and their relationships. This is made apparent in the secondary level, in which the meanings of the objects change, in that they no longer possess the ability to signify patriarchal origin or authenticity. The photograph and the stadium blanket function as hypercoded stage props on a theatricalist level, detached from dramatic meaning. Their ability to signify meanings about the family's origin has been lost and they become, not cryptograms, but vacuous conundrums. The Others in the play, however, cling to their desire to make symbolic sense of the props.

Unlike the photograph and the blanket, which metadramatically question the audience's ability to understand the family's history, the knife, which is the play's most central prop, deludes characters and audience into believing that it carries decipherable meanings. When Donny asks Del if he knows the "Meaning" (64) of the knife, if he knows "what it's for" (65), he gives a simple answer: "To cut things" (65), as if it were merely a utilitarian object with only a practical, everyday use. The phrase "to cut things" could establish the knife as a phallic metaphor that both literally and symbolically penetrates "things," enacting a form of rape that could also be murder. This is certainly the case in Eugene Ionesco's *The Lesson* (1951), in which a Professor tutors a Pupil in an absurdist repetition of "knife . . . kni . . . fe . . ." (73) as he brandishes a knife at her.[6] This repetition builds until he stabs her and she falls onto a chair, "*legs spread wide*" (75), as if she has been raped, as well as murdered, by the knife. Ionesco's stage directions allow the director a choice between "*a big knife, invisible or real*" (73), recalling Macbeth's "dagger of the mind, a false creation" (2.2.38). If an imaginary knife is used, the action becomes focused almost entirely upon the lack of meaning in the word "knife," and the rape-murder becomes a theatricalist abstraction that illustrates the power of language to murder; as the Professor observes, "the knife kills" (74). The knife, then, signifies language itself in Ionesco's play, and, in the Maid's estimation, "philology leads to crime" (76). This formulation could be said to be the underlying logic in most of Mamet's drama and cinema, in which language betrays.

In *Three Uses of the Knife: On the Nature and Purpose of Drama*, Mamet conceives of the knife as providing a "drive-to-resolution" (67) in dramatic structure. Quoting Leadbelly (also Huddie Ledbetter, see epigraph), Mamet reasons that the first two uses, "to cut the bread . . . [and] to shave" (66), were to please a lover, whereas the third use, "to cut out her lying heart" (66), was to "ensure she gave her love to no one else" (67). This obvious phallic rape-murder is justified by various male mythologies that call upon men to take control of women as property. Mamet, however, veils the type of power-motivated murder symbolized by the knife in romanticism, writing that "the appearance of the knife is the attempt of the orderly, affronted mind to confront the awesome" (67). The "orderly, affronted mind" is obviously male in Mamet's lexicon, and he goes on to claim that "the awesome, the inevitable are the province of theater and religion" (67), the purpose of which "is to inspire cleansing awe" (69).

Here, Mamet seems to invoke Aristotelian notions of the positive effect of tragic purgation in order to mystify the violence encoded in male myths of the knife, imbuing it with vague religiosity. This religious mystification surrounds the recitation of a story of murder, told in the voice of a fake spiritualist medium, in *The Shawl* (1985). The male medium represents the voice as a woman's, who says that she provoked the murder by begging her lover to take her with him when he leaves: "How can you leave me in this room—clung to him, threatened, his fierce, my mistake, threatened with the . . . you say that I reaped the desired result, that I won, stabbed, stabbed in the belly, ripped out with his dirk, bloodied the sheets, wiped it on the wall . . . when he'd killed me"(23). The incredulous voice says that "his fierce" was "my mistake" and goes further to suggest that it was suicide, saying, "I reaped the desired result," in which she

"won" a stab "in the belly." Mamet makes the equation between the knife
and the phallus in the phrase "ripped out with his dirk," in which the
dirk/knife clearly stands for "dick."

In *The Cryptogram*, the knife functions as a phallic signifier of male
mythology, said to be a "War Memento, with 'associations'" (87), as if to
promise that it is a conduit for the father's heroic war stories. The knife
is an antique, a phallic weapon of the father, which carries the weight of
two male myths in the play. The first myth of the knife is recounted by
Donny as a story that would seem to establish the authenticity of Bobby's
masculinity, in which the knife is said to be a "combat trophy" (84), a
"German Pilot's Knife" (83) that he brought back from the "War."

> Donny: It's a *pilot's* knife . . .
> Del: . . . yes. I know that . . .
> Donny: If he was forced to *parachute* . . .
> Del: Yes.
> Donny: The pilot would use it to cut the *cords*. If his parachute snagged.
> Del: Huh. If it snagged. On, on what?
> Donny: On a tree. (65)

This reading of the knife is reminiscent of the knife in Mamet's play *Edmond*, in which the knife is identified as "*a survival* knife. G.I. Issue.
World War Two" (77). In both of these plays, the stories that attach the
knives to a historic war and to the notion of survival represent the symbolic, idealized level of male mythology. These speeches romanticize the
past, expressing the nostalgia for origins represented by the father for
whom both John and Edmond are searching.

The characters are faced with the task of decoding the meaning of
this myth at greater length, however, producing a slippage between the
symbolic and "real" levels. As Del reflects: "When he was forced to
abandon his . . . (*Pause.*)" (66). In the space of Del's pause, the unspoken
word "family" could be inserted. He continues, "He looked for *safety*,
and the knife, it cut . . . It '*released* him'" (66). When Del considers
Bobby's "Odd Gesture" (64) of giving him the knife as a sort of "going-
away present" (64), the potential for the knife (male mythology) to release him from his family bonds becomes resonant, if unspoken, in the
cryptic dialogue. Del then proceeds to tell his narrative of the gift of the
knife, which is a nostalgic myth of male friendship that seems to romantically forget the myth's proscription against homosexuality. His
fictional account of his fishing trip with Bobby imagines that Bobby's
gift of the knife is a "sign" (68) of his symbolic initiation—as a gay
man—into the world of men and its codes. He says: "It's funny for two

grown men to go camping anyway. (*Pause.*) I don't care. (*Pause.*) Huh. I
was born a *city* boy. (*Pause.*) (*He displays knife.*) And now I'm a Forester.
(*Pause.*) I'm a Ranger . . . did you know there's a Fraternal Group called
the Catholic Order of Foresters?" (68).

In making up this lie about the knife, which he displays as a badge
of honor, Del nostalgically reveals his own desire to become an "official" man, a member of a "Fraternal . . . Order," and in doing so, exposes the nearly medieval fictions of male mythology. As Donny
continues to probe for specifics, clearly disbelieving him, Del finally
breaks down, violating the masculine ethos by telling the truth to an
outsider—a woman. He says: "We didn't *go!* Do I have to *shout* it for
you . . . ? We stayed *home.* What do you *think?* He'd traipse off in the
wilds . . . with *me* . . . ? To talk about *life?* Are you *stupid?* Are you
blind? He wouldn't spend a *moment* with me. Some poor geek . . ."
(74). In substituting the word "geek" for "queer," Del frames his status
as a homosexual in a world of straight men as being equivalent to a
sideshow freak, for whom there is no possibility of being anything than
Other. Their common betrayal by Bobby could (in someone else's play)
unite them in a common bond of anger. But these marginalized characters are like the collection of objects in the attic who reference their
identities to the male mythology of the father-subject.

This scene recalls the "mock duel" (75) in Pinter's *The Collection,* when
Bill picks up a "splendid cheese knife" (72) and James grabs a "fruit knife"
(74) for his attack on Bill, the gay "bloke." The knives are referred to by
their utilitarian names, indicating that they are not antiques, but they
nevertheless function as warlike phalluses. The metatheatricality of the
"mock duel" emphasizes the symbolically homoerotic nature of their gestures and wounds, as the two ask each other if they "swallow" knives.
James throws the "fruit knife" at Bill's face, missing it, but producing a
"scar" (75) on Bill's hand. While Pinter appears to be more concerned
with the sexual level of *The Collection* as yet another narrative to be un-
spun, Mamet's *The Cryptogram* seems to be fixated primarily upon the
narrative mythology of the father.

With the destruction of the nostalgic myth of male friendship, Donny
challenges the myth of heroic authenticity attached to the knife, revealing that it is not a souvenir from the "War," but that Bobby simply bought
it "From a man. On the street. In London" (87). Similarly, in *Edmond,* the
real history of the "*survival* knife," for sale in the pawn shop, is equally
fuzzy, even though it is said to be the "best knife that money can buy"
(57). While the war story attached to the knife in *Edmond* goes unchallenged, in *The Cryptogram,* the (apparent) truth would seem to debunk
the knife's masculine "associations," severing its symbolic link with male

heroism and history and decoding it as a fraudulent "story" purchased in a capitalist exchange. Donny uses Del's lack of knowledge of the "real" story as a weapon, attacking him with Mamet's arsenal of invective, calling him "You 'fairy'" (86) and "You faggot" (94), ostensibly removing him from his role as surrogate father and husband and homophobically reinscribing him as an Other on the margins of the family.

The overlapping metadramatic stories connected to the encrypted objects in the play increasingly point to its tragic end, as John questions, "Do you ever think things? . . . Do you ever wish that you could die?" (78). John's "think[ing] things," in his attempts to decode the blanket and the knife, have been blocked, and he can only cling, childishly, to the meanings and outcomes he desires—his father's return and a trip to the "Cabin" (80)—that are still encoded for him in the knife's mythology. He seizes upon the knife as a symbol in his own version of a masculine "story," and, hearing "voices" (100) calling him, he constructs a fiction about why he wants it, saying that he needs it to cut the twine wrapping the blanket, as if to unravel his family's history. In the end, Del tells him to "Take the knife and go" (101), as if it were an invitation to take all of the associations with masculinity the knife carries and do the only thing he can do, which is to exit from the family and life. John's suicide seems to reverberate with one of the last lines in Clifford Odets' *The Big Knife* (1949), in which the lead male is said to have "killed himself . . . because that was the only way he could live" (76).[7]

The end of *The Cryptogram* suggests that John's death occurs at a symbolic level, almost without his use of the "real" knife, but an imaginary one. In *Edmond*, also, the knife seems to wield itself as Edmond stabs Glenna, saying to her "*now* look what you've done" (78). Edmond's act of murder, that is, killing the "stupid fucking *bitch*" (78), is defended when Edmond acknowledges he "doesn't feel like a man" because his "balls were cut off. . . . A long, long time ago" (25). After the murder, when he claims he had the knife "for protection" from "everyone" (83), it is suggested that, suffering from castration anxiety, he could not discover that his "real" manhood/penis resembled the symbolic phallus. He metatheatrically acts out a male myth with the prop/knife by killing Glenna, who represents a figure of castration in the world, which Edmond perceives as a "shit house" (71). He wants to return to the "Theatre. . . . [where he may] *ask respect*" (71) for himself. As Edmond sits in prison awaiting emasculation by homosexual rape, he says, "Every fear hides a wish," (89), suggesting an awareness of homoerotic desire underlying his homophobia. While *Edmond* is an expressionist journey play, it keeps a masculine silence, as the audience is not permitted to witness the interiors of any of its characters.

The Cryptogram would seem to suggest that in Mamet's drama of the
1990s there is no exit from the crippling fictions of male mythology. Although the deconstruction of the knife's symbolic value reveals the unstable, fictional quality of those myths, the marginalized characters of this
"family play" are so deeply invested in defining themselves in relation to
the patriarchy that the play could hardly be said to be a critique of the
masculine ethos. It is, rather, a tragedy of delimited vision that ultimately
can only continue to reinscribe those myths. At the play's end, Donny rationalizes the failure of the myths, claiming that "Things occur. In our
lives. And the meaning of them . . . the *meaning* of them . . . is not
clear. . . . But we must assume they have a meaning. We must" (79). Despite her crucial role in exposing the myths as lies, she can only reinvest
her identity in them. Using the vernacular of the masculine ethos, she
writes Del off as "You faggot. [Like] Every man I ever met in my life . . ."
(94). Del participates in this fag-bashing, saying "Who am I? Some poor
Queen. Lives in a hotel" (94), and "I'm pathetic. I know that. You don't
have to tell me. The life that I lead is trash. I hate myself" (88). This language of self-pity and self-loathing—which is some of the most direct,
least cryptic verbiage in the play—does not seem to be spoken by the
voices of a woman and a gay man, but rather by the voice of a heterosexual male, just as the voice of the murdered woman in *The Shawl* emanates
from the fake male spiritualist. The male voices in these plays, speaking
from behind Mamet's wizard-curtain, manifest a basic belief in male
mythology that reinscribes the woman as "cunt" and gay man as "fairy."
And that is the tragedy.

NOTES

1. Robert Vorlicky has observed that Donny's identification of Del as "You
   fairy" and "You faggot" recall the labels applied to Williamson in *Glengarry Glen Ross,* when, after he breaks the male codes of salesmanship,
   Roma calls him a "stupid fucking *cunt,*" a "fairy" and a "fucking *child*"
   (96–97)—names which could, ironically, be applied to the characters of
   The Cryptogram. (See Robert Vorlicky, review of *The Cryptogram,* Westside Theatre, New York, May 28, 1995, in *The David Mamet Review* 2
   [Fall 1995]: 3–4).

2. For a discussion of Poe's use of cryptograms to demystify myths (as opposed to Mamet's use of them to mystify), see Terence Whalen's "The
   Code for Gold: Edgar Allen Poe and Cryptography," *Representations* 46
   (Spring 1994): 35–57. Also see Michael Williams' "'The language of the
   cipher': Interpretation in 'The Gold Bug,'" *American Literature* 53 (January 1982): 646–60.

3. Lord Alfred Douglas wrote of the "Love that Dare Not Speak Its Name" in "Two Loves," *The Chameleon* 1 (1894): 28.

4. For a different reading of Baudrillard against Mamet, see Elizabeth Klaver's "David Mamet, Jean Baudrillard and the Performance of America," *David Mamet's Glengarry Glen Ross: Text and Performance*, Ed. Leslie Kane (New York: Garland, 1996), 171–83.

5. See, for example, Mamet's *American Buffalo, Glengarry Glen Ross, House of Games* and *Things Change*.

6. For studies that relate Ionesco's *The Lesson* to Mamet's *Oleanna*, see Verna Foster's "Sex, Power and Pedagogy in Mamet's *Oleanna* and Ionesco's *The Lesson*," *American Drama* 5:1 (Fall 1995): 36–50; and Craig Stewart Walker's "Three Tutorial Plays: *The Lesson, The Prince of Naples* and *Oleanna*," *Modern Drama* 40 (1997): 149–62.

7. Clifford Odets' *The Big Knife* contains very few similarities with *The Cryptogram*. It is, by Odets' description, a "melodrama" (Rhodes) about a Hollywood actor's descent into suicide. It contains no knife or allusion to one, but in an interview with the *New York Times,* Odets explained that "the big knife is that force in modern life which is against people and their aspirations, which seems to cut people off in their best flower" (Peck). Like so many of Odets' plays, therefore, this becomes a play about the struggle of an individual against social forces, ultimately critiquing society. Arguably, that is also an aspect of Mamet's drama, although the comparison would seem to end there.

WORKS CITED

Baudrillard, Jean. *The System of Objects.* First published as *Le système des objets.* Paris: Editions Gallimard, 1968. Trans. James Benedict. New York: Verso, 1996.

Dolan, Jill. *The Feminist Spectator as Critic.* Ann Arbor: U of Michigan P, 1991.

Douglas, Lord Alfred. "Two Loves." *The Chameleon* 1 (1894).

Foster, Verna. "Sex, Power, and Pedagogy in Mamet's *Oleanna* and Ionesco's *The Lesson.*" *American Drama* 5:1 (Fall 1995): 36–50.

Ionesco, Eugene. *The Lesson.* 1951. *Eugene Ionesco: Four Plays.* Trans. Donald M. Allen. New York: Grove Press, 1958, 43–78.

Klaver, Elizabeth. "David Mamet, Jean Baudrillard and the Performance of America." *David Mamet's "Glengarry Glen Ross": Text and Performance.* Ed. Leslie Kane. New York: Garland, 1996, 171–83.

Lacan, Jacques. *Ecrits: A Selection.* Trans. Alan Sheridan. New York: Norton, 1977.

Mamet, David. *The Cryptogram.* 1994. New York: Vintage Books, 1995.

———. *Edmond.* 1982. New York: Grove Press, 1983.

———. *Glengarry Glen Ross.* 1983. New York: Grove Press, 1984.

————. "In the Company of Men." In *Some Freaks*. New York: Viking, 1989, 85–91.

————. Interview. *The South Bank Show*. October 1994.

————. "Kryptonite: A Psychological Approach." In *Some Freaks*. New York: Viking, 1989, 175–80.

————. *Sexual Perversity in Chicago and The Duck Variations*. 1974, 1972. New York: Grove Press, 1978.

————. *The Shawl*. New York: Samuel French, 1985.

————. *Three Uses of the Knife: On the Nature and Purpose of Drama*. Columbia Lectures on American Culture. New York: Columbia UP, 1998.

McDonough, Carla J. "David Mamet: The Search for Masculine Space." In *Staging Masculinity: Male Identity in Contemporary American Drama*. Jefferson, NC: McFarland & Company, 1997, 71–101.

Odets, Clifford. *The Big Knife*. New York: Dramatists Play Service, 1949.

Peck, Seymour. "An Angry Man from Hollywood." *New York Times* February 20, 1949.

Pinter, Harold. *The Collection*. 1961. *Three Plays*. New York: Grove Press, 1962.

Radavich, David. "Man among Men: David Mamet's Homosocial Order." *American Drama* 1:1 (Fall 1991): 46–60.

Rhodes, Russell. Interview with Clifford Odets. *New York Herald Tribune*. May 1, 1949.

Savran, David. *Taking It Like a Man: White Masculinity, Masochism and Contemporary American Culture*. Princeton: Princeton UP, 1998.

Sedgwick, Eve Kosofsky. *The Epistemology of the Closet*. Berkeley: U of California P, 1990.

Shakespeare, William. *Macbeth*. *The Complete Works of William Shakespeare*. Ed. William George Clark and William Aldis Wright. New York: Grosset & Dunlap, 1864, 979–1006.

Silverman, Kaja. *Male Subjectivity at the Margins*. New York: Routledge, 1992.

Vorlicky, Robert. *Act Like a Man: Challenging Masculinites in American Drama*. Ann Arbor: U of Michigan P, 1995.

————. Review of *The Cryptogram*, dir. David Mamet. Westside Theatre: New York. May 28, 1995. *David Mamet Review* 2 (Fall 1995): 3–4.

Walker, Craig Stewart. "Three Tutorial Plays: *The Lesson, The Prince of Naples* and *Oleanna*." *Modern Drama* 40 (1997): 149–62.

Zeifman, Hersh. "Phallus in Wonderland: Machismo and Business in David Mamet's *American Buffalo* and *Glengarry Glen Ross*." *David Mamet: A Casebook*. Ed. Leslie Kane. New York: Garland Press, 1992, 123–35.

MAMET'S NOVELISTIC VOICE

ILKKA JOKI

"'You can't ask equipment to do more than's in its nature.'"
—*David Mamet*, The Village

In an interview with David Mamet, Melvyn Bragg introduces a parallel to Mamet's first novel, *The Village* (1994), in Thornton Wilder's celebrated play, *Our Town* (1938), and Mamet readily agrees (*DMI*).[1] To be sure, the strength of both works stems from their idea that the spectacular cannot be and is not more important or representative than the ordinary. The everyday, the seemingly commonplace, can aesthetically suggest something essential and unique in the human condition, as these American authors demonstrate. *Our Town* concludes with a cavalcade, a funeral scene that emphasizes the place of the individual in the grand scheme of things. *The Village*, too, provides a "false ending" in a scene at a cemetery, but with a strong military accent. Moreover, the penultimate tone of the novel brings home the unexpected, "always the unforeseen" in human existence: "Everything changes except War" (*V* 231; 230). The voice here is Lynn's, the oldest and arguably wisest of the male characters, the consummate hunter, but Mamet emphatically endorses the idea through his choice of Lynn as the focus in this crucial scene.

To emphasize the parallel further, *Our Town* is a highly novelistic drama, and *The Village* is a novel whose form and structure reflect the dramatic genres of the theater and the cinema, exhibited most strikingly by the almost violent economy of its segmented format. The common ground for these two works is the overarching speaking persona, the narratorial voice. What is at issue here is the "dramaticality" of drama and the "novelness" of the novel, their generic distinctiveness. In this context, Mikhail Bakhtin's theories of the various genres of speech, such as the "ordinary" and the "artistic," their times and lives, provides an enlightening heuristic.[2]

I

Bakhtin's insistence on the "monologicality" or absolute authorial control characteristic of "pure" drama is well known and much debated. Obviously, playwrights create characters who are, potentially, temporarily or "constantly," the playwright's "spokespersons." As a foregrounded example of this device, Manfred Pfister mentions the "epilogue" to Brecht's *Der Gute Mensch von Sezuan*—an after-the-event account external to the represented world (Pfister 110). By contrast, Pfister argues, the authorial voice internal to the imagined world can be brought forth by the choir or by a directorial character. According to Pfister, the Stage Manager in *Our Town* is exactly such a trusted agent. Characters of this latter type have the task of mediating between the world that the playwright (re)presents on stage and the audience. The remarkable thing about the Stage Manager, and by extension about Wilder's authorial voice, is that this character is at times rather overbearing and "monologizing," although still highly sympathetic (Joki 64). The authenticity of the Stage Manager's speech authority is underscored by our knowledge that Wilder himself played this very role (Gould 212). What is generically most striking here, however, is the fact that by pressing the novelistic device of the narrator to its limits, Wilder has deliberately monologized his prototypically Western drama.[3] If one were to take Bakhtin's word at face value, such a move, novelization, or testing and pressing the generic boundaries, as he calls it, might rather have been coupled with the opposite discourse phenomenon, dialogization, or the (relative) liberation of the dramatic characters' voices in general. In other words, there appears to be something inherently monologic to the narrator institution, no matter what literary genre offers to host it. Dialogization seems to be brought about despite this given monologism—or the author may deliberately capitalize on the extra edge of knowledge attached to the narrator. The latter one is the choice that Wilder and Mamet have made.

In *The Village*, the narrator elects to report and show how one of the characters, Henry, learns about an auction within a comfortable distance from his home, gets there in time to secure seating that will afford him an overview of the audience and the "scene," and lets himself be sucked into the interchange. The narrator lets his true opinions be seen through foregrounding Henry's admiration for the auctioneer's performance: "It hung in the air. And the crowd waited. There was no 'going Once'. . . . It was the auctioneer's pleasure to extend or stop the bidding at will" (*V* 41). Henry's observations on this subject are acceptable for the narrator as such, without question or coloring comment of his own. Indeed, this narrator does not care to hide his pleasure in, will to, and power over, his function as narrator. He dispenses knowledge at his discretion, and he segments and reshuffles the storyboards in ways that capture the reader's primary interest. This ordering and organizing activity is what the Russian Formalists, such as Victor Shklóvsky, called "plot."[4]

In the case of Mamet's first novel, the analogy of cutting, splitting, stacking, and burning logs is close at hand—an image highlighted in the novel itself. The story of *The Village* emerges from the yarns the characters constantly spin in order to plot their bearings in varying situations with each other and within themselves. This content or *sjuzét* of the work is not a particularly difficult problem.[5] The characters and their plotted tales and their themes or various *sjuzéts* we can deal with. The narrator has allowed that. One's more difficult task in *The Village* is to come to terms with the narrator "himself" and "his" plotting. But why all this foregroundedness? The narrator meets the reader halfway by revealing that some of the characters' stories are not entirely "based in facts" or "valid," but one cannot really be so sure of the status of some of them. Also, the narrator maintains an ironic distance from certain characters and the grasp of the world he shares with a few others (Lynn, the role model and focalizer, Marty, and Henry). In other words, the narrator takes the reader into his confidence, but not unreservedly, not consistently. The instances when this unequivocally happens are invaluable as ways of getting at the elusive narrator. The momentarily careless narrator may have revealed more than he had intended. Yes, this is a pursuit; the hunt is on.

For example, the narrator records what takes place inside Beth's head (she is the daughter of Marty—one of the more skilled hunters) at the dinner table: "'Nobody knows what I'm thinking,' she thought" (*V* 74). The narrator thus sportively shows that he knows all about the reckless self-confidence of the young, as well as their fundamental insecurities, but this sphere of experience cannot engage him for long, since he has more interesting emotional areas to explore.

For Marty himself, entering into the woods is like a homecoming. He takes his position in a rocky landscape, anticipating targets, sitting "'In a cleft of the rock,' he thought, and, 'Then the Lord shielded him with His hand,' and he laughed softly and shook his head, as if to discount or disavow a grandiose comparison" (*V* 28). Here the narrator both sympathizes with and is made slightly insecure by the self-revelatory vista that Marty willy-nilly opens: the question of a supreme being and the role of language in shaping existence. This insecurity shows in the choice of expressions such as "discount" and "disavow," culled from an awkwardly literary register or speech genre. Marty himself makes an attempt to balance the diction by resorting to a "manly" speech genre: "'Oh, God, I could just explode,' he thought, 'it's so fucken beautiful'" (V 30).

The narrator moves toward the other speech extreme while reporting a flashback Marty has in the rock country: "And he thought back to his climbing the rock face, and the time he'd gotten up there, two hundred feet up, and could not get down, frozen, just below the top of the cliff, and couldn't get a grip, over, on the grass, or a root, to pull himself up, and couldn't find the projection, to start his way down, eviscerated by fear, until he had forced himself into a state of balance sufficient to start him down the cliff" (V 31).

Now, the phrasing "he'd gotten," in the first half of this initially exhausted and then recomposed sentence, stands for an index of Henry's idiolect. But toward the close of this descriptive report the diction turns more literary again. Above all the passive participial form "eviscerated by" is impossibly out of character for Marty, who runs a small workshop doing repairs on vehicles. He would probably talk about "cutting out the innards." And all the other villagers, too, with the possible exceptions of Henry and the Minister, would have to look up "eviscerated." In other words we are dealing with a double-voiced and more accurately a hybrid utterance, whereby the narrator forces the reader, through paying attention to Marty, to return to an awareness of that narrator.

Two readings would be feasible here. In the first place, the scene might be interpreted as a script in a cinematic sense, the phrase "eviscerated" being a neutral directive for a "medium shot," showing both Marty's distressed facial expression and the positions of his numbed hands and the rest of his body. But a second reading would harmonize with the first, spiritual example above. The narrator's surgical diction here is a sign of slight insecurity and imbalance, the apparent coolness of the tone again a mask for sincere empathy. But a man like Marty, who edits even thoughts and words about God's acts that have been with him since childhood, would himself be liable to get embarrassed at overt, strong displays of sympathetic emotion from another person. The near silence between Marty and Carl and later the markedly restrained tone of the exchange between Billy, the State Trooper, as the news about the death of Marty's son has to be broken, suggest such emotional reticence on his part (V 219–220). Thus, this apparent breach of style actually suggests a delicate sensibility on the part of the narrator.

Henry has a house and a cabin at a pond. He is a writer of some sort. Now, this knowledge alone reverberates with literary associations, such as the "Henry" persona of Henry D. Thoreau's *Walden*. Mamet's Henry, unlike the nineteenth-century observer, has a woman in his house on the hill; but for him, too, the cabin is a celibate sanctuary. Like Marty, Henry, too, is a hunter and a fisherman, but unlike Marty's (and *Walden's* Henry's), his childhood memories are not related to the woods. He does not stay within the village sphere and repair other people's cars, for instance, but he drives around, from auction to auction, like *Walden's* Henry, to view what Thoreau's persona cynically calls "effects" that go to show that "life had not been ineffectual" (*W* 67). "Effects" suggest interaction, which Mamet's Henry relishes; for him "effects" also suggest private treasures whose possession may nullify time (*V* 20). As *Walden's* Henry puts it, openly hostile toward this sort of sentimental affection for "trumpery": "When a man dies he kicks the dust" (*W* 68). In his essay "The Cabin," Mamet accurately analyzes the kind of superiority auction attenders feel over "that person whose goods are out on the lawn" (*TC* 49). Thus Mamet shows understanding for both views toward "leavings," although he seems to be inclined to follow the "sentimental" one.

Mamet's Henry is much more of an outsider than Thoreau's Henry and more in need of private treasures, safe anchorages in time. *Walden's* Henry will remain a presence in his village; his separation from the village is brief and will only intensify the connection. But Mamet's Henry is aware that for the villagers—despite all their friendliness—he will always be a newcomer whose name will not linger after his departure. The natives are going to call him merely "[that] 'fellow lived at the old Bailey place'" after his effects have been disposed of in public (*V* 216). This will never become *his* village.

The narrator is also an outsider, not an active agent in the village, although he penetrates its life and reports at will. Partly for this reason, one suspects, Henry is the one character for whom the narrator reveals greatest affection and affinity. He reports Henry's activities and troubles in detail both as an observer and as the narrator. For example, in chapter four, while driving to town along a mountain road, Henry is forced to follow, at a snail's pace, a truck with a heavy load, without a chance of safely overtaking it. He decides to lag behind at a roadside diner, entering into a conversation the context of which he can only guess (just like the reader). But the narrator still registers Henry's perceptions in every particular as he takes in the setting inside the diner. "There were several cardboard signs, with the usual sayings, up on the wall over the grill" (*V* 71). Firearms provide the balance of the other interior decoration. Limiting description of the signboards to the phrase "with the usual sayings," the narrator implies a similarity between himself and the reader, who is assumed to be familiar with the interiors of diners in the Northeast, just as Henry is.

In effect, the technique labels Henry as the central figure of the novel and defines the ideal audience for the novel as a knowledgeable reader. Certainly sex and gender also play a role in Mamet's idealization of such an audience. When Henry tells his wife about the diner scene later in the evening, he fails as a narrator, for his thoughts are elsewhere; the situation does not engage him. The narrative runs its course on automatic pilot, and the whole thing strikes him as "empty and horrible" (*V* 81). This horror is a stark contrast to the "rapport" between Henry, the narrator, and the ideal audience apropos of the diner; ironically, the contrast comments on the relationship between Henry and this less than perfect audience, this woman who happens to be his wife.

Toward the end of the novel, a mountain lion jumps across the road right in front of Henry's car. While Henry drives in the direction of the village, he thinks about the best way to tell this story to the men at the hardware store. Debating between three possible openings, he finally imagines an elaborate beginning gambit: "[Henry] shook his head, and smiled, with that private knowledge of those who have been there" (*V* 215). Like "the usual sayings" discussed above, this scene confirms the narrator's and the audience's liaison with Henry.

Here Henry the writer dramatizes the mountain lion story for himself as well, deliberately dialogizing his inner speech. "Two parts of his mind spoke," the narrator reports appreciatively (*V* 215). One part of his mind pictures building a community consensus on a person's credibility. At that, ready, having mustered the required courage, rehearsed and "pleased with himself," (*V* 218) like a writer or an auctioneer should be, he arrives at the shop door. But the hardware store has been padlocked by a foreclosure. Henry is thus locked out of the "theater" of speech and deprived of his audience. The death and burial of Marty's son is another chance event that prevents Henry's telling his story of a spectacular sighting. From now on, Henry has to go to town to buy the supplies he needs, but the town will not supply him with the proper audience for his mountain lion story. On his way to town, Henry chances to pass the funeral procession of Marty's son. He drives out of the village and out of the story.

Cut off by the mountain lion, Henry suddenly yearns for a life "'in a pure state,'" "as he phrased it to himself." The narrator reports these thoughts as emerging from "another part of his mind . . . forming the story he would tell down at the store" (*V* 214). The expression "pure state" is typographically distanced, for at least three voices and three different types of addressee intertwine here, and the voice of Thoreau's Henry is not the least important one. In *Walden*, "pure state" is associated with Nature, with beauty, simplicity, beneficence, curativeness, equilibrium, shelter, promise, innocence, inexhaustibility, variety, vastness and strangeness. Another aspect of pure Nature is its merciless presentness and truth to itself: "Nature puts no question and answers none" (*W* 282). A mortal can approximate this miracle, according to *Walden*'s Henry, only by achieving total honesty: "Say what you have to say, not what you ought. Any truth is better than make-believe" (*W* 327).

The past winter, Henry had aimed at achieving this pure state of immediate presentness, but with near disastrous consequences. This incident results in another failure as storyteller for Henry. He is hunting alone, following a deertrack. "There's no one here but me. My wife is not here. Nothing in my life is here except me. In the woods. A Man in the woods. And if I'm strong enough to navigate in this snow, then I am. And there's no further analysis you need" (*V* 201–202). But violating this "pure state," soon two voices struggle within him, one scheming for the destruction of the deer, the other one urging him to return home, for night is falling fast. This inner dialogue leads gradually to uncertainty and obstinacy.

Curiously, Henry is being acutely self-conscious at this time. Like a Dostoevskian character, he is aware that sometimes humans, perhaps out of pride (or "willfulness," to use a key phrase in *The Village*), commit themselves to an action they "know" to be the worst possible choice in their situation. Henry's feeling of loneliness overpowers him, so he personifies and addresses his own compass, *but* refuses to act upon the knowledge that his intuition is taking him straight away from compass North (true North), where, as he knows, his home lies. Henry loses his compass, and even the spare compass he keeps sewn under a badge on his coat slips through his fingers into the snow. Now truly on his own and lost, he blindly, desperately runs through the woods, panicked. Luck or chance or *whatever* saves him when he stumbles upon the North Road, so close to his home and wife, and yet completely alone.

Walden's Henry speaks beautifully and at length on the overall benefits of losing one's way:

It is a surprising and memorable as well as valuable experience, to be lost in the woods any time. Often in a snow storm, even by day, one will come out upon a well-known road, and yet find it impossible to tell which way leads to the village. . . . not till we are completely lost, or turned around . . . do we appreciate the vastness and strangeness of Nature. Every man has to learn the points of compass again as often as he awakes, whether from sleep or any abstraction. Not till we are lost, in other words, not till we have lost the world, do we begin to find ourselves, and realize where we are and the infinite extent of our relations. (*W* 170–71)

As an example of such educational shocks that afford novel points of departure, *Walden*'s Henry tells of going to his village to get a shoe mended, but being thrown into jail because he had refused to pay state taxes (*W* 171).

The narrator of *The Village* reveals a great deal to his audience through his description of Mamet's Henry's response to potentially fatal Nature at such close quarters: "And there's no further analysis you need" is Henry's starting point, but ensuing events force Henry to analyze his situation. Finally, he flees from death like an animal does, but his encounter with Nature results in an impure and senseless state of ugly fright, because, after all, he does not have full animal instincts about him. And when he *did* have all his senses, before his panic, they had failed him. What is strange is not his loneliness in the face of Nature, but his survival despite everything. Still, this distantly hopeful note is balanced by Henry's vision of a homecoming. The section ends with a cinematic zoom shot, "closing in" on Henry's home: "Down below, far below, he saw the bend; and below the bend he saw his house, and the yellow light in the kitchen, and the shadow which was his wife, moving down there, cooking and talking on the telephone" (*V* 210). What Henry sees here in terms of human "themes" in the Proppian sense, or "relations," as *Walden*'s Henry would put it, is a shadow of a dialogue, a distanced reflection of a dialogue with somebody else, most likely over something or somebody else. The first version of Henry's story had failed him completely, and the second one leaves him solitary.

II

In *The Village*, the narrator is constantly more aware of other generic— that is, formally representational—possibilities than the purely narrative ones, and sometimes he has chosen a representational option for "bringing into focus," rather than a more straightforward telling. He frequently accentuates or closes scenes by "showing" a character enter or exit the imagined field of vision of the focalizing character. The restless, sexually charged girl, Maris, often functions as such an eye-catcher in *The Village*, a collector of the "male gaze," as film students like to put it. When the funeral procession for Marty's son walks into sight, Henry's car simultaneously approaches from the opposite direction. The procession yields to Henry's car, which, in turn, slowly glides out of view. Imagistically, Henry is labeled "dead" as a novel character. The observation position proceeds from the general via Henry's eyes to a focus on the procession, and it remains with the mourners. Then there is a quick shift to Lynn's view of them at the cemetery (*V* 227).

Sometimes the narrator pictures what might result if a cinematic "auteur" happened upon the scene. Showing Henry preparing tea in the woods, the narrator comments that it has grown so dark that nobody observing Henry could identify him as anything but "[t]he man" sitting on a log and sipping his tea (*V* 170). When Henry drives home from the Gun Show, having decided to attach the patch he bought to his jacket, he pictures himself "in the woods in the jacket, turning, as to some sound, as to some sense not yet a sound" (*V* 192). Henry is here something of an "auteur" himself. At home, he goes on making and watching this mental movie. The "shots" he projects are not described any longer in such detail, but now Henry is shot, in turn, sitting on the kitchen counter, a spectator of his life, "with the coat across his lap, his hands resting upon it lightly, as if it were a stadium blanket, and he sat very still" (*V* 193).[6]

Similarly, when the State Trooper, Billy, is fishing, alone, at first he sees the scene from his perspective on board the boat, but then suddenly his observation point shifts much further away: "From the shore, someone looking on would have seen a man in a black slicker and a floppy green cap, sitting low in the boat which drifted slowly inland with the wind" (*V* 102). In the next instance, the narrator provides a generic statement about such shifts in perspective. Describing the Trooper, he notes: "He sat in the boat, in a pose that might have looked like a man thinking. But he wasn't thinking" (*V* 105). Here, the narrator indirectly shows what the cinema can do and what it cannot do. Another example occurs when the State Trooper spends an evening at a bar with friends: " . . . the three sat silently for half a minute which each might describe as 'lost in my thoughts,' but which was only another way to enjoy each others' company" (*V* 157).

The narrator twice more uses a similar combination of pictorial representation and contrasting narrative comment. The Minister holds a Sunday school class, relating a parable known to the pupils from the local lore: "'Now, here's a vision of a man. Wet, cold, and *angry*'" (*V* 148). Having made his point (the story is about instinct versus visibility), he moves on: "He got down from the desk and walked to the blackboard. Five words were written, one over the other, and he pointed to the third of them. 'Now,' he said" (*V* 149). There is no way of indicating cinematically that the Minister is pointing at the third of five hierarchical words on the blackboard without revealing what these words actually are, as the narrator chooses to do here (" . . . [P]leasure to extend and stop bidding at will").

And in a "definitive" example, the narrator indicates that the "auteur" should not even contemplate such an undertaking. After Marty's son's death, "Marty looked across the street, at the three people at the entrance of the hardware store. If they had glanced at him they would have seen him quiet and calm. And, although not impertinent, he would not have acknowledged their gaze" (*V* 213). The auteur could not document such interior comment without introducing the awkward voice of the narrator, and thereby compromising generic purity. In *The Village*, marked cinematic shifts between introspection and focused external views only occur in connection with male characters, with the single exception of Maris. But the narrator handles her "differently."

III

Just as Henry pre-dramatizes how he would tell other men about the mountain lion, or pictures how he will look in the woods wearing his patched jacket, Maris toys with a pet plan of hers, about castrating, blinding, and mutilating her mother's boyfriend. This introspection is coupled with Maris's view of a group of villagers, taking her in, discussing her. But the narrator keeps an ironic distance from Maris throughout. According to his report, Maris is fond of her torture plan, because it gives the man just enough time to suffer, and at the same time always keeps her one step ahead, "because she reasoned that given more time than the four seconds, the man might attempt to 'psychologize' her, as she puts it to herself" (*V* 138). The narrator here factually "places within quotes" the way she imagines that a male speech plan might turn out—i.e., the narrator does not subscribe to the scheme but distances himself from it. He would never subject Marty's or Henry's speech to such an openly sarcastic treatment.[7] The tone of the narrator regarding Maris thus also colors his cinematic handling of her.

A similar distrust of male speech is reflected in the inner speech of the "Town girl," the mistress of Billy, the State Trooper. She says something casually hazy, unclear, and even pointless to the Trooper, whose job and public image require deductive powers: "'And I don't even know what I *mean*. . . . but let *him* figure that out'" (*V* 68). Billy's mistress is antagonized by persons who employ such deliberately confusing language as a rule. Men above all stand accused. "Someone *gets* there, n'then they want to pull the *ladder* up" (*V* 68–69). This utterance echoes Carol's virulent condemnation of higher education and learning as an enterprise, as an industry, in *Oleanna* (or as a "racket," as Saul Bellow's protagonist/narrator phrases it in *Humboldt's Gift*).[8]

The image of the missing woman also personifies a communicational dilemma in *The Village*. By the end of the novel, both Maris and the Trooper's girl will be missing, and one of them has probably met with a violent death. The Trooper's wife discovers the existence of the girl Billy had attempted to hide, and either one (or both) of the two women will have to go. Maris has either left or been taken away or she has been killed by one of her sex partners. And then there is Henry's wife, who seems to be no more than a shadow on the kitchen wall.

Feelings between the sexes in *The Village* range from mutual uncertainty to outright suspicion. Carl's question—or story—about what "whores" do when they step out of the room foreshadows this early on in the novel. That dramatized story is clearly a lesson both in the art of storytelling and a case study pertaining to gender borders. The addressees are Marty and his son. The narrator gives a detailed account of the addressivity involved.

"In a *whorehouse,*" he [Carl] began, elaborately indicating that his speech was a lesson geared down for the uninitiated. "In a *whorehouse,* whore comes in, y'choose her, or, whatever, if y'got to take what you get; n'you *tell* her, mm? You go to her *cubby,* n'you *tell* her what it is you *want,* n'she goes *away.*" Marty craned his neck side-to-side, to relieve the stiffness. He took the rag and wiped his hands. He sighed, and sat on the bumper of the bus. Carl sat by him.

"N'*then . . .*" he said, elaborately not including the boy in his speech, "they *stay* away awhile, n'y'r wondering: 'Th'hell are they *doing?*' or 'Is it just *me . . . ?*' N'then they come back, and . . . but *later,* mmm? Y'r wondering: 'Where did they *go,* what were they *doin',* for the love of Christ?'" He made an appeal to Marty. "What could they've been doin'?" (45)

The question is left, and has to be left, open. Both Carl and the narrator indicate that this is one of the eternal, unresolvable issues, a mystery one stops to ponder in silence. And this is the proper way to tell about it, the appreciative narrator hints by relaying the reactions of Carl's addressees. And so it goes on, throughout the novel's regulated shower of story-sparks. The absence of any interface that would perform a faultless "gender change" is evident even between Dick and his wife, who are brought closest to each other by the ruin of their hardware store, their joint venture. "Yes. She could come here, or I could go to her, but there is a *world* between what she is, and me," Dick thinks, when there are just the two of them left (*V* 174).

Even the female characters feel this way. "A fork's a woman, and a knife's a man," Mrs. Bell says (*V* 21).

IV

The intertwining of two stories of solace, the dialogized monologic speeches of the Minister and Dick, at the Church, is the clearest instance of the typical novelistic narratorial work in *The Village*, along with its ending.

In this novel there is also a prototypically absent man, the Banker, but he is absent only physically. He is as present as an emblem of the Town and its economic power over the village; he signs the fate of Dick's business. He is like the Mitch and Murray characters in *Glengarry Glen Ross*, or like a manipulating representative of the "dream of industry" in *The Water Engine*. Dick's dramatized inner speech is addressed to the absent Banker, made present as a captive audience in this imagined encounter. Its subject and location is the hardware store, the same dramatic space for which Henry later rehearses his account of the mountain lion. The goal of Dick's monologic discourse is to destroy the Banker's arguments, to devastate his person, and to rid himself of the store while protecting and restoring his dignity. Dickie, like Henry, tries his hand at being an "auteur."

The Minister's monologue is a sermon, about change, life, and death, about accepting them without despair or pride. Curiously, the principal addressees of this monologue, too, seem to be the men in the congregation. The Minister at first turns to "those of you who have seen a *woman*, who have been blessed, to see a woman giving birth" (*V* 161). Then, almost as an afterthought, he also includes, without mentioning blessedness, "those of you who have given birth," and who have to bear the pain, even though protesting against it and wishing to escape it (*V* 161). The Minister actually comes close to blaming women for doing a poor job at facing this essential task of life that has been assigned to them.

Mamet's orchestration of the two speeches resembles the interactive, simultaneous, hidden telephone dialogues he used in *The Verdict*. But here the novelistic genre allows much greater ease in the alternation between the Minister's out-loud speech and Dickie's inner speech. The speakers are able more clearly to indicate and shift their choice of audiences, make real or imagined pauses in their discourses, rehearse and enjoy the unfolding of their speech plans even in advance. These processes are intimately coupled with reports of the effects these speeches have upon the real and imagined audiences and the corresponding reactions of the real and imagined speakers. In its ability to accomplish all this with such ease, as a unified artistic utterance, the novel would indeed seem to be superior to the dramatic genres, at the same time as it shamelessly borrows its scenic, dramatic structure from them.

Mamet has always proven himself to be a master at marrying the High and the Low, in particular hortative oratory and the demotic, as for instance in the one-acters *A Sermon* and *Cross Patch*. But seldom has he been so subtly successful in going about this as in the church scene of *The Village*. He alternates in foregrounding these two voices, the overt and the inner ones, and the possibility of visualizing the unheard helps him bring out fresh psychological nuances through one of his best-loved dramatic devices. This is what Bakhtin calls dialogized polyphony:

> "And God was sending peace. And yet they fought it. As it is our nature to fight. To resist. To confuse death with life, and life with death; for we are always growing, and dying, and . . ."
> " . . . ten thousand cocksuckers named 'Bob,'" Dickie thought. "And I'll be damned if I have to explain it. What the *hell,* what in the fucking *hell* do they expect is going to happen to this country?"
> " . . . of the search for peace," the Minister continued; and cleared his throat and glanced down at his notes. (*V* 162)

Even in fiction, though, Dickie cannot come up with a bomb-proof speech plan that would convince and convert Bob the Banker and undo the foreclosure. Dickie has to skip this part of his imagined persuasion, and cut straight to a scene with the shame and regret of the Banker as a fait accompli. This gap in the argument is the reason why his fiction ultimately fails to satisfy him. In other words, not even a fantastic dialogue is omnipotent. What about the sermon, then? The juxtaposition of these two monologues seems to suggest that we are in fact more reassured by the theme, the *sjuzét,* the authoritatively decreed speech situation between people with definite roles, than by the words delivered by even a preacher. However, in the context of the novel's narratorial processing, this should perhaps not be seen as a piece of devastating criticism. It is these speech situations and processes themselves that are beneficial.

The final duologue of the novel takes place between Lynn and Billy the State Trooper, at Lynn's hunting cabin. The subject is memory, mementos, stories as mementos, and mysteries, the correct way of telling a story, that is, the right way of dealing with memory and mystery. In the presentation of this dialogue, the narrator himself shows "the right way to tell a story." Likewise, Mamet's novella entitled *Passover* turns upon the right way of telling *the* family story about their miraculous survival during a pogrom in Russia; the right way of baking *their* Passover cake. Indeed, the key word of that story, too, is "right."

In *The Village,* Marty has found a badge in the woods, and given it to Billy as a potential piece of evidence that can have a bearing on the disappearance and suspected murder of Maris. From the description, the reader identifies the Minnesota Fish and Game patch that had belonged to Henry. For Billy and Marty this is on the one hand just a badge that has surfaced in the woods, but on the other hand it is also a mystery to them.

Here, one more time, it is the Auctioneer-Narrator that calls the shots, oversees the bids. He leaves (forever) unresolved the mysteries of Maris and the final story, retold and analyzed by Marty, about a dead man found in the woods. He—doubtless authorized by the narrator—argues that, if true, the story should either have been left untold, or then told simply and modestly, without any guesswork and speculation attached, as a true mystery should be told. The narrator, however, in his telling of the master story, does reveal a track that we know to be false, but that the two characters do not. Henry's patch is an innocent thing, not calling for an analysis, as we know. This last piece of shared knowledge can be regarded as part of the bargain struck between the narrator and the ideal addressee, a reward for the reader for bearing with the "difficult," hard-to-get narrator this far. The sign that Henry had perhaps rashly appropriated and consequently lost is thus pinned onto the reader, for he or she has truly worked for it, having been there all the way.

In sum, the narratorial ideology of *The Village* is of a more modest dimension than the grandiose vista of the universal mind in *Our Town*, created through the novelistic device of the narrator. Nonetheless, even though the events and the plotting of *The Village* bear witness to the dictum "always the unforeseen," the narratorial strategy also hints that persistence and perspicacity, coupled with honesty, can and do pay in the end, if one's expectations are not unreasonable. In the words of *Walden*'s Henry, "With the liability to accident, we must see how little account is to be made of it. The impression made on a wise man is that of universal innocence" (*W* 318). *Walden*'s Henry, too, is dead against speculation over mystery. And as Mikhail Bakhtin puts it, " . . . chance is but one form of the principle of necessity and as such has a place in any novel, as it has its place in life itself" (Bakhtin 97). In the light of *The Village*, what is important is the time shared with other like-minded participants in the presence and the presentness of the correct way of storytelling, a human voice, an image of a speaking person. Such a sharing presents itself in *The Village* as nothing less than the way of regaining and redeeming one's innocence, analogous with public confession.

According to Bakhtin, the present, the actual now, in all its messiness and incompleteness, is the dimension with which the novel is in constant contact. The participants of the novel, and the genre "itself," are fully aware of the fact that it is impossible ever to get the full picture of such a vast gamut of eventualities. But the novel makes radical use of the recognition of such unfinishedness, especially through the situations and possibilities of narrativity. Bakhtin calls it the only genre in which language is both a medium and object of representation, always simultaneously busy with these functions ("the auto-criticism of discourse" [Bakhtin

412]). In Mamet's novel this shows in the massive foregroundedness of the narratorial agency.

Provocatively, Bakhtin repeatedly sets the novel apart from other literary genres, here due to the understood "aloofness" of the author from the genre: "In other genres (the drama, the lyric and their variants)," he argues, "the most contiguous possible position of the author, the point of view necessary to the shaping of the material is dictated by the genre itself: such a maximal proximity of the author's position to the material is immanent in the very genre. Within the genre of the novel, there is no such immanent position for the author" (Bakhtin 161). Because of this necessary aloofness, Bakhtin suggests, " . . . the novelist stands in need of some essential formal and generic mask that could serve to define the position from which he views life, as well as the position from which he makes that life public (161)." In Mamet's case "novelness" and narrativity themselves serve as such masks—the correct way of telling a story. Without this dimension, one might be tempted to call *The Village*, a strikingly scenic and segmented piece of writing, a "dramatized novel." There is, though, an extra bonus to this generic choice: the naturalness of the novelistic voice. One can label the surgical shifts of voice in *The Village*'s church scene nothing else but "natural." Nonetheless, Bakhtin is too categorical in his generic absoluteness. Arguably, the church scene could be staged, perhaps even successfully, for instance, by using spotlights, and a narratorial character or a narratorial voice. But, to give Bakhtin his due, such a spectacle would doubtless smack of "experiment." And this is in fact one more reason to admire the delicate balance between drama and narrativity in *Our Town*.

The Village deals with the vicissitudes of chance but also with necessity from the peculiar and enviable position afforded to and assumed by the narrator. If we accept the position of Mamet's narrator, it will have to be granted that if we were deprived of enforcement and necessity, we would be left with very little except the story and its telling. Under such daunting circumstances, the story will always have to be told the correct way even in the meantime, as a precaution. And along this line there seems to come a point at which we move from the domain of imagination into that of perception—or vice versa. That would seem to be a point very much worth striving for.

NOTES

1. Elsewhere Mamet refers to the novels of Elliott Merrick, who "lived in and wrote about my town in Vermont" ("The Northern Novel," *M-BT*

87) as points of reference as well as to the work of Sinclair Lewis, and "[Theodore] Dreiser and Willa Cather, whom I denominated the Two Greatest American Writers. Thirty-five years later I still think so" (*M-BT* 88). Further Mamet lists Sherwood Anderson, Philip Roth, Saul Bellow, Anzia Yerzierska, Ernest Hemingway, as novelist but especially as a short story writer, and the "non-Beat" work of Kerouac. However, these listings have more to do with the Northern "aura of foreboding" (*M-BT* 90) than with narratological choices, with the obvious exception of Hemingway.

2. On speech genres, see the essay "The Problem of Speech Genres," pp. 60–102, in Mikhail Bakhtin,1986, *Speech Genres & Other Late Essays*, trans. by Vern W. McGee, ed. by Caryl Emerson and Michael Holquist, Austin: U of Texas P. Bakhtin presents a typology of the novelistic or prosaic word in *Problems of Dostoevsky's Poetics*, (1984), ed. & trans. by Caryl Emerson, Manchester: Manchester UP. Bakhtin deals with the particulars of the novel vis-à-vis "the rest" of the literary genres, above all in the essays published in the collection entitled *The Dialogicmagination* (1981), ed. by Michael Holquist, trans. by Caryl Emerson and Michael Holquist, Austin: U of Texas P. ("Epic and Novel," "From the Prehistory of Novelistic Discourse," "Forms of Time and Chronotope in the Novel," "Discourse in the Novel"). The literature on Bakhtin and the various types and situations of discourse is considerable and growing fast. The Bakhtin database—led by Professor David Shepherd at the University of Sheffield, England—is the most comprehensive reference source (Bakhtin Centre, Department of Russian and Slavonic Studies, The University of Sheffield, Sheffield S10 2TN, United Kingdom; Email: bakhtin.centre@Sheffield.ac.uk).

3. In classic or ancient Chinese theater, with which Wilder was reasonably well acquainted, the narrator who sets the stage is a standard device (Gould 212).

4. Shklóvsky takes a parallel from chess. *Sjuzéts* correspond to gambits or classic chess moves. *Plots* can be seen as variants or individual or idiosyncratic realizations and attempted resolutions of these prototypical clashes (cf. Sklovskij 60).

5. According to Vladimir Propp, *sjuzét* or "theme" can be defined through the subjects and objects in a sequence of events (e.g., who, what, or whom?, and so forth), through the actants and patients—the dramatis personae, as he calls them—more than through the connecting predicates used (a dragon kidnaps a princess, for example, or a banker deprives a storekeeper of his livelihood) (cf. Propp 113). Propp's idea is that the number of themes and functions (as represented by the dramatis personae) in the folktale is fixed, whereas there can be almost any number of variants to them. Also, he claims that this (perfected) genre rather effectively constrains the actual performance of the storyteller. It is more the genre than anything else that speaks. This is one of the main reasons why Bakhtin calls the epic a monologic genre: "In its style, tone and manner of expression, epic discourse is infinitely far removed from discourse of a

contemporary about a contemporary addressed to contemporaries. . . .
This boundary . . . is immanent in the form of the epic itself and is felt
and heard in its every word" (Bakhtin "Epic and Novel," 1981, 13–14,
16). By contrast, the fictive narrator, especially under postmodern uncertainty, will find all "predicative" or compositional constraints already broken. Therefore, narrative themes and situations become the other focus of
interest, something semi-tangible, in addition to the very possibility of
narrativity itself. Such is the case in *The Village*.

6. Henry buys at the Gun Show a 1946 Minnesota Fish and Game Authority patch. The patch is something purchased secondhand, but not
paid for in full in terms of invested life. Consequently Henry loses his
sign as he fails as a tracker under the winter cold. At the show, Henry had
longed for a "badge" that could clear the way for him in the crush of the
people, something like a reporter's badge. But instantly he assures himself
that it would be "'the worst lie . . . to claim another man's experience'" like
that: a most unmanly thing to do (*V* 182). A similar item at the auction
catalogue had drawn his attention on a previous occasion: "a 1948 'Minnesota Fishing and Hunting Club' badge" (20). This self-labeling orien-
tation of Henry's is, among other things, a token of his desire to belong,
to gain acceptance as a male inhabitant of the North.

7. At Marty's garage, Carl has just finished his "what-did-the-whore-do?"
story. "[Marty] and Carl sat there, smoking. After a bit Carl nodded.
They sat there for a while more. 'Well,' Marty said, as if the word were in
quotes. Carl turned slightly toward him" (*V* 46). The narratorial mode "as
if" triggers off overt double-voicedness. Marty is about to launch into his
"monkeys" story, in reply to Carl's tale, and the generic way he signals this
is caught by Carl, the narrator of *The Village* and, by implication, the
competent audience. In this instance, the narrator's employment of
quotes is inclusive and appreciative; giving and sharing—the opposite to
the utterances and speech plan of Maris.

8. "The Ph.D. racket is a very fine racket but I want no part of it," says
Charlie Citrine to Rinaldo Cantabile the gangster, whose wife and mistress are both in the academic industry (Bellow 106).

WORKS CITED

Bakhtin, Mikhail. *The Dialogic Imagination.* Ed. Michael Holquist. Trans. Caryl
Emerson and Michael Holquist. Austin: U of Texas P, 1981.
Bellow, Saul. *Humboldt's Gift.* London: Penguin Books, 1983.
"David Mamet Interview" [*DMI*]. *South Bank Show.* LWT Productions, October
1994.
Gould, Jean. *Modern American Playwrights.* New York: Dodd, Mead & Co., 1966.
Joki, Ilkka. *Mamet, Bakhtin, and the Dramatic: The Demotic as a Variable of Addres-
sivity.* Åbo (Turku), Finland: Åbo Akademi UP, 1993.

Mamet, David. "The Cabin." In *The Cabin. Reminiscence and Diversions* [*TC*]. New York: Vintage, 1993, 41–50.

———. *House of Games*. New York: Grove Press, 1983.

———. "Northern Novel." In *Make-Believe Town: Essays and Remembrances* [M-BT]. London: Faber and Faber, 1996, 87–91.

———. *Passover*. Illustr. by Michael McCurdy. New York: St. Martin's Press, 1995.

———. *The Village. A Novel* [*V*]. Boston: Little, Brown and Co., 1994.

Pfister, Manfred. *Das Drama. Theorie und Analyse*. Uni-Taschenbücher 580. 4. unveränderte Auflge. München: Wilhelm Fink Verlag, 1984.

Propp, Vladimir. *Morphology of the Folktale*. 2nd rev. ed., ed. by Louis A Wagner. Austin: U of Texas P, 1968.

Sklovskij, Viktor. *Theorie der Prosa*. Frankfurt am Main: S. Fischer, 1966.

Thoreau, Henry D. *Walden* [*W*]. Ed. J. Lyndon Stanley. Intr. Joyce Carol Oates. Princeton, NJ: Princeton UP, 1989.

Wilder, Thornton. *Our Town*. New York: Vintage, 1957.

"A SMALL PRICE TO PAY"

SUPERMAN, METAFAMILY, AND HERO IN DAVID MAMET'S OEDIPAL *HOUSE OF GAMES*

CHRISTOPHER C. HUDGINS

"Use your head, can't you, use your head, you're on earth,
there's no cure for that."
                                        —*Samuel Beckett*, Endgame

David Mamet's *House of Games* (1987) garnered both high praise and puzzled resentment from its reviewers. Roger Ebert labeled it "The year's best film," while Vincent Canby called it "a wonderfully devious comedy." Molly Haskell, on the other hand, called it "a surprisingly savage treatment of a repressed heroine," which "at end, leaves us suspended in helpless disbelief" (146). Articles and books that discuss Mamet's first directing effort also vary widely in their judgments. At one extreme, Katherine Burkman suggests that Mamet's treatment of Margaret Ford (Lindsay Crouse) is misogynistic, with Mike's (Joe Mantegna's) judgment of her as thief and whore an accurate summation: "Mamet does not give us the melodrama of the good girls versus the bad guys, but rather the melodrama of the bad guys . . . versus the worse women."[1] On the other extreme, several critics read the film's conclusion as implying that Margaret has discovered her identity as a woman, that she has "successfully treated herself," though typically offering few specifics about the nature of that "cure" (Brewer, Van Wert).

Scholars concentrating on the ambiguity of *House of Games* either praise it as fruitfully complex or criticize the film's omission of an obvious moral.

In his *Playboy* interview, Mamet suggests that critics who find his plays and films unclear actually mean that they are "'provocative.' That rather than sending the audience out whistling over the tidy moral of the play, [the ambiguity] leaves them unsettled" (52). Most criticism about ambiguity in *House of Games* has centered on how we are meant to understand Margaret Ford at the film's conclusion. In her insightful essay, Ann C. Hall suggests that "By the end of the film, Ford is enigmatic, but in charge, 'gotten-away-with,' illegal, neither idealized nor condemned. . . . We cannot read complacently, for [Ford's] gesture [with the cigarette lighter] forces us to reconsider, reread, and reevaluate. The [film] . . . violate[s] our own tendency to place female characters on one of two stools [Madonna or whore]" (149). Hall's suggestive reading in effect recognizes that the film's concluding coda has two dominant motifs. The first implies that Ford "has forgiven herself. . . . she is not the same woman," which for Hall inverts the typical film noir plot, revealing Maggie's murder of Mike "as a feminist triumph" over male oppressors. Since the second motif, the theft of the lighter, undercuts the "positive" feminist ending, we wonder about the implications of Maggie's sphinxlike smile (148).

That process of questioning in retrospect is what interests me about this film, its implicit call for us to "reconsider, re-read, and re-evaluate" its ambiguity. Broadly, I approach film analysis by extending reader-response theory; specifically, my heuristic blends Walter J. Ong's insights about authors writing for audiences that they envision or "fictionalize" for themselves with Hans Robert Jauss's well-known ideas about "intended audience response." I recognize the notion of subjective response, but agree with Jauss that a writer includes indicators within his or her work that point toward a trans-subjective horizon of intended response. I'm most fascinated, in that context, with ironic and ambiguous modes and how an artist suggests intended response to such ambiguity or irony. Given the ambiguity of Mamet's work, guardedly using his expository statements of his ideas in his essays and interviews to help "read" such indicators or "labels" seems appropriate, so long as we do no violence to the aesthetic structure of the work itself.

Certainly, *House of Games* is ambiguous, but a careful retrospective reading reveals both scripted and "performative" indexes of intended response to the murder and to the double coda that follows. Such a reading must struggle with the film's ambiguous representation of psychiatry and with what it is that Margaret Ford *wants*, a recurring motif that comically recalls Freud's famous query. Mamet has suggested that screenwriting should be structured around "several very basic questions: What does the hero want? What hinders him from getting it? What happens if he does not get it?" (*On Directing Film*, xv). From this perspective, Mamet structures his plot for *House of Games* around Margaret's pursuit of a life beyond the sterility of her work, around her attraction to Mike, and around her "chance" discovery of Mike's betrayal of the best that is in him, another imaginative recasting of Mamet's central "Oedipus plot."

In his 1988 interview with Henry I. Schvey, Mamet reminds us that for Aristotle "what we celebrate with the audience is the capacity for strife, the capacity for revelation and the capacity for self-knowledge" of the hero, which implies that we celebrate it in ourselves (91–3). Famously, in *On Directing Film*, Mamet posits that "the job of the film director is *to tell the story through the juxtaposition of uninflected images*—because . . . the nature of human perception [is] . . . to perceive two events, determine a progression, and want to know what happens next" (60). He concludes that "The real artistry of the film director is to learn to do without the exposition; and, so, involve the audience" (86). In his conversation with Schvey, Mamet says that, just as in Aristotle's estimate of Greek tragedy, writing for movies is "about . . . when and how you reveal information," and that "what the hero is following and what he ends up with may be two very different things. . . . Oedipus wants to find out why there is a plague in Thebes and then ends up finding out that he killed his dad and screwed his mom. . . . as Aristotle says, the protagonist undergoes both recognition of the situation and a reversal" (93).

Mamet suggests, here, that "things change" suddenly and shockingly for Oedipus, and that his original goal transmutes into a courageous search for self-knowledge. That first search, though seemingly noble, is conditioned by *hubris*, by Oedipus's conviction that he can "outwit" the gods, that he's "exempt." That second search, for Truth in the face of the recognition that he has failed in his initial goal, Mamet writes, celebrates the capacity for self-knowledge. The central conflicts in Mamet's canon erupt when some new revelation or event disrupts a relatively pleasant status quo: Teach's temptation of Don, the sudden life-changing turns of events in *Things Change* (1988), the arrival of disruptive Karen in *Speed-the-Plow*, the revelation that Laura is duplicitous in *The Verdict* (1982), the divorce in *The Cryptogram*, the serious illness of Levene's daughter in *Glengarry Glen Ross*: the plague arrives, the shepherd returns, things change. "Father Brown's" sermon in *We're No Angels* (1989), articulates this idea as Jim echoes the final choral ode in *Oedipus Rex*, summarizing the world as a place where man is completely alone in a dangerous place with nothing to rely upon. The notion of a successful life, he concludes, is "all in your head. They could take the money from you. They could take the position from you. . . . They can whip you. People turn their back on you. Everything happens to everybody. . . . Nothing can stave it off" (108).

Mamet writes in "Self-Help" that "strife is our natural condition," but that many religions and "self-help" systems promote obedience to their precepts to stave it off, offering the secret fantasy of the child, "that every desire is right now within one's wish . . . [in short] that he is God" (164). As he suggests in "Guilt," such systems depend on the "individual's knowledge of his or her own worthlessness. The system holds itself out as the . . . redeemer of the guilty individual" [but] the state these systems profess to cure—anxiety, guilt, nervousness, self-consciousness, ambivalence—is the human condition . . . and, coincidentally, the stuff of art. . . . Psychoanalysis hasn't been able to cure them in a hundred years" (86–87).

In sum, Mamet's well-known statements that we all seek love and community in our world of strife, in conjunction with his devotion to the Oedipal plot and his denigration of psychoanalysis, point toward an "intended retrospective" reading of House of Games, one of his most beautifully structured works. As he points out in "Second Act Problems," in the second act "the previously unsuspected must emerge . . . sink[ing] the protagonist (and the artist) into the slough of despair. . . . Out of this despair must come the resolution to complete the journey. . . . Part of the hero journey is that the hero . . . must revamp her thinking about the world" (37–38)—as Maggie does. Citing Tolstoy, Mamet adds that we "correctly identify the advent of this phenomenon as a 'midlife crisis' and strive to live through it so that we can return to our previously less troubled state" (38–39). This is what Mike insists on doing, abandoning any real attempt to change his life, despite his momentary recognition of the possibility of "communion"—and that kills him. Like many Mamet cautionary figures, Mike rejects love in favor of "business."

In "Kryptonite: A Psychological Appreciation," we find perhaps the most revealing gloss on both Margaret's and Mike's initial refusal of love. The fear of Kryptonite, writes Mamet, "the remnants of [Superman's] destroyed childhood home . . . rule[s] Superman's life. The possibility that the shards of that destroyed home might surface prevents him from being intimate—they prevent him from sharing the knowledge that the wimp and the hero are one. The fear of his childhood home prevents him from having pleasure" (178). That's because Superman fears that revealing his weakness will allow his enemies or his lover, including Lois Lane, who represents Superman's fear of women, to kill him, to triumph over him. By taking on the disguise of Clark Kent, Superman thus "presents to the world two false fronts: one of *impotence* and the other of *benevolence*" (179). Such disguises destroy any possibility of true intimacy, of family, of belonging.

In essence, Mamet suggests that those who are insecure cannot love; thus they either desperately seek power or control over others or avoid "communion" altogether, unwilling to risk intimacy. That insecurity springs from "destroyed" childhood suggests either the fear of adult "power" or the guilt of not living up to adult expectations, as we'll see with Margaret Ford. Consistent with many Mamet characters, Mike desires intimacy, but his fear of women's control and of admitting such "weakness" to his peers leads him to "front-off" about not caring for Margaret, implicitly asserting that he was only in it for the money. Margaret, in contrast, risks seeking communion, despite her own insecurity, but discovers herself and new strength instead.

Beneath its film noir trappings, then, *House of Games* is about the nature of love in the time of midlife crisis—or "two people at odds—each trying to fulfill his or her frustrated sexuality," just as Mamet suggests is the case in *The Cherry Orchard* (xv). Mamet structures the film around Margaret Ford's evolving understanding of her world, using her like an unreliable narrator for most of the film. Thus we come to understand the sources of her frustration with her, and we admire her courageous attempts to "square the circle," to change her life by seeking love (Mamet, "Between," 114). Mamet's structure or "point of view" is so successful that we are shocked with Margaret, bewildered at our sudden recognition that what she and we have thought to be a new joyous potential vanishes with Oedipal suddenness and irony. The moral contemplation that Mamet requires of his audience begins in earnest after our discovery with Margaret of the long con, a retrospective struggle that parallels her own.

The first scenes of the film serve as subtle exposition, revealing Maggie's emotional state before she meets the con men. Despite her recent success, she is dissatisfied, not handling very well that "midlife crisis." The opening shot of a mottled surface gradually revealed as pebbles and stones embedded in a concrete wall is one of several "barriers" we associate with Maggie. As people purposefully stride to work, we see a woman at a coffee stand, leather case under her arm, impeccably dressed in a dark suit, white blouse buttoned to the neck. A shot of a woman in red follows, then a closeup of the book she carries, *Driven: Compulsion and Obsession in Everyday Life*, by Margaret Ford, M.D., her photograph on the jacket identifying the figure at the coffee stand. When the fan asks Margaret to sign her book, Ford pastes on a phony stage smile as she says behind her severe dark glasses, "Of course" (6). The book's title labels much of what follows as obsessional or compulsive, ironically characterizing both Margaret and Mike. Several awkward pauses where Margaret could easily speak more humanely suggest that Ford lives her life much as she practices her therapy, refusing any significant, risky interaction, beyond the most "ordinary" of "scripts," cold, distant, impersonal. After Margaret strides away, the film cuts to her hand, writing on a tablet. The camera pulls back to reveal her with a young female patient, the uninflected cut suggesting a parallel of "performance" between the first and second scenes.[2]

The film's opening scenes belittle the effectiveness of psychoanalysis and self-help books, providing a thematic label. The patient's first line is " . . . and I saw the face of an animal—and I said, we all try to run from experience." Ford keeps writing, as the woman, in frustration, says "I'm *talking* to you. Do you think that you're exempt?" Calmly, Margaret replies "Do I think that I'm exempt . . . that I'm exempt from what . . . ?" The patient replies, "*Experience,*" centering our attention with, "Well, you'd better be assured you're not" (7). Ford, looking at her watch, insists on returning to her patient's animal. Perched on a high bed, the patient is above Ford in her low chair, and by traditional implication, above Ford in her insight. Together, the first and second scenes suggest that Maggie typically runs from experience, that she avoids the idea that the catastrophe, Oedipal surprise, can come at any moment; she relies on, instead, unthinking, narrow obsessions with work and schedule, all at the expense of "communion."

The uninflected cut to the restaurant scene with Ford's friend, Dr. Maria Littauer, reinforces these ideas. Maria wants to know how Maggie is, setting up the contrasting echo in the concluding restaurant scene. Here, Margaret replies, "I'm fine. Listen to this," urgently reading her notes to her friend about that patient. Recounting for Maria several lines we haven't heard, she reports that the patient finally calls the animal a "lurg"; telling Maria that by inverting "lurg" we get "girl," with a little grin of triumph, Ford concludes that thus the patient, like the animal, is saying that *she* is just trying to do good (7–8). Though ambiguous, the simplistic inversion of "lurg" to "girl" is intended to satirize psychiatry as meaningless claptrap, a conclusion that Ford later comes to herself.

Here, when her friend congratulates her and asks her to eat, Margaret says, "I don't have time," pulling out a cigarette that, in the film, Maria lights with her gold lighter. Taken with its quality and beauty, Maggie says "it looks like someone gave it to you," adding, "Sometimes I think the only pressures in my life . . ." (8), which Maria calls to her attention as a Freudian slip. Maria advises her to "Slow Down" after the "confusion" her success with her book has brought, to give herself some rewards, to buy a gold lighter for herself, to eat lunch with her friend. In the film, she adds, "Try to enjoy your success," but Margaret looks at her watch again, asking for forgiveness. Maria says in the film, "Goodbye. Go. Work," and we cut to Ford's hand, writing, again, as she keeps her appointment with Billy, the "compulsive gambler."

In retrospect, this ambiguous scene contains a number of indicators or labels, bits of revealing information that we initially don't recognize as such. Maria accurately reads Maggie's slip as pointing toward her need for joy in her life, but she misses the central implication that Maggie is envious that someone cared enough for Maria to make her such a fine gift. Ford's rushing from appointment to appointment negates the possibilities of human relatedness, her unfiltered Camels labeling her behavior as self-destructive, obsessive or compulsive—in popular terms, "workaholic." At the same time, the lighter is the first of a series of Mamet's playful Freudian symbols. We're meant both to laugh at the "easy" symbolism of the lighter, the cigarettes, the guns, even the leaking ones, the keys, cigars, knives, and so on, *and* to understand that they do serve as emblems for Margaret's desperate need for power and control. In popular usage, obsessive or compulsive individuals cannot be flexible, cannot express pleasure spontaneously, tend to get caught up in details rather than pursuing fruitful actions. As a variety of critics have suggested, Margaret is herself an obsessive/compulsive personality in the popular sense—in her smoking, in her reliance on her rituals of writing and distanced observation, which reflect her inability to experience "pleasures." But more basically, Margaret Ford is obsessive about systematizing human personalities, putting them in neatly defined boxes, anathema to Mamet.

Mamet's frontispiece for *True and False* embodies in the words of D. W. Winnicott the preferable alternative implied by the film: "The scientific approach to the phenomenon of human nature enables us to be ignorant without being frightened, and without, therefore, having to invent all sorts of weird theories to explain away our gaps in knowledge." For Winnicott a bland, conforming, symptom-free person "with no spark of life, no authenticity or originality, [is] tantamount to a dead person." In contrast, an "authentic person" feels in touch with others and with her own body and can pursue a creative, innovative life (Grolnick 32, 35). "Authenticity" results from confronting one's insecurity, a gloss for Maggie's progress and Mike's failure. Winnicott writes that insecurity often springs from the fact "that all individuals (men and women) have in reserve a certain fear of *woman* [which is] responsible for the immense amount of cruelty to women" (Brink 195). Men typically form obsessive defense mechanisms to avoid confronting that fear and to avoid acknowledging their vulnerable, "soft" sides, occasionally refusing emotional involvement with women altogether, finding refuge in work, in the club, the locker room—or in the metafamily that frequents The House of Games.

The cut from Maria's telling Maggie to "Go. Work" to Ford's hand taking notes on Billy Hahn furthers our impression of Ford's escapist or compulsive rituals, but, in retrospect, we know that Billy's presence in Ford's office is a part of the "long con." From that perspective, Billy's lines, like the murderess's, point to truths about Margaret's life—that she thinks she's exempt, that she's living in a dream world. The con men, ironically, have relied on Ford's not identifying Billy as a "phony" patient and not being able to refuse Billy's challenging request for help. As he pulls out that gun, Margaret swallows the hook by taking the .45, and the film cuts to Ford alone, reviewing her notes from the day.

Mamet's first "soliloquy" for Margaret tells the story through images, a fortunate Mamet obsession.[3] In retrospect, we know that Margaret has begun to recognize that she's not helping her patients. In the filmed scene, we see her notes: "Help me. No one will help me," followed by "The character of MIKE—The unbeatable gambler. Seen as omniscient, who doles out punishment" (11). Attracted both by the idea of helping, and perhaps curious about a dangerous man, Margaret sees the address of the bar, looks at her watch, pauses, and sighs; she closes Billy's folder, takes off her glasses, places her hand, cigarette smoldering, to her head, sighs again; we see her gold watch, which reads 5:30, in conjunction with the gun reminding us that the mob will kill Billy tomorrow. In effect, in this "soliloquy" we admire Margaret's courageous decision to break out of her ivory tower even though it is consistent with her compulsion to work "beyond quitting time."

In conjunction with those sighs, the cut from Ford's "safe" office to the dark, steaming urban streets, half in light, half in shadow, the very bricks eaten up, the doors worn and grimy, emphasizes how bold her decision has been. Margaret reaffirms that decision several times, opening the door to the House of Games, heading up the stairs, vulnerable and out of place in the business suit she's worn all day. Without flinching, she confronts the bartender, Mike himself, the room full of men. And she agrees to do Mike his "favor" in order to help her client. Ironically, performative elements in the bar scene suggest that Ford is playing a part on several levels. She has decided that she must appear even more forceful and "in charge" in this hostile environment. Identifying with her discomfort, we see the place from her perspective, through her "gaze," a point of view different than the male "gaze" Laura Mulvey's use of the term suggests. Almost empty, the bar at first seems aglow in the red reflection of a neon Budweiser sign, the bartender in a red shirt, the doors to the poker room apparently red in this light, which makes the place seem foreboding.

When the bartender asks if he can help her, Margaret replies, "Yeah. I need a match," Crouse's delivery implying Ford's intention to sound tough, in control. The bartender's "You lookin' f'ra *partner*. To *play* something?" emphasizes the double entendre on "match" for the audience, and Margaret's no-nonsense response, "I'm looking for *Mike*" (12), continues the suggestion that she is *both* courageous *and* looking for something "to light up" the sterile life she leads.

In retrospect, we know the bartender is part of the set-up, as is Mike's initial "performance." But with a "Say Bull" sign in the background, as Mike offers to show Maggie Billy Hahn's IOU, *both* faces are half lighted, half in shadow, suggesting the traditional noir blend of good and evil in both characters. Through Maggie's gaze we see Mike as attractive, well-dressed, but with a day's growth of beard suggesting earthiness; her eyes and expression are newly engaged. Mike tells her that he's showing her the notebook "because I *like* you . . . 'Cause you got blond hair" (14). In short, in performance the scene suggests a *mutual* attraction beneath their assumed roles. In retrospect, we may recognize that Mike tells Margaret he likes her both to explain this part of the con, that Billy Hahn has lied and only owes $800, *and* because he does like her, his skilled improvisation a reflection of what he actually feels for Margaret, perhaps to his surprise.

Such "double" labels for Mike continue as he tells Ford he wants a favor. She replies "What do you *want?*"[my italics]. Describing the idea of the "tell," he concludes, "I want you to do me this *favor*. I want you to be my 'girlfriend' for a while, come in the game, you stand *behind* me, watch me *play*" (15–16). "Be my girlfriend" includes overtones of comfort and support; "come in the game" carries associations of "action," "gambling" and, in retrospect, being conned. As they stare into each other's eyes during Mike's demonstration of the coin "tell," magnetism oozes off the screen, Maggie close to smiling, then smiling broadly as he explains her "tell," that she points her nose slightly toward the appropriate hand. She gazes steadily at Mike as she agrees, a marked contrast to what we've seen in all of the expository scenes; even with her old friend, her gaze is not intense, not energized, not direct and personal like this. Dennis Carrol observes that "In his direction of Joe Mantegna, Mamet achieves the effect of a slight italicization, a roboticization of speech, as if the character is guarding his litany of statements against an underlying feeling which might betray them" (182). While critics typically read Mike as a melodramatic "macho" business figure of evil, occasionally commenting on why Mike-as-prole-existentialist might be attractive to Ford, Carrol suggests that *Mike* is genuinely attracted but that "business wins out because of a betrayal of genuine 'communion' and attraction on Mike's part" (181).

That's largely correct, but both Mike and Maggie gradually let down their guards before Mike's betrayal. When Mike goes out, as arranged, leaving her behind to watch for the tell, Margaret and he exchange significant glances, Margaret smiling back at him in complicity, agreeing to cheat with him as he exits. She lights a cigarette, using his lighter, and goes to Mike on his re-entry, their faces close, almost as if about to kiss. She whispers that the mark played with his ring. She has lit a cigarette from his pack on the table and now lights one for him from her lit cigarette, burning from his lighter, which he accepts, gazing into her eyes. She tells him that he should call the bet, serious about the game, energized by this new life, and by that comic, Freudian ring and finger; he in turn takes a spark from her. Ironically, we discover that the exchange is part of the initial con, which we take, at first, to be the only con. Still, beneath that "business" surface, we see Mike as attracted, almost as if against his will.

Margaret's behavior remains courageous during this scene; we admire her moxie as she responds to the leaking squirt gun and her amusement at her initial discovery: "You guys are fantastic. What, do you, do this for a living . . . ?"(25). We are pleased, too, at Maggie's joyful interaction with the "guys" from the House of Games in the scene that follows. In the film, she smiles as the gang reveals to her the secret of the "flu," laughing at the empty envelope, at their ability to victimize an innocent, and then laughing again when Joey reveals how he has palmed the twenty. In retrospect, we know that she's played into the hands of the con men, but both the contrast with her joyless behavior in the exposition scenes and the old notion that a woman's laughing at a man's jokes implies that she's interested in more than the punch line suggest to the audience Maggie's attraction to Mike. For the moment, though, she jumps back on her guard, formally asking Mike for her friend's IOU; in the film, when Mike asks, "What's your name by the way?" she says, "Thank you for a lovely evening" and pulls away in her cab, refusing to reveal herself (27).

The film cuts to Margaret Ford's second major soliloquy after a long take of Mike's response to her leave-taking. The cut from Mike, alone in the street, to Maggie, alone in her home, encourages the audience to make the connection that both are lonesome, isolated, despite their business metafamilies. Maggie wears a baggy dark cardigan over a white night gown, ironically echoing the one her patient wears in her cell. In the script, Ford gets into bed in her apartment; the film shows us an elaborate home—"more pathetic," as Mike says about the aunt in the flu scene—Maggie alone on her living room couch, tasteful, light gray furniture, the room neatly arranged, sterile, a stone and glass coffee table, an elaborate silk flower arrangement on the hall table, mail orderly to the side. Revealingly, there are no photographs of loved ones. In her severe glasses, Maggie sets down a tea tray in her kitchen, switches off a light at the curved stairway that leads, we imagine, to the lonely bedrooms, and goes to the work she's been doing in the living room. Arranging her materials neatly, she huddles on her sofa, pulls up a quilt, the fireplace dark, not aglow with warmth. Our concluding that the room's cold decor reflects its owner's personality allows us to recognize a change in Maggie: jarringly, she can't bear going upstairs this night to that big empty bed. As she stubs out her cigarette in a tasteful ashtray, ten butts suggesting how long she's worked, we see her pick up the souvenir House of Games chip, and laugh affectionately.

The film cuts from Margaret to the murderess in her equally sterile, confining cell. The soliloquy at Maggie's sterile home, then, prepares us for her return to the relatively joyful life of the con men, implicitly suggesting how much Maggie longs for something beyond her workaholic, ordered existence, how much she wishes for that sense of belonging and love as she contemplates the emblem of her experience with the con men. Almost girlish, thirty-nine and infatuated, Maggie still feels exempt, optimistic, at least in part because of Mike's ingratiating behavior before and during the flu scenes. We may conclude that she's thinking about Mike after Joey and George walk back to the House of Games, leaving them alone together, about his affirmative answer to her questions about whether or not he's an "honorable man," a "Man of your word" (27), about his saying, "You're a lovely woman," framed in the window of the cab's door, his eyes warm, glowing, a smile on his face. She's thinking about his line, in Mantegna's delivery sincere, a marked contrast to his playfully stilted lines in the poker game, "Come back anytime you'd enjoy some more excitement" (27). With Maggie, we have assumed that Mike is romantically interested, and we typically want it to "work," because, like Maggie, we see Mike as interesting, articulate, attractive, a sympathetic rogue.

In retrospect we know that Mike, in part, wants to set the hook, wants to use his attractiveness to lure her back for the long con. But the cut to Mike, alone in the street, staring after that cab, suggests, even in retrospect, that he, too, longs for something more fulfilling than the tavern across the road. First turning his head, then his whole body as he walks into the middle of the noir street, Mike thoughtfully flips a coin two times, as if betting with himself whether or not she'll return—as if to say, "she loves me, she loves me not." Miming the coin-in-the-hand tell he's shown Maggie earlier, smiling, he walks across the street toward the glowing windows of the House of Games, his refuge in the night. Mike's smile, during his only "soliloquy," suggests how much he wants her to return, *both* for the primary goal of the con *and* because he longs for something other than that shoddy gambling hall where he expends his works and days.

The cut from Margaret's face in her home, looking to the left of the screen in her white gown, to the murderess, looking toward the left of the screen in her similar gown, suggests a parallel between Ford and her patient. Now in a light gray suit with a purple blouse open at the neck, already more feminine than we've seen her before, Margaret is not taking notes, but gazing into her patient's eyes with real compassion. Typically, the scene gives us information we use to read the rest of the film without our being aware of it. The patient tells Ford, "He said, 'I can make any woman a whore in fifteen minutes'"(29), and that she responded that he couldn't make anyone a whore that wasn't a whore to begin with. The murderess describes the man telling her that she *is* a whore, though "he didn't realize what he had done." Beginning to break down, the patient says "You know, I know there are people who are normal. . . . But I don't know what those people . . . do . . ." Maggie goes to her and embraces her, comforting her, not looking at her watch this time, prominent on the arm embracing the patient, as the murderess concludes, "How can you live, when you'd done something . . . when . . . ?" (29). In retrospect, we recognize the similarity of this scene to the finale in which Mike tells Margaret that *she* is a whore and the parallels between this scene and the one in which Ford asks Maria outside her classroom, "What do you do? What do you do when . . . when . . ." (56). Neither Margaret nor her patient know. Shot through the bars as she exits the prison through doors that won't open easily, Ford is profoundly shaken at her recognition that she cannot help this woman.

In the next scene, frustrated, human, Maggie tells Maria that what she does is "a sham. It's a con game" (30), echoing both Billy's accusation and her evening with Mike. Her emotional life emerging from its hiding place, she makes the second of her three Freudian slips: "That poor girl, all her life my father tells her she's a whore, so all her life she seeks out . . ." (30). Maria's calling her on the slip centers the audience's attention. The line implies that at least part of Margaret's "driven" personality springs from her attempt to live up to parental expectations. That is, Ford's achievements are never enough to make her feel other than disowned, condemned, unable to return to Krypton, and thus unable to show love without fear of being destroyed. Implicitly, perhaps, Margaret also needs to revolt against authority. When Maria expresses her pleasure that Maggie will do something enjoyable this evening, Ford focuses on her $6,000 check, another souvenir of her evening, as she turns down Maria's dinner invitation. Though uneasy at Maggie's duplicity, we're pleased with her brave decision to return to the House of Games, aware only in retrospect that she is naively venturing into a trap. This doubleness of response to Ford's actions continues as the film cuts to Margaret later that night in the darkness across from the House of Games. For the first time, we see her in informal clothes, tan jacket and slacks, a soft ecru blouse; she's "changed" from her tailored business suit. On her way to Charlie's Tavern, she opens her collar a bit, a natural gesture that still suggests that she wishes to be alluring; she orders scotch, emblematically wishing to participate, to imbibe the culture, as she had not the night before. Charlie's, though, like the House of Games, is predominantly red in "aura," the tavern sign glowing red neon, red tablecloths, again subtly ominous. The song on the jukebox serves as another important label, "This True Love Stopped for You (But Not for Me)." The lyrics that we hear in the film are not in the published script, but they suggest that the female singer is doomed to a life of loneliness because her true love, the man, will pass by, saying, " we're still friends." A perfectly believable country tune to be on Charlie's jukebox, the song comments on Margaret's previous night, alone at home, sitting and staring, isolated in her safe environs out of fear of emotional risk. The second half of the verse, though, implies that this "love" that she now courageously pursues will not work. Mike appears with her scotch just as we hear the lines about the end of true love. Our primary response, nonetheless, is to Ford's delighted grin when Mike arrives, cheerfully impersonating a waiter, and to Mike's equally delighted smile, though she still refuses him her name.

But after the Western Union scene in which Margaret plays the role of Mike's wife and the mother of his child, perfectly willing to cheat the young Marine, she finally reveals what she wants. Gentle music comes up in the film as Maggie and Mike draw close, their reflections in the glass behind a barred window, a beautiful shot that implies how imprisoned Maggie has been, encouraging us to approve of her apparent honesty when she does tell Mike that she wants to make love. Mantegna's delivery is movingly believable as he clasps her hands, telling her: "The things we want, we can do them or not do them, but we can't hide them" (38). In response to Maggie's initial reticence, in the film's dialogue, Mike says he thinks she wants "Somebody to come along, somebody to possess you, to take you into a new thing. Do you want that? Would you like that?" After a pause, Margaret replies, "Yes," Mike's fingers gently at the blouse she's opened on her way to Charlie's, caressing her lower neck, thumb softly on her chin. He whispers, "What is it?," and she repeats "Yes," music still playing, as she makes what we think is the courageous decision, finally risking.

The hotel room sequences include several of the most convincing labels of Mike's affection for Maggie. After the wonderfully comic scene in the hotel lobby, Mike once more offers her a chance to renege, holding up the key he's palmed at the desk; "In or out?" he asks in the film, staring into her eyes with anticipation. Smiling, she takes the key and easily inserts it in the lock, another lightly comic Freudian emblem. In retrospect, we know that this is a part of the long con, which depends on Mike's assuming that he can persuade Margaret to sleep with him in the room they've "dressed," presumably to encourage her loyalty later. Once in the room, though, Mike passionately urges the affair along. As they embrace, she turns away from him; his hand pulls out her blouse and inches into the waist-band of her skirt, caressing the flesh of her belly. She turns to him, deeply kissing him, the scene fades out, the audience convinced that Mike is sincere, not over-the-top as he has been in the poker scenes.

Mantegna's delivery of Mike's lines suggests both introspection and affection as the camera cuts from the fade-out to Maggie in the chair, a feminine camisole, no bra; subliminally, we may suspect, she has dressed for the occasion. In response to Maggie's implying that he's an interesting man, Mike says, in the film dialogue, "I'm a con man. That's what I am. I'm a criminal. You don't have to delude yourself. You can call things what they are. You can call yourself what you are." Margaret asks him, "What am I?" (41), which implies both that she is uncertain during this midlife crisis and that she is intensely interested in what Mike thinks of her. Again, just slightly different than in the published script version, in the film Mike tells her, thoughtfully genuine, "there's many sides to each of us: good blood, bad blood, and somehow all those parts have got to speak. You know what I mean. The burden of responsibility's just become too great."

On initial viewing, like Ford, we take this line seriously, recognizing that Maggie's "bad blood" has spoken up this evening but that on one level, ironically, that is healthy. Mike's linking such a notion to the "burden of responsibility" implies that "duty" has overwhelmed individuality, inhibiting such extemporaneous, unconsidered actions too radically. Even in retrospect, Mike's conversation alone with Maggie suggests that he *does* like her and that he dwells on "responsibility" because he now has mixed feelings about carrying through with *his* job. After Ford agrees that "responsibility" has become too great, Mike tells her that he's read somewhere, "if you're fired from your job, take something, take a pencil, something, to assert yourself, take something from life," for in his mind revolt is the right way to live. Sincere, pleased with himself, he tells her, in the film version, "And I think what draws you to me is this: I'm not afraid to examine the rules. And to assert myself. And I think you aren't either." That leads to Margaret's brief third soliloquy as she contemplates herself in the mirror while Mike is washing up. Her gaze tracks over cigars, change, a nice pocket*knife*. As Mike returns, she guiltily puts *it* in her pocket. Again, we watch her make a decision to break out of her former responsible life of "living and partly living."

Our response to Margaret's morality, or lack of it, during this exploratory stage continues to be at least ambivalent as we watch her beg to participate in swindling an unsuspecting "business man," happily playing the role of Mike's wife. In retrospect, we clearly recognize that outside that intimate room, Mike is once more insincere. Mantegna's delivery of his lines becomes stilted, as in the film's, "Oh, my god, we've got to get her out of here." At first, though, along with Ford we're so caught up in the suspense that we typically don't notice; indeed, during the struggle at the door, we fear that Maggie has been shot, sighing with relief when the "cop" is the one who drops to the floor. Mamet's manipulation of his audience's sympathy with Maggie's perspective is so accomplished that we are pleased when a "police officer" dies.[4]

Our ironic sympathy continues as we admire Maggie's courage and loyalty during the escape scene, when she steals the "get-away" car and sacrifices her money for "the good of all." As she crosses toward that emblematically red Cadillac, if we're very observant we notice a large pair of dice dangling from the mirror. Those dice, the car's color, Mantegna's stilted delivery of the final hooks—"Where's the briefcase?," "You have that kind of money?," "Then, for god's sake, *get* it" (52–3)—*may* make us suspicious. Typically, though, we continue to see this world from Maggie's conned perspective.

The following scene with Mike and Joey in the cab outside the bank is central to our understanding of Mike's doubleness. On first viewing, Mike's line, "Funny how things happen sometime" (53), seems to refer to his amazement that their con has gone awry and that Maggie can save them. In retrospect, though, Mantegna's melancholy delivery and his unwillingness even to look out the window as Maggie approaches with her money, his ostensible goal, seems puzzling. Given Mantegna's heartfelt sincerity in the seduction scenes, the line makes a different kind of sense, revealing, briefly, that something *has* gone awry in Mike's plan to con Maggie. He's been distracted from his primary goal, from wanting to con Maggie out of her money, by his attraction to her. Alone with his best friend, Mike has the courage to hint at the idea that he recognizes the attractiveness of "communion," but Joey, typical of many Mamet "third wheels," doesn't want to hear about it, and Mike drops the subject, ashamed of such "weakness."

Alone once more with Maggie after Joey leaves, Mike's affection resurfaces. He puts his arm around her as soon as she gets in, moving closer, advising her not to yield to her urge to confess. In retrospect, we know that the con men only need to keep Ford from confessing immediately; they know that she will tumble to the con as soon as she realizes that the morning papers carry no headlines about a murdered policeman. At that stage, they are counting on Ford not to lodge a complaint because it would prove too embarrassing for her national reputation, as Mike reveals at the airport. But once Mike has fulfilled his "responsibility" as con man, Mantegna's delivery again becomes sincere, less obviously "actorly." He whispers in the film, "I, I just wish . . ." licking his lip as he pauses, then urgently pulling her to him, caressing her face, kissing her on the cheek with farewell passion, embracing her. On first viewing, we fill in the blanks with Margaret, understanding that Mike wishes they could be together. The kiss, the whispered lines of affection, are unnecessary for the con. We think them real at the time, and we may think that in retrospect, if we struggle with Mamet's provocative conclusion.

Ford's desperate sadness as Mike's cab pulls away prepares us for the cut to Maggie's third scene with her mentor, where a central theme emerges. In contrast to the Freudian jargon Maria dispenses to her note-taking students, deeply disturbed for her friend, Maria offers difficult but vernacular advice. When Maggie blurts out, "What do you do? What do you do when . . . when [you've done something terrible] . . . And if you reveal yourself you betray someone else, and . . ." (56). Echoing the murderess asking for Maggie's advice, the lines reveal that Maggie is still being loyal to Mike. Maria says in the film, "When you have done something unforgivable, I'll tell you exactly what to do. You forgive yourself." Fleeing down the dark hall, in shadow, then in light, then in shadow again, ironically, Maggie only thinks that she has killed somebody, but she will hug Maria's advice to her heart when she actually has killed someone.

Unable to accept this advice yet, reverting to her former defenses, Margaret isolates herself in her shuttered office where a fourth major soliloquy shows her painfully disowning her former life, recapitulating the plot for us as she destroys evidence of her crime. Sighing, Ford stares at her book, hurling it from her to shatter the glass over her framed diploma, which she rips out and crumples. With Maggie, we focus on her painfully extracting shards of glass from her bloody palm, empathizing with her pain as she stanches the flow and opens Billy's file. We see her crumple the yellowed IOU, open the drawer and take out Billy's gun. She removes the House of Games chip from her purse and discards it on top of the folder, along with pages from her notebook on the House of Games. She adds Mike's pocketknife to the stack, unzipping her jacket and seeing the blood on her blouse from this same morning. Shocked all over again, she rips off jacket and blouse, revealing the camisole from her evening with

Mike before disaster struck, before things changed. Grabbing a red sweatshirt from a gym bag, she pulls it over her head. As she holds the bloody blouse, a knock comes at the door. Straight out of Kafka, via Pinter, the knock seems threatening to Margaret. The red sweatshirt, consistent with those previous evocative reds, suggests that she's on edge, emotionally vulnerable, dangerous, as those first drops of blood on Billy Hahn's file foreshadow. When Billy appears at the door, his red T-shirt further associates Margaret with the immorality of the House of Games, here, and for the rest of this third evening.

The central Oedipal irony in the film is that Mike assumes that Billy will not alert Margaret Ford to the truth when he sends him to check on her, that he can continue to manipulate her. That's an act of hubris which leads to Margaret's recognition and to his downfall. In an extremely high angle shot of Margaret stuffing her bloody blouse on top of the other evidence in the trash can, the camera briefly holds on *Driven*, reminding us that Margaret is still an obsessive, cleaning up her messes; the shot from the ceiling traditionally suggests that we "look down" on Margaret Ford for not confessing to her "crime." In sum, by "chance," Margaret happens to take the evidence to the dumpster just in time to see Billy Hahn on the phone. Ironically, she has emerged from her back door, marked "No Deliveries," and Billy's precaution of parking the red Cadillac out back proves catastrophic. As in the Greek drama, this "chance," or "fate," in retrospect seems inevitable, just as surely as Oedipus's fleeing Corinth the result of character, of Mike's hubris and of Ford's obsessive personality. Following Margaret's point of view, we catch a glimpse of the fender of the red Cadillac and, with her, trash can full of her life clutched to her red sweatshirt, we watch Billy pull off in full view, dice dangling from the mirror. For us as for Margaret, the "messenger" suddenly reveals radical truth beneath previous appearances. In this classic recognition scene, Crouse's wonderfully expressive eyes register both painful discovery and determination, a strength in her jaw much different than the trembling, nearly hysteric features we've seen when she visited Maria's classroom. Margaret's response to dawning recognition, like Oedipus's, is both anger and a determination to pursue the truth of her situation no matter how painful.

The camera cuts to Maggie's face against a dark brick wall, her face wet from the weather, perhaps a tear trickling down. Maggie's first descent into this underworld was a courageous attempt to help a patient; her return on the second night was a courageous search for joy beyond sterility. But this final dangerous visit in search of truth ironically reveals only a part of the reality behind Mike's betrayal. The scene embodies Maggie's fifth significant soliloquy, for she is unobserved, almost as if invisible, once she passes the red Cadillac glistening in the rainwater and enters the rear entrance of Charlie's Tavern, with its "Delivery" sign perhaps a label suggesting final truths or "deliverance." Opening the barred gate, then the door, Margaret sees "Mr. Dean," the tuxedoed black man from the hotel, on the phone, overhearing in the film "What?! Well, that's good news. I'm always glad to hear that." Under a Carta Blanca sign, holding a cigar from the "dressed" room, "Mr. Dean's" introductory lines ironically label the scene. The truth that Margaret will hear will not seem good news to her, but the Carta Blanca sign suggests that the con men think that anything goes here, that they are "exempt" from observation or interference in this retreat, the sound of a cash register emphasizing their central concern.

By "chance," "Mr. Dean" doesn't see Maggie as he brushes past, because he's in a rush to boast to his cronies that he's just won $5000 on a baseball game, which characterizes the boasting that follows, especially Mike's, as a pose, a claim to prowess, an affirmation that one is beating the world. From Maggie's point of view, through decorative turned-wood bars, we watch the men at the booth as they tell "war stories" about the con. At Joey's urging, Mike tells the story of "the broad" stealing his pocketknife, and "Mr. Dean," full of praise for the leader of this pack, says admiringly, "Took her money, and screwed her, too." "A small price to pay," replies Mike (62).

The camera focuses on Maggie's face on *this* line, in profile, half in shadow, as she lowers her head and closes her eyes, neck exposed, hood down, vulnerable, hurt. This is the third major shock to Maggie's equilibrium: her recognition that she cannot help her murderess despite her proud reputation; her "false" recognition that she has committed a murder and that Mike is gone; and now this. Crouse's eyes, here, and her recoiling into the shadows, suggest that this is the most difficult shock for Margaret to deal with, that what she has really *wanted*, love, a vibrant environment, a new "family," is not to be, because her "love" has betrayed her. With Maggie, then, we rapidly reconstruct what we understand about the con, appalled at the con men's callousness, and distraught at Maggie's despair and pain. But we know more than Maggie, and in retrospect must struggle with *our* assumptions that Mike has been sincere during several of those love scenes, that his "Funny how things happen sometimes" line, which Maggie has not heard, now seems explicable only if Mike had "fallen" for Maggie. In short, we should recognize Mike's claim not to have been affected by making love to Maggie as macho posturing. Mike's "a small price to pay" is intensely ironic, the opposite of what he truly feels, a boast uttered to bolster his "place" among his cronies as a "superman" above such emotional, weak responses, the "Ring-Tailed Rounder" *and* the "King Kong" of con men as one calls him (62). The men accept and depend on such posturing; but Maggie, the "outsider," does not understand it. The final irony is that Mike's boast, "a small price to pay," his hubris, will lead to his death. He is convinced that he is "exempt," that his "atrocious" behavior will not be discovered or punished. Still, we should perhaps remember that King Kong was looking for love.

The film's previously identifying Ford with the murderess implies what is to follow, and that Margaret's actions are wrong, though horrifically understandable. Complexly, the scene at the airport also suggests that Ford's plot to con Mike evolves as she wishes, so that she can kill him. As the scene begins, from Margaret's perspective we see an affectionate father and his young son, then two couples, the communion that she's missed, and then Mike. Ford begins her pitch seemingly to humiliate Mike, to beat him at his own game, Crouse's delivery clearly "actorly," baiting her con with that quarter million dollars. As Margaret allows Mike to lead her into the baggage room, she reveals her name for the first time, apparently giving him her confidence. When she concludes, "It was fate I found you" (65), Mike agrees that they can make it together, but we in the audience recognize that ominous Greek reference. In that context, Margaret's third Freudian slip emerges as an integral part of her con. In the film, she says, "No, I knew that I was bad. You know why, you know when I knew? Because I took your knife. That's when I knew." Ford's two earlier Freudian slips prepare us for this one, another revelation of the "hidden" that the speaker wishes to surface. "Your knife" alerts Mike that Maggie knows of his duplicity and betrayal. That Margaret has brought Billy Hahn's gun with her implies that she has come prepared, "if, God forbid, something inevitable occurs," to use Teach's phrase. Aware now of Maggie's con, but not of the gun, Mike's repeated question is ours, echoing Mamet's structural motif: "What do you want. What do you fucken *want* from me . . . ?" (67).

Tension and hostility building inexorably from this point, Margaret catalogs her complaints, beginning to whip herself into a frenzy. Pulling the gun when he contemptuously dismisses her, Maggie shoots Mike the first time after his suggestion that she's bluffing, finally revealing her real goal: "I want you to beg me" (69). Though Mike still thinks that Margaret won't give up "that good *shit*" she has, "that 'Doctor' stuff, that 'money,'" up against the wall under another ironic sign, "SECURE AREA," Mike is wrong, for Margaret has set out on her adventure because she has found that "stuff" so unfulfilling. Her search for love and vitality fruitless, Ford maps out for Mike that she won't be discovered because it's not her gun and "I was never here." Shooting him a second time, she reiterates, "Beg for your life. Or I'm going to kill you," adding "I can't help it—I'm out of control'" (69). Crouse's delivery achieves the equivalent of the quotation marks, implying both self-mockery and a mockery of popular psychological explanations. In the script, Ford has written about Billy Hahn: "*Compulsive succeeds in establishing a situation where he is out of control*" (11). She has created just such a situation with her Freudian slip and by bringing Billy's gun, a "rationalizing" of what she wants to do instinctively.

Ford knows that Mike will not beg, that she will need the gun she rescued from the trash, because Mike cannot bear not being "in control"; he will not allow himself to beg or to yield to a woman, to be less than macho. His character, in short, leads to his "fall." Telling Margaret, in the film, "I'm not going to give you shit," he spits at her. When Ford shoots again, Mike, in agony but with a twisted courage and humor, says, "Thank you, sir, may I have another?" (69). A jet loudly takes off as Margaret shoots him three more times. The sound emblematically suggests the building, turbulent force of Maggie's mental state while also providing the narrative rationale for, "by chance," no one hearing these shots.

The film's beautiful double coda, the aftermath of the real murder, suggests that the revenge Margaret has plotted does not provide her satisfaction. Ironically, it is Ford's confrontation with herself *after* the murder that allows her to progress toward a more fulfilling life. Once more shot from the ceiling, the camera captures Margaret exiting the baggage area, Mike's bag, solitary on the floor, poignantly commenting on this couple's not taking a journey together, the extreme angle labeling Margaret's behavior as terribly wrong. Our sharing her pain of recognition at Charlie's Tavern still encourages our sympathy, but in Mike's early moments of rational explanation, he has actually apologized to her, saying it wasn't personal, and, "funny as that sounds, I'm sorry that it happened." The money has won out over the affection implied by that "funny as it sounds" line, but Mike concludes his apology with: "And you learned some *things* about yourself that you'd rather not know. I'm sorry for that, too" (68). Margaret's final shots ring out over Mike's accusations that she's a whore and a thief, implying that this new self-knowledge has disturbed her profoundly. She's condoned stealing from others; she's stolen herself; she's been willing to cover up her involvement with a murder; and she's been a "whore," atypically yielding to the adventure of sex with a rogue stranger.

Killing Mike, then, embodies both vengeance and a momentary rejection of self-knowledge. Still, the confrontation with the self, the recognition of what one has done, can potentially be healing. The film implies that later, after another "journey," Maggie becomes more "authentic." Maggie's killing Mike is not the source of her "renewal" or rebirth, as some have claimed. The source for that renewal is the courageous seeking after truth, which we see Maggie begin as she heads for Charlie's Tavern on the third night, refusing to ignore the messenger as Jocasta would do; the continuation of that struggle to confront the truth about herself takes place offstage, as is traditional. The final scene of the film celebrates the results, which do not suggest that Margaret Ford has "cured" herself, as some critics have maintained; neither do they suggest that she has become Mike, has internalized the values that he represents, as others have argued. Rather, these final moments imply that we should recognize that Maggie has come through her long dark night of the soul and has taken a few steps toward becoming a healthier person, toward being able to work and being able to love with some degree of balance. Margaret has suggested that Billy Hahn should seek to cure himself (9), but that was during her salad days.

The scene at the airport ends as the sound of gently flowing water replaces the sound of the jet over the shot of Maggie's pushing past Mike's body, which fades out as a much different shot of Maggie fades in. We see her back as she contemplates the peaceful water of an elaborate fountain flowing over another wall, this one of marble pleasingly varied in structure, framed by lush fronds gently swaying in a light breeze. The image labels the scene, contrasting with the rough pebbled concrete of that undifferentiated wall we've seen as the film opens and with the artificial floral arrangement in Maggie's cold apartment. Maggie's flowing dress suggests a changed, healthier persona; she wears more casual earrings, an attractive floral print, predominantly deep green with contrasting pale yellow and pink flowers, a mixture of darkness and light. She's sipping a drink, the back of her dress open to the waist, modest, but sensuously revealing her bare back, as she turns to us, easy, graceful, relaxed, her hair less coifed, looser.

The first part of this coda emphasizes how very much Margaret has changed for the better. A formal, off-camera voice asks "Are you Dr. Margaret Ford?" (70). The music subtly suspenseful, she turns, removes her sunglasses this time, easily replying, "Yes. I am."[5] We think for a moment that the official voice may be that of a detective; we laugh in relief at the stiffness of this autograph seeker in his dark suit. Continuing the reversal of the first autograph scene, much more gracious here, Maggie writes "Forgive Yourself" in her book, announcing the topic of this scene, labeling that which is to follow just as Maria arrives. With a hug and a wonderfully warm smile, Maggie responds to Maria's "How are you" this time with "I'm fine, really fine," and, smiling, answers Maria's "Are you?" with a heartfelt, "Yes. I absolutely am." With clearly genuine pleasure, Maria says, "Good." Emphasis through repetition here serves as another label. Maggie can easily reveal her name to a stranger; she is taking a drink for the first time in the film, not just ordering one as at Charlie's Tavern; she will actually eat lunch with her friend, not rush off to work.

When Maria tells Maggie how frightened she was for Maggie before her trip, that is, during the aftermath of the murder, Maggie stops her, saying "and you said, when you've done something unforgivable, forgive yourself, and that's what I've done, and it's *done*" (71). Again, with delight, Maria responds, "Good. Good." The scene's dominant note is that Maggie's "forgiving herself" *is* good. Maggie is better, not because of revenge but because she has recognized her immoral behavior, struggled with it. One cannot forgive oneself, in short, unless one recognizes one's "flaw," that one has something to be forgiven for. Though it may sound like a self-help cliche, forgiveness of self, in this context, requires the same strength of will to recognize one's actions as evil or immoral that classic recognition implies.

But Maggie is not "cured," since recognition does not imply a miraculous, total revision of character. Thus, the final scene, the second part of the coda, in which Maggie steals that cigarette lighter, is a reflection of Mamet's stringent realism—that is, people may change significantly after courageous confrontation and struggle, but they don't emerge as perfect. When Maria, ironically, is briefly called away by "business," Maggie glances up from her menu to see a woman lighting a cigarette with a gold lighter, haughty, unsmiling, stiffly tailored. When the woman turns to look at the buffet, coldly polite, Maggie calmly reaches into her purse and purloins the lighter. We watch Maggie's hands caress the lighter under the table, then light her cigarette, enjoying the heft of her new prize, the precision of its mechanism. We see a closeup of Maggie's face, Crouse's eyes vaguely pleased as a slight smile begins on her lips. Gently triumphant music rises, Maggie exhales, her smile broadens, her lips open, her face now in full light, black curtains on the left of the screen. Blackout.

In the context of this basically positive concluding image, we recognize that Maggie has stolen, hearing an echo of Mike's "The bitch is a born thief" (62). But we also hear in retrospect Maria's advice to buy a similar lighter, to find some joy in her life. And we hear an echo of Mike's advice that one should "take something from life," not be abused, which Maggie can do with new skill and confidence. In other words, the theft of the lighter represents another side of what Maggie has become; her healthy new joy in life includes this side, an embodiment of Mike's noting that good blood and bad blood pumps in our veins, that each must express itself. In Mamet's world, characters are not "either/or," "white hat/black hat," macho Superman or wimp-sensitive Clark Kent; they are "both/and."

This final image of Maggie, healthy and happy in a flowered dress, about to take the time to enjoy a good meal with a good friend, and caressing a stolen lighter, smoking those unfiltered Camels, is puzzling, "provocative" at first, but it encourages us to make connections in retro-spect and to celebrate Maggie's coming to self-knowledge through her capacity for strife and striving. In a Richard Covington interview, Mamet suggests that film noir is much closer to tragedy than the Hitchcockian "light thriller," for "at each step, the hero seems to be doing the correct thing, but at the end of the movie ends up assigned to perdition or death, or disgrace, because of some internal flaw." Unlike Arthur Miller, Mamet emphasizes the notion of tragic *recognition* in such reversals. In this con-text, though, we should remember that in *Oedipus at Colonus* the hero is finally redeemed both by his nobility in suffering and by his recognition of the truth that *he* is the culprit. Maggie, in short, emerges as a nearly re-deemed tragic figure in what Mamet has called his film noir. She has suf-fered the punishment of recognizing her sin for what it is, of recognizing herself, as Mike says, for what she is, of being disgraced in her own eyes. But it is the confrontation with the self, not the murder, the recognition of failure, not gloating triumph, that has enabled her to progress.

Just as Maggie is not a totally virtuous figure at the film's conclusion, neither is Mike a totally heinous villain. We admire his tenacity, but Mike is deeply flawed, like Superman. He recognizes his need for love, but he is too frightened to give up his "power," and consequently must take second best, the company of men, for he cannot risk love and aban-don the arena in which he feels secure. Many have misconstrued the darkly optimistic ending of this film because, as Mamet suggests about *The Woods*, it is "about heterosexuality, which is . . . a subject that people would rather not address—why men and women have a difficult time trying to get along with each other" (Schvey 94). In sum, in Mamet's world, only those with sufficient self-esteem can resist such urges toward domination of others; and only the "autonomous" can risk any possibil-ity that self-revelation may lead to control by another.

Mamet's evocative limning of such themes through his presentation of "provocative," ambiguous, "morals" is so reverberant because he projects the fears and wishes of many in his audience, the zeitgeist of children of divorce and bewildered participants in a revised battle between the sexes. In his 1998 review of *Lakeboat*, Michael Billington writes that Mamet's men are "lost souls" and that "Mamet's real genius is his understanding of the fear, isolation and fantasy that hermetic male groups camouflage through language of bullish bravado" (27). That's an accurate description of the bravado of Mike's "A small price to pay." In retrospect, the line ironically emphasizes the magnitude of Mike's loss, which occurs because he has not had the courage to love, as Paul Tillich would have it.

The brilliance of this gem of a film lies not only in Mamet's subtle portrait of the isolation and false bravado of hermetic male groups, but also in his equally subtle portrait of a woman courageous enough to venture beyond the confines of her own hermetic refuge, a profession that Mamet regards (for the most part) as a different kind of con game. At the film's conclusion, we are encouraged to think that Margaret now does have that "courage to be" in a world of strife—an intensely ironic, and celebratory, finale. That *may* be the opposite of misogyny, but it is certainly subtle, sophisticated art that makes the process of our identification with a complicated female heroine on a journey nearly mythic in its accomplishment so wonderfully enjoyable.

NOTES

1. My thanks to Katherine Burkman for sending me her paper, "Web of Misogyny: Mamet and Pinter's Betrayal Games," presented at a special session on Pinter and Mamet at the MLA Convention in 1993.
2. Where Mamet's published script and the film's dialogue or "business" are the same, I will cite the script version. Where they differ, I'll cite my transcription of the dialogue, so indicating with "In the film."
3. I find 16 scenes in the film in which Maggie is alone, emphasizing how much of this film is from her "point of view," how central her actions are to the work as a whole. Five of these scenes are so delicately wrought as to be the cinematic equivalent of the soliloquy, revealing a character's thoughts, much as the dramatic term suggests, but primarily through images.
4. That's true for a variety of reasons beyond our identifying with Maggie, for "businessman" and "cop" are remarkably unsympathetic.
5. Film buffs will recognize the allusion to the concluding scene of *The Lavender Hill Mob* (1951), in which a previously stiffly correct businessman is captured in a tropical bar after robbing a bank.

WORKS CITED

Billington, Michael. "Souls Cast Adrift." *Guardian Weekly.* February 22, 1998, *ARTS* 27.

Brewer, Gay. *David Mamet and Film: Illusion/Disillusion in a Wounded Land.* Jefferson, NC: McFarland, 1993.

Brink, Andrew. *Obsession and Culture: A Study of Sexual Obsession in Modern Fiction.* Madison, NJ: Fairleigh Dickinson UP, 1995.

Burkman, Katherine. "Web of Misogyny: Mamet and Pinter's Betrayal Games." A paper presented at the MLA annual convention, Washington, D.C., 1993.

Canby, Vincent. "Mamet Makes a Debut with House of Games." *New York Times.* October 11, 1987, 94.

Carrol, Dennis. "The Recent Mamet Films: 'Business' versus Communion." In *David Mamet: A Casebook.* Ed. Leslie Kane. New York: Garland, 1992, 175–90.

Covington, Richard. "The Solon Interview: David Mamet." *Salon,* October 24, 1997.

Grolnick, Simon A. *The Work and Play of Winnicott.* Northvale, NJ: J. Aronson, 1990.

Hall, Ann C. "Playing to Win: Sexual Politics in Mamet's *House of Games* and *Speed-the-Plow.* In *David Mamet: A Casebook.* Ed. Leslie Kane. New York. Garland, 1992, 137–60.

Haskell, Molly. "Psychotherapy." *Vogue.* September 1987: 140, 146.

Jauss, Hans Robert. "Levels of Identification of Hero and Audience." Tr. Benjamin and Helga Bennett. *New Literary History* 5 (1973–74): 283–317.

Jordan, Neil (Dir.). *We're No Angels.* Screenplay by David Mamet; Robert De Niro, Sean Penn, Demi Moore, Hoyt Axton: 1990.

Mamet, David. "Between Men and Women." *Make-Believe Town.* New York: Little Brown, 1996, 109–16.

———. "Guilt." *True and False: Heresy and Common Sense for the Actor.* New York: Pantheon, 1997, 86–92.

———. *House of Games: A Screenplay by David Mamet.* New York: Grove Weidenfeld, 1987.

———. *House of Games,* Dir., Screenplay; Lindsay Crouse, Joe Mantegna, Mike Nussbaum; 1987.

———. "Kryptonite: A Psychological Appreciation." *Some Freaks.* New York: Viking, 1989, 175–80.

———. "Notes on *The Cherry Orchard.*" *The Cherry Orchard by Anton Chekhov: Adapted and with an Introduction by David Mamet.* New York: Grove Weidenfeld, 1985, vii-xv.

———. *On Directing Film.* New York: Viking, 1991.

———. "*Playboy* Interview." April 1995: 51–60, 148–50.

———. "Second Act Problems." *Three Uses of the Knife.* New York: Columbia UP, 1998, 42–61.

———. "Self-Help." *Make Believe Town.* New York: Little Brown, 1996, 161–66.

———. *We're No Angels: A Screenplay Written by David Mamet.* New York: Grove Weidenfeld, 1990.

Mulvey, Laura. "Visual Pleasure and Narrative Cinema." *Screen* 16 (1973): 6–18.

Ong, Walter J. "The Writer's Audience Is Always a Fiction." *PMLA* 90 (1975): 9–21.

Price, Steven. "Disguise in Love: Gender and Desire in *House of Games.*" *Gender and Genre: Essays on David Mamet.* Ed. Christopher C. Hudgins and Leslie Kane. New York: Palgrave, 2001, 41–59.

Schvey, Henry I. "Celebrating the Capacity for Self-Knowledge." *New Theatre Quarterly* 4 (1988): 89–96.

Van Wert, William F. "Psychoanalysis and Con Games: *House of Games. Film Quarterly* 43 (1990): 2–10.

Man Without a Gun

Mamet, Masculinity, and Mystification

Diane M. Borden

The question, "What does it mean?" jabs itself into the dialogue of Mamet's plays and films like a taunting signifier, the phrase itself posing a dilemma of signification. The question appears not merely as an interrogative query that moves dramatic and narrative action, but as an imperative longing, an urgency related to desire. The meaning of "meaning," however, is always contextualized, in part, through Mamet's preoccupation with discursive communities—or communities bonded by what John in *Oleanna* calls "terms of art" (*Oleanna* 3).[1] Mamet's plays and films do not attempt to resolve the provocative question, "What does it mean?" but rather to remystify the moral, psychological, and philosophical closures that come all too pat in a system where rational discourse (literal, bound, essentialist) is privileged (Worster 384). The desire for knowledge, both experiential and theoretical, leads paradoxically to unknowing, a slippage from what characters think they want to know to what they can't seem to figure out. Fascination with meaning can lead to ravishment, or, as Mike in *House of Games* tells Margaret, "You want someone to come along, to possess you, to put you into a new thing." Similarly, the drive to speak, the aggressive compulsion so characteristic of Mametian dialogue, ultimately masks what is unutterable.[2] At the core of Mamet's project is a kind of *mysterium tremendum*, a phenomenological concept related to Freud's theory of the uncanny or Heidegger's notion of unconcealment. I suggest that Mamet's work, in particular his two films *House of Games* and *Homicide*, disclose the sublime, where meaning is constructed by, yet ineffably lost in, language. Such knowledge is both awful and awesome.

In this essay I will first address mystification as a practice and consequence of language systems, whether visual or verbal, word or sign. In *House of Games* and *Homicide* the process of mystification follows three parallel paths. At the most simple level, both the protagonist and viewer are caught up in a mystery. At the level of authorial practice, Mamet artfully designs a managed process of obfuscation. Finally, at the level of signification, the work results in an aporia; though the "crime" may be solved, the mystery not only remains, it is compounded. In both films, a network of codes evokes a complex phenomenology of secrecy. The hardboiled "man-to-man" talk of cops or the Yiddish and Hebrew languages of Jews, the learned, elevated jargon of psychoanalysis or the low-life argot of con men, represent various modes of language that lead ostensibly to secret knowledge while at the same time undermining that knowledge. Parallel to this code network is the notion of a secret society, whether the camaraderie of thieves or the politics of a religious sect. In each film, an initiate is seduced, gives himself or herself over to the Other in a state of eroticized desire, only to be conned, defamiliarized just at the point when he or she thinks they are about to be part of the family.

I have already asserted that Mamet's project of mystification can be understood as a category of the sublime, but I also want to argue that the sublime is linked with psychological defense mechanisms and transference love, phenomena fused in a peculiar response to cliques with mystique. The narrative drive of suspense in Mamet's psychological thrillers promises but ultimately subverts conventional solutions; elaboration defensively wards off both terror and closure. At the same time, secrecy excites the pleasures of transgression. We will test how fellowship in a discursive community constructs an alternate "family" whereby transference love, a reactivation of powerful desires centered around parental or sibling figures, drives a subtextual psychodrama. Idealization of and submission to a secret society constitute a radical rendition of sublimation. The classical notion of the sublime—contemplation of the lofty, elevated, and beautiful—shifts in post-Burkeian articulation to an engagement with mystery, one characterized by a paradoxical enmeshment of desire and dread.

In the second half of this essay I will contextualize *House of Games* and *Homicide* within the genre of film noir, with the suggestion that Mamet's work signals a transformation of the genre and its conventions. Film noir, in its original evolution through the 1940s and 50s, had an often intentional subversive agenda that destabilized the rational, scientific premises of traditional detective fiction that sought to unravel and solve the "mystery" in the mode of Sherlock Holmes. Film noir, on the other hand, while often using the machinery of detection and investigation, would at the same time disclose the complex connections among larger unrealized mysteries. Mamet takes the destabilizing energy of traditional film noir, both reclaims and disclaims its conventions, then invigorates the genre through idiosyncratic aesthetic, psychological, and narrative strategies.

As a related focus to Mamet and mystification, I intend to explore how constructions of gender emerge in film noir representations, and how Mamet modifies notions of the masculine through his preoccupation with men in groups and the semiotics of the gun as an instrument of masculine empowerment. The problematics of the gun, who has it and when it is used, play off of classic noir conventions of dominant and subservient masculinities within the postures of men in groups. But just as often men are threatened by a femme fatale, that is, a woman with a gun. However, the conventional sexual powers of the dangerous woman become sublimated in the Jewish mother and black mama of *Homicide* and in the butch style of Margaret Ford. In both these films, the gun acts as a free-floating signifier: it operates in a system of gift exchange while carrying the obvious phallocentric implications. However, as Lacan (un)cannily suggests, "You can either have the phallus or be the phallus." We might add that you can either give the phallus or lose the phallus. In Mamet's textual elaborations it would seem that gender and genre reciprocally construct a kind of mystification whereby the gun operates as an awesome (awful?) signifier that cannot be subsumed within a given discourse, cinematic and/or psychoanalytic.

My purpose is to explore Mamet's art, and his particular craft as a filmmaker, through dialogue, visual style, and narrative structure. But I also wish to uncover how this art poses the question, "What does it mean?," as a strategy of mystification. "Terms of Art," the *sui generis* speech (and acts) of a discursive community, generally lack intimacy, are impersonal, and constrained within boundaries. Yet the illusion of intimacy (familiarization) motivates Ford and Gold to a sublime surrender to the very discursive communities that will ultimately betray them. Language operates as a weapon and/or defense within a forum of desire, power, and gender.[3] Signification is both scattered and withheld; elaboration leads to aporia.

LANGUAGE, MYSTIFICATION, AND THE SUBLIME

Two dominant discourses intersect and parallel in *House of Games:* psychoanalytic frames of reference and con man argot. In the opening sequence of the film, Margaret Ford is asked to autograph her book *Driven,* a work on obsession and compulsion. The book title, in close-up, initiates a system of psychoanalytic terminology. At the same time, Mamet play-fully introduces a subtext of signs that arise out of advertising.[4] Here the Ford who (which) is driven is not a car but the doctor herself. In a fol-lowing sequence, Dr. Ford speaks with a patient, a young woman who with difficulty describes a dream in which the word "lurg" appears.[5] Mar-garet suggests that the dreamwork, in the censoring, encoding ways dreams emerge from the unconscious, has transposed "girl" for "lurg." Hence, psychoanalytic discourse, through Margaret's interpretation, at-tempts to access the hidden meaning of the patient's conflict.

The film's sequential continuity follows with a third rapid narrative immersion into the discursive apparatus of psychoanalysis. Margaret speaks with her patient Billy. The question is asked, "What does it mean?" He answers, "Just talk. The whole thing is a con game." Here, the dynamic between analyst and analysand, and the language of therapy is linked with the other specialized discourse of the film—the language of the confidence man. At this point, Billy displays and threatens with a gun; but ultimately, through the persuasive powers of the doctor's lan-guage within the analytic hour's performative of secrecy and enclosure, he hands over the gun to Margaret. This exchange activates then inter-meshes the mysteries of the marginalized world of crime with the esoteric world of psychoanalysis. Later, Margaret expresses her frustrations with clinical practice, when she tells her mentor, Maria, the same thing, "That it is a sham. That it is all a con game."

House of Games plays with a number of Freudian symbols, standardized objects that, in the lexicon of film rhetoric and postmodern self-reflexivity, share a system of repeated, now conventional, references. For example, when Margaret is in the hotel with the con man, in postcoital caress, her hand in close-up lingers over a box of cigars on a bureau. This comes just before her decision to steal a pocketknife positioned next to the cigars. One cannot doubt that Mamet must have been amused by this visual joke, knowing that "sometimes a cigar is not just a cigar." The joke has fuller im-plications when we understand that the con man, at the hotel reception desk, takes the key of a black man (a fellow con artist), registered in the hotel as Richard White. Dick White, transposed in the idiom of the un-conscious, becomes white dick; the exchange of the hotel room key (from White to Mike to Margaret) visually signals a circuit of desire. Margaret takes the key, opens the door, and once again crosses a dangerous thresh-old: here to sexual intercourse. Margaret even wears a Freudian "slip," a satin teddy, strikingly feminine, at odds with her otherwise tailored mascu-line clothes.

A series of Freudian slips access key insights into Margaret's uncon-scious motivations, drives that apparently "drive" her to yield to the allur-

ing dangers of the underworld. This system of parapraxis not only borrows from psychoanalytic notions of language and the unconscious, but
allows Mamet a narrative mechanism in which the revenge of the feminine finds its final voice—speaking with a gun. The first slip of the
tongue occurs when Margaret in a restaurant tells her mentor, Maria,
about her current case, reporting the girl/lurg transposition and also saying, "My father said she is a whore." Maria catches the pronoun switch
that should have been stated "*her* father," not "*my* father." Also, Margaret
slips when she uses "pressures" to mean "pleasures."

Finally, when Margaret attempts to con Mike at the airport, she gives
herself away by another pronoun unmasked by unconscious eruption. She
says "*your* knife"; this slip tells him that she is aware that she was framed.
What psychoanalytic discourse calls parapraxis, con man argot describes
as "cracked out of turn." Just as the psychoanalyst is trained to read the
unconscious of the language of the patient (what Lacan calls broken discourse, meaning hidden in ruptures and slippages), so too the con man
reads the speech behaviors of his "tell." Mike has Margaret's number, so
to speak; of course, he has had it all along. Strikingly, at this turn in the
struggle to master the situation, he calls her a "bitch" and a "whore." "You
come back like a dog to its own vomit," he says. Mamet now portrays the
con man simultaneously speaking a discourse of the hard-boiled criminal
while unwittingly triggering a psychoanalytic frame of reference. Margaret is emotionally charged, angered at a betrayal based, not on taking
her money, but on taking her sexual favors. Once again she hears herself
being called a whore. Her unconscious discourse is connected in some
way with fathers calling daughters whores. When Margaret shoots the
con man, in effect, she unconsciously shoots the father. For Mike has become an object of transference love, someone who would "possess her and
carry her away" in a kind of sublime swoon, a defensive move toward
reparation and transformation of the verbally abusive father trapped in
Margaret's unconscious memory and/or fantasy. Margaret, from a therapeutic perspective, experiences a failed transference. Rather than confront
the return of the repressed (activated in the seductive powers of the con
man, who stands in for the rejecting father), Margaret's love turns, not to
understanding something about herself, but into hatred toward the of-
fending love object.

The discourse of psychoanalysis enters into the film in other pointed
ways. Maria, Margaret's older mentor, lectures on functions of transformation: inversion, projection, elaboration, compression. Like a mantra,
the set of terms is repeated, at a time in film continuity when Margaret
attempts confession, with flashbacks to the murder she thinks she might
have committed in the hotel room. In effect, she needs to speak to her

therapist, who inadvertently gives her permission to act out transgressional behaviors. "When you've done something unforgivable, you forgive yourself." The Epilogue sequence recapitulates this dictum, for Margaret, again approached by a fan for an autograph, writes in the book jacket "forgive yourself."

Someone familiar with the clinical practice of psychoanalysis might question the authenticity of Mamet's representation. However, Mamet is not concerned with realistic representation in the narrow sense, but rather in the way that psychoanalysis, as a discourse, both uncovers meaning and evokes mystery. Mamet has found in the psychoanalytic system of language something akin to what his characters, and surely many in his audience, receive as meaning, something that is both knowable yet overdetermined, transitory yet grounded, fixed yet interminable.

The discourse of the criminal world is, curiously, initiated by Margaret, who enters the House of Games talking tough. Margaret's transition from professional woman to gangster moll is marked by passage through the club door. A long-held close-up on the threshold, as the door closes and masks Margaret's body, suggests a signifier of transformation and/or transportation. A liminal space is encoded in cinematic rhetoric; and the phenomenology of the sublime is activated, for both danger and bliss come together in the sequence to follow. With this entry into the House of Games, the discourse of crime argot is introduced. Margaret, at the poker game, is explicitly mentored in the first con strategy. Mike explains to her the dynamics of "the tell." Enraptured, seduced, called into a mode of being both risky and exhilarating, Margaret willingly plays the role of the girlfriend as she watches for the card player's "tell." At the conclusion, when she "calls" the poker player's "bluff" after seeing the leaking (not smoking) gun, she speaks (so she believes) from a position of power.

Familiarized and eroticized by the secret society of con artists, she now strives to solidify her place in this alternative mode of being. In a following sequence, set in the dark urban streets of noir convention, the brotherhood of thieves describe for her the operations of "the flue," a strategy, comparable to a magic-show trick, that rips off money from the gullible. Another con operation, called "the mark," is enacted when Margaret and Mike target an unsuspecting soldier in a Western Union office. Yet another discursive community, the Marine Corps, allows Mike to tap into the language that bonds a group, gaining access to a shared experience. The con man ironically subverts corp group identity, stating "semper fi." Through this posture he tricks (or would trick) the gullible soldier.

Mike educates Margaret in the fundamental philosophy of the con: an implied contract of trust. Confidence is shared in an intimate engagement that breaks through the ordinary distance of human interaction.

Mike says, "Everybody gets something out of every transaction." One might loosely compare the transference of psychoanalysis with the transaction of the con, both performatives of language enmeshed with desire. At the airport sequence, when Margaret "cracks out of turn" and Mike catches her, Margaret says, "I gave you my trust." She has now set him up with her suitcase of money, an attempted "sting" she initiates, one that parallels the "bait and switch" operation carried out by the con men with the hotel conventioneers. Then the psychoanalyst, unmasked by parapraxis, fails in her attempt to revenge her betrayal. Language has betrayed her so she reverts to and asserts power through the speech act of the gun. The sign "SECURE AREA" ironically comments, through mise-en-scene, as Mike is gunned down. Thus in *House of Games*, Mamet devises an intertextuality between the discourses of psychoanalysis and con-man argot, both significant loci of confidentiality, both implicitly secret, and both requiring a process of initiation.

Homicide likewise schematically presents, then decenters, two parallel though seemingly less comparable modes of discourse: professional cop talk and various languages of Judaism—Yiddish, Hebrew, and Kabbalistic. At various points a triangulation of racial, religious, and political speech complicates and mystifies meaning. The question, "What does it mean?" finds its rhetorical companion in "Who are you?" Identity is tied up with knowledge; but when identity is bifurcated (to be a good cop or to be a good Jew), Gold (as good as) finds that he ultimately is betrayed by (and betrays) both communities; identity and meaning fracture into problematic mystification. At the end of the film a powerful look of recognition is shared between Gold and the domestic killer, who tells Gold at the beginning of the film that he will show him the nature of evil. In that wistful look of narrative closure, an essential aporia opens up, for it is difficult to know just where and how evil exists.

The discourse of ethnic wrangle and gender derogation, with terms such as kike, faggot, nigger, and pussy, battle it out with the stychomythic "fucks" that punctuate cop speech.[6] Brutal but vibrant, such language grounds the initial sequences of the film. A narrative shift occurs when the compassionate, humanized speech of mourning, spoken in Yiddish, both beguiles and mystifies Gold. He initially thinks it is Hebrew, thus calling into question the authenticity of his Jewishness, since he cannot distinguish between two very different languages. As he gradually falls into the sublime of Jewish Otherness, he is beset by a double bind in not knowing what faith to keep: the brotherhood of cops, in particular his bond with his partner Sullivan, or his Jewish heritage, with focus on a guerilla secret society countering defamation. Like Margaret Ford, eroticized by engagement with the transgressional con world, Gold too is beguiled, indeed swiftly infatuated with the transformational rush of the Jewish underground and its illicit activities.

Gold, as a cop, mediates between discourses; he negotiates through virtual "terms of art," whether they be to a beleaguered colleague, a Black Mama, or a Jewish saboteur. However, Gold does not fully realize the problematic position of mediation: for the mediator is always part of the terms of his or her own discourse, part of the negotiated transference. Ultimately, Gold gets caught in the mystery of his own desires, for transference love usually operates in an illusory unilateral communication. One might say Gold submits to the sublime of the Jewish Other precisely to defend against guilt for having failed to keep the faith, for having failed to know the meaning of Judaism. At the same time he fails to keep the other faith, the professional fidelity to the brotherhood, inadvertently betraying his beloved brother/partner by forgetting to arrive on time at the final crucial showdown shoot-out.

Mamet brilliantly elaborates a system of codes, words, and signs to visually render a mapping of mystification. This system of visual signifiers functions in some ways like a cinematic palimpsest (Lacan 70). What can be written, can be written over; superinscribed and layered, messages are sent in a hidden encoded language. In *Homicide* a threefold elaboration process rotates the signifier, which is foreshadowed, enunciated, then erased. Mamet finds in the particular nature of cinematic rhetoric the ability to compress image and word in a complex formulation. We understand that "language erases even as it creates" (Belsey 55).

The core image of *Homicide*, the star, illustrates just such a problematic signifier wherein rotational elaboration creates a palimpsest. The five-pointed police badge, a pentagram, is written over by the Mogen David, the six-sided Star of David. In naturalistic presentation, part of the fictional real of the shot, we see Gold's badge and later the murdered Jewish woman's necklace, a close-up on a gold Star of David. The image of the Mogen David quickly passes yet functions as a liminal foreshadowing, later to be enunciated by the Jewish scholar's lecture in the library. Gold's police identity, to protect and serve, is destabilized by the scholar's interpretation of the pentagram as a sign of threat. He asks, "Are you a Jew?" Gold's affirmative is undermined when the inquisitor challenges, "What are you then if you can't read Hebrew?" Further, the scholar explicates the name Esther to mean "conceal"; but it is also a pun on star.

The two emblems—cop badge and Mogen David—visually represent the two primary discourses of the film, as well as the bifurcated loyalties of Gold. However, this clever visual palimpsest is in turn overwritten to chilling effect: two stars are visually erased in yet another variation—the spinning star of the swastika, boldly seen in the Christian rightist's propaganda office. Such a triangulation of signs, each bearing a powerful emotional charge, each connecting discursive communities that either embrace or denounce them, destabilizes any easy this-for-that signification. Finally, in the shoot-out sequence, Gold enters an apartment underground (set in contrast to the roofs in the first third of the film) and sees the fragmentation of a star, an enigmatic rendering on a concrete wall. Mamet has uncovered something uncanny, both disturbing and enlightening, yet difficult to speak of, within both the film's realistic setting and critical discourses that might explicate the film.

Jarring juxtapositions of signifiers fracture commonly held politically correct or sentimental views. Think about Mamet's choice of dog breeds: Rottweilers and Dobermans guard the Jews. Note they are *police* dogs of *German* breeding. Consider the word HOMICIDE, in bold capitals on the police station door that frames Gold at the end of the film. Homicide is not only a legal category of murder, it is also a *corps d'esprit*, a family of bonded colleagues in the police hierarchy, a locus in space and a habitus of being. Also, we see Gold and his boss stand in medium shot in front of a door signed with the word MEN. HOM and MEN aesthetically frame and conceptually assert male institutional space where "the power of a masculine ethos . . . insists on the presence of hierarchical authority" (Vorlicky 45).

Polarized signification is visualized in the palimpsest of the Jewish grandmother's photograph. Gold examines a framed picture taken in the woman's youth in a sentimental pose. From underneath, another photograph slips out; we now see her as a gun-toting, gun-running subversive. Mamet forces the viewer to consider the implications of overdetermined signs, particularly those that trigger apparently uncomfortable registers of emotion.

The mapping of mystification in *Homicide* takes other forms. The word GROFAZ initially appears on a bag of bird seed set beside a pigeon coop on the apartment roof of the Jewish family. Gold, in pursuit of an enigmatic shooter, passes the bag without seeing it. However, in close-up we the viewers do *see*, in a kind of forced, ironic inner-frame montage. The peculiar word, foreshadowed here, is seductively enunciated in a three-stage elaboration. When leaving the roof, Gold finds a torn piece of brown paper written in bold capitals with the six letters. Later, at a repair store (Gold needs to fix his gun strap), an old Jewish man says the letters are an acronym for Hitler. And when Gold visits the library, the hidden name of the Fuhrer is actualized through propaganda posters that spell out the acronym in German. However, at the end of the film, the esoteric acronym, GROFAZ, is revealed as no longer esoteric but as a brand name from a bird-food label. Gold, who has not known this reference, is bewildered. We ask, with the same disenchantment as Gold, what does it mean? How could an acronym for Hitler be the name of pigeon feed? Who put the inscribed piece of paper on the roof and how would he or she know Gold would pick it up? Such rational queries are deconstructed in Mamet's map of mystification, for the narrative drive of the film is not situated in detective fiction's solving of a crime, but rather in the unfolding of mystery as a given of human experience. The call of the Jewish Other seduces Gold, draws him into a transference love, sweeps him into a sublime of awe, where he gives over allegiance to Jewish identity. But awe couples with the dangerous and unattainable, and Gold is left bereft and unknowing. In the idiom of *Homicide*, to be starstruck is to be awestruck.

A broader look at the philosophical history of the sublime, along with connections I see in psychoanalytic thinking, can help us grapple with Mamet's particular engagement with mystification. Two parallel paths forge a phenomenolgy of the sublime in *Homicide* and *House of Games*: desire as unfolded in the subjectivities of Gold and Ford, and experience as a dimension of aesthetic reception. The world, as represented in each film, is dominated by the subjectivity of Gold and Ford, who manifest a complex and ambivalent psychic reality in a world that otherwise appears single-minded. The aesthetic properties of each film, including the organization of subjectivity, manipulate the viewer to participate in the psychological "thrill." Enraptured by narrative disclosure, the viewer experiences unconcealments that bring a simultaneous mixture of horror and delight.

At first association, many readers/viewers of Mamet's work would resist a connection with the sublime, the concept laden with notions of nature, grandeur, and transcendence. The gritty world of men in groups, talking tough, competitive, and, in particular, the noir vision of an urban underworld, seem unlikely sources of the sublime. But, as we shall see, the ongoing interpretation of this category, from Longinus to Burke, from Kant to Cassirer and Lacan, offer a metaphysical resource for hermeneutical investigation of Mamet's texts.

In the history of debate on the sublime, a long hiatus follows Longinus's initiating position that the sublime constitutes an aesthetic inquiry into the contemplation of beauty. A radical shift occurs in the eighteenth century with Edmund Burke's swerve from beauty to the contemplation of mystery. For Burke, whose work follows psychological categories, the ego finds exaltation and liberation in the breaking of boundaries; pleasure is grounded in fear, "a sort of delight full of horror, a sort of tranquility tinged with terror" (qtd. in Cassirer 330). Further, as Cassirer summarizes Burke, the individual alters and transgresses the limits of social boundaries:

Not only the inner freedom of man from the objects of nature and from the power of destiny is expressed in the sense of the sublime but this sense releases the individual from a thousand ties to which he is subject as a member of the community and of the social and civil order. In the experience of the sublime all these barriers vanish; the individual must stand entirely on his own feet and assert himself in his independence and originality against the universe. (Cassirer 330)

Both of these fundamental Burkean notions of the sublime characterize how Ford and Gold, as embodiments of subjectivity, respond to the pleasures of the dangerous. As enraptured respondents, they are moved, with an excess of desire, to cross boundaries, to move beyond limits. We should recall that liminal means threshold, and Mamet's intuitive genius overtly suggests doorways and passages as key image patterns in both *House of Games* and *Homicide*. Both Ford and Gold go outside the law, literally and psychologically, embracing a breakage with social order in order to succumb to boundlessness. That such boundlessness is transitory and illusory confirms Burke's revisions of ongoing philosophical debate around aesthetic response.

A confluent way to understand operations of the sublime in Mamet is to relate the process to psychoanalytic categories. The sublime can be connected to the falling-in-love phenomenon; the subject, in this case Gold and Ford, is (or may be) powerfully moved, swept away, to alternate states. In particular, the sublime swoon enacts a transference love, in which the object of desire is encoded with familial traces, in both cases tainted (Ford) or divinized (Gold) with the paternal metaphor. Ford falls for both the con man and the society of thieves; Gold's seduction is not so much located in one individual (though the Jewish woman radical with a briefcase bomb could function as the mediating figure of transference) but in the whole tradition of an idealized Judaism. Surrounding these transference loves, both Gold and Ford, significantly *without* biological or socially constructed families, psychically live out familiarized substitutions. A maternal/sororal dependence appears in Margaret's relationship to her teacher/mentor Maria. And the bonds of fraternity bind Gold and Sullivan in an interethnic marriage of respect and loyalty.

A second reading of Mamet's evocation of the sublime as a psychological function can be seen in the dynamics of defense mechanisms. As a way to ward off rejection, to defend against a pattern of loss, the subject gives himself or herself over to a counter force. They subjugate themselves, in a state of mesmerized awe, to the seductive forces of the Other, replacing (unconsciously) what has been lost. Destructive feelings (hate, guilt, revenge, contempt, dismissal) are recharged, in a defensive

reparation, to exaltation, idealization, and rapture. As the phenomenal
world opens up in such a state of bliss, Mamet simultaneously starts to
pull the magic carpet from under ungrounded feet. The return of the repressed breaks loose, overturning the illusory ties that Gold and Ford
have momentarily forged with new families. Ford reverts to revenge, in a
pathological acting out of hostility, while Gold fails to protect Sullivan at
the final shoot-out, left finally to the denigration of the police fraternity.

Rudolf Otto in his discussion of the *mysterium tremendum* comments
on the element of awfulness as a phenomenon marked by a particular
dread coupled with the numinous. He compares the experience of the
sublime to the shudder in a ghost story, and talks about the notion of the
Wholly Other. The two esoteric discourses of *Homicide* and *House of
Games*, Kabbalistic Judaism and psychoanalysis, fit Otto's notion of the
numinous and the awe-full. The numinous reveals itself in the otherwise
concealed inscriptions of the Kabbala or in the manifestations of the unconscious. Both of these concepts, the Wholly Other and the ghost, can
be linked with the return of the repressed and the exotic Other of psychoanalytic theory.

Otto makes a very important distinction between solving a problem
and accepting a mystery:

> . . . the mysterious is something which is and remains absolutely and in-
> variably beyond our understanding, whereas that which merely eludes our
> understanding for a time but is perfectly intelligible in principle should be
> called, not a "mystery," but merely a "problem." (Otto 28)

Such a formulation underscores the privileging of mystery in film noir
in general, and in these two Mamet films in particular. Thus, Rudolf
Otto, speaking from a theological position, links the sublime with mystification. In contrast to Kant's delineation of the sublime with grandeur
and immensity of scale located in Nature, Otto dematerializes the object
of the sublime and locates it in the contemplation of the Wholly Other.
However, Mamet's films reflect a postmodern sensibility in which both
Transcendence and Nature have been erased; for Mamet, the constructions of subjectivity and relationship relocate the object of desire in the
immanence of the all-too-human. Here then is the site of the sublime:
not Schopenhauer's "transcendence beyond will," but immanence within
the demands of subjective desire.

Frederic Jameson has called the postmodern sublime "hysterical."
While enunciating it, he does not, however, explain it (Jameson 34).
Rather, I would suggest that "mystique" be offered as another elaboration
of the mystification process of the Mametian method. A mystique might

be understood as an artificial sublime, "terms of art" as a pontification. The creation of a mystique (a clique [im]posturing special knowledge, a *cognoscenti* of neon halos) functions as a mode of power within a discursive community. To access the sublime in a postmodern era is to feel, not only a manic terror, but a terrible mania. The subject, in a state of suspended pain/pleasure, momentarily arrested by the numinosity of the beloved object, asserts the need, as an outsider, to become familiar with and a participant in a secret society. Such a position strides an ironic threshold: to go in the door of the House of Games means you come out the door of Charlie's, or out the door of the Homicide office, not older and wiser, but in a state of toxic enchantment. Perhaps an inversional response to what Jameson calls the "hysterical sublime" might be described as the *mysterium infandum.*

Guys and Guns:
Gender, Genre, and Mystification

In both *House of Games* and *Homicide,* the image of the gun provides a chain of signifiers that (re)mystifies issues of gender and genre. Mamet contextualizes the gun within psychoanalytic associations of phallic representation and/or substitution and within conventions of film noir as they navigate the politics of desire, power, and gender.[7]

A barrage of rifles, elongated in shadows, silently penetrates the stairwell and corridor in the opening shots of *Homicide.*[8] An overcompensated macho ambience is (humorously) signaled by this hyperbolic ballistic metaphor. Mamet positions Gold as a man with a tenuous hold on his gun; the tool of his trade appears as a psychological metasymptom of Gold's transitory potencies. Sullivan initially tells Mike, "Don't forget your gun." Immediately following, Welles, the man who has shot his family and would teach Gold the nature of evil, grabs the detective's gun, breaking the holster. A struggle ensues. This breakout of male violence over the instrument of power triggers (so to speak) the breakdown of Gold's control over professional, and that means for Mamet personal, confidence and competence.[9] The agonistic struggle over the gun reappears in Gold's basement pursuit of Randolph, the cop killer. Unaware that he has dropped his instrument, Gold hunts down the criminal, only to be taunted by Randolph's comment that if you forget your gun "death is calling." Randolph's rhetorical question, "Do you want to beg for your life?" plays out the same commanding sadism seen in *House of Games* when Margaret, with gun pointed at the con man's body, orders, "Beg for your life." When Gold is shot he lies prone on a flat cart, soon to cradle the targeted body of Randolph. The two men, in medium shot, form an ironic pieta, parallel to the earlier pieta of the dying Sullivan in Gold's arms. Mamet suggests that the power of the male bond, of a would-be brotherly love, is destabilized by the exchange of the gun, a free floating signifier of virility that asserts a harsh dynamic of submission and domination.[10]

At the scene of the candy store crime, Gold at first leaves his gun in the squad car; a delayed montage edit shows in close-up that the murder victim, an elderly Jewish woman, packs her gun in a cigar box. (Freud's cigar dictum again asserts itself in a not so unsubtle visualization of phallic exhibition.) Later, Gold discovers in the basement a box containing documentation on rifles. And, as we have already noted, the Jewish matriarch, distantly viewed in an old photograph, is portrayed as a gun-toting political guerilla. Here then is encoded a cinematic archetype of the woman with a gun, a characteristic representation of film noir's dangerous woman. As noted above, this begs the question of the sexual prowess of the femme fatale. However, the deconstructed representation of an aged, apparently helpless, and visually unseen victim destabilizes the tough broad style. Jewish mothers would seem unlikely femme fatales; perhaps, however, the dialectics of mystification play with, not a mixed metaphor, but a mixed stereotype.

The gun bears its phallic signification in other key narrative junctures of the film. The double enunciation of MEN and Men on the bathroom door provides a backdrop for Gold and his boss, with gun at holster emphatically foregrounded in an expressive mise-en-scene. Sullivan, half in jest, half in seriousness, raises the issue: Why must Gold always be the first at the door in a raid? Gold, in a later explanation, sees this as compensation for him being an outsider, that "I was a pussy because I was a Jew." The effeminized man must therefore carry the most ready/steady gun so as to continually enunciate his manhood. Such phallic exhibition contains a hyperbolic irony, particularly telling when Gold in close-up double hands the butt of the long-stemmed metal only to meet a deadpan old black Mama.

Gold significantly drops and loses his gun while chasing the rooftop prowler at the Jewish family's apartment building. Momentarily, the gun lies next to the GROFAZ bird seed: two signifiers meet in the night, to form a compound sign, then go on their way through respective chains of signification. The broken gun holster brings Gold to a repair shop, which in turns sets him on the continuing chase for the meaning of GROFAZ. At the Jewish secret society meeting, an old patriarch says to Gold, "See that gun. I had one just like it." The gun becomes linked to the discourse of the Kabbala when the Jewish scholar responds to what Gold thinks is concern when he sees the gun in his holster. "The gun is a tool. The badge is a symbol." However, we might provide a corrective to the scholar's categorization: sometimes a gun is not just a gun; sometimes it is a symbol.

The phallometric cycle of the gun operates in a different but equally compelling and inventive way in *House of Games*.[11] Mamet conflates the image of the gun with corresponding objects—cigarettes, lighter, knife, poker chip. A series of exchanges, some as gift exchanges, others as theft, imbue the objects with talismanic properties of power. Indeed, the objects carry with them an eroticized as well as gendered inflection.[12] Sex and gender piggyback the phallic signifier in a way that underscores the erotic charge of danger and transgression often represented and experienced in film noir. Margaret first "gets her gun" when she negotiates with her patient Billy. She puts the weapon in her desk drawer. Later, in another sequence, she opens the drawer and we see in close-up a telling composition, for a cigarette is juxtaposed to the gun at a contiguous angle. Margaret is a compulsive smoker (soon to be gambler) and here the double signifiers team up to exhibit the fantastical props of the phallic woman. We should also note that the cigarette is an accessory of erotic charge, particularly prevalent in classic Hollywood film noir, often "worn" by the femme fatale as part of a performative allure. In contrast, Margaret consumes rather than displays her cigarette, which tells us something about her restrained sexuality.[13] Further, that Mamet uses a close-up on these objects, the gun and cigarette, sets in motion a pattern of italicized gazes upon talismanic objects.

The poker game can be read as the master sequence of the film, one that references the game of chance as a recurring site of desire and competition in film noir.[14] Margaret, performing as a kibitzer, enters the ring of men at battle, in the guise of the woman who would bring luck. Instead, she is asked to cover the bet (with her own money). The "winner" puts out a gun, asserting his authority, in order to complete the transaction. But the transaction becomes complicated in a series of ironic exchanges. As Margaret is about to hand over a check, she sees that the gun is leaking. The jig may be up, but in fact, it is really down (so to speak). Or, given that this is a con, it seems that the gun does, in fact, do the necessary job—not to threaten, but to seduce. As a souvenir of "the escape from a con man," Mike gives Margaret a chip. Then, with the exchange of Billy's paper IOU, the transaction is complete—from gun to check to chip to IOU.

Margaret's keen observation of (and psychological disposition toward) guns surfaces once again when she sees the supposed agent's gun in the hotel bathroom, reflected in a mirror. She alerts Mike and his partner that a police agent is present. But what follows implicates Margaret in a struggle over the phallic signifier. In attempting to flee the scene of the crime, she inadvertently becomes the shooter in that scene. Denigrated as Mike's "square John broad," Margaret at this moment is trapped in an imaginary trope, that male fantasy that believes Woman only brings trouble when entering Man's domain. Keys likewise function as phallic signifiers. Recall the difficulty with which the guard attempts to open the hospital prison door, as the metal bars mask the anxious Margaret. That anxiety is momentarily relieved when the doctor assertively opens the door to the hotel room of Dick White. The conflation of the key, cigars, and a pocketknife occurs in the postcoital gaze at the bureau, the camera positioned in Margaret's subjectivity. The key appears again when Margaret momentarily dupes Mike at the airport; she opens a storage container to retrieve a briefcase of nonexistent money.

The association of gun with other talismanic signifiers occurs in a series of shots at Margaret's office when she attempts to erase all mementos of both her careers—as psychoanalyst and as criminal. In a destructive rage she shatters her diplomas. Then we see in close-up the gun and chip; the continuity continues with the crumpled-up IOU, the knife, the gun in the garbage can, and cigarettes. The souvenirs of her brief crime spree spread out through a cinematic roll call of recapitulated imagery.

The shift of Margaret into the femme fatale of noir nostalgia is signaled by a close-up on her high heel shoes, at the beginning of the airport sequence. Mamet appropriates another accessory of dangerous women with the implication of dominatrix power.[15] At the same time, another transformation occurs: Mike, embodiment of the *homme fatal*, shifts to a man without a gun, fulfilling the fear of imaginary Woman as castrating bitch. (Ironically, throughout the film the *homme fatal* is often a man without a gun.) Showing no remorse, Margaret guns down her "rapist," as she calls him.[16]

The theft of the lighter in the epilogue of *House of Games* completes the cycle of phallic signifiers. A fetishized object, the lighter, hard, always ready to be lit, as good as gold, fulfills the phantasy of phallic woman. From a mythic standpoint, Margaret triumphs, a Medean figure who succeeds in her revenge of the feminine. However, the problematics of right action complicate the poetic justice of narrative closure. An unstable ethic would seem to feature yet another Mametian mystification. Yet this ambiguity of moral responsibility pervades the ethos of the psychological thriller, and, in particular, film noir. Margaret fulfills a threefold performative: victim, criminal, and detective. The same can be said of Gold (though his degree of "responsibility" for Sullivan's death does not fit the same category of criminality as Margaret's shooting of Mike). Trust and confidence, deception and betrayal are for Mamet axial virtues and vices; they provide the shifting sands on which characters speak and act. The gun is, ultimately, nothing more than a prop, an accessory of empowerment. The problem of the phallus, whether leaking, smoking, shooting, or disappearing, is not who has it, but does it have you? That is, *con* you. In both *House of Games* and *Homicide*, it is Woman who holds the gun, while Mike and Gold are men without a gun. Does Mamet merely repeat the femme fatale fantasy, or does he overturn the very suppositions of that fantasy? What is suggested, in a tragic and ironic way, is the position that (wo)man is always without a gun. The very nature of power, like the nature of evil, is at question here. Ultimately, the gun, as a free-floating phallic signifier, beguiles and stymies in a delusional enmeshment of gender and genre.

As we draw to conclusion we need to reconsider issues of gender and genre with regard to Mamet's process and thematics of mystification. Mystification operates on three simultaneous levels: aesthetic, ontological, and linguistic. While the noir genre engages in a narrative of mystery-solving, Mamet manipulates genre expectations by a parallel track of obfuscation. Like Gold and Ford, we, the viewers, follow a yellow trick road, the managed mystification of authorial wizardry. But Mamet doesn't dazzle us with smoke and mirrors simply to let us know he's a gifted kid. Facility and precocity are emphatically *not* Mamet's style. Rather, through mystification—with its links to discursive communities and the psychology of the sublime—Mamet uncovers a profound, perhaps tragic, insight into the fact that the signifier is never completely reducible to any one meaning. Hence, knowledge is always trapped in an endless circulation of power and desire. Transference love, emerging out of unconscious familial needs, risks disenchantment when transferred to the mystique of a virtual politique, an artificial family bound by specialized language. If the sublime experience means being caught up in the strange, then estrangement is the price one pays when the hero realizes that the signifier grants no payoff, that the promise of meaning is nothing but a con.

Ultimately, Mamet demystifies mystification, for we are left with a specious numinosity, absence as the presence of power, and the underlying tyranny of gender constructions. In part, this is what Julia Kristeva means by the powers of horror, for the sublime creates an alternate (and delusional) moment of subjective expansion, a moment of unbounded ecstasy; but such embellishment leads to a position of abjectivity (Kristeva 11–12). Yet such horror is part of the delight in works such as *House of Games* and *Homicide*. If terms of art will get us nowhere, that is precisely where we like to be, for to relish Mamet's vision and aesthetic is to enter the doors of a *mysterium infandum*.

NOTES

All quotations from *House of Games* and *Homicide* are from my transcription of the films, not the published screenplays, which differ occasionally from the films' dialogue.

1. MacLeod examines the concept "terms of art" in regard to the acquisition of linguistic power in discussing the politics of gender, language, and hierarchy (209).

2. For a full discussion of the "unutterable" in modern drama, see Kane, *The Language of Silence*.

3. Vorlicky examines the relationship between power, language, and masculine postures in *Glengarry Glen Ross*. His comments on American male mythologies as encoded in Mamet's dialogue shed light on my examination of men in groups through the discursive communities of cops in *Homicide* and con men in *House of Games*.

4. Consider the advertising signs "Say Bull" and "Budweiser" behind the bar in the pool hall. As expressive mise-en-scene they can be read analytically. Speaking "bull" might be understood as both the discourse of the con men and the psychoanalytic community. But are we any wiser? That is the fundamental Mametian question.

5. Mamet explicitly states that "psychoanalysis is a great storehouse of information about movies," suggesting that "All film is, finally, a 'dream sequence.'" We know that Mamet *consciously* (that is, intentionally) evolves a psychoanalytic signification because he further recommends works by Freud, Bettelheim, and Jung. See *On Directing* (7).

6. Language, like the gun, is used both as a weapon and as a posture. The noir hero excels in the hard-boiled idiom of confrontation; verbal sparring advances masculine narcissism. Krutnik defines a "closed circuit of male-male communications" (43). When a woman appropriates language (or thinks she does), as does Margaret, she finds herself trapped within a system of male power plays (and that means language plays).

7. Interestingly, in an interview regarding techniques of filmmaking, Mamet refers to a gun sequence in *House of Games* to illustrate a broader discussion of *homage*. That Mamet chooses a "gun" sequence to speak to his best in filmmaking, further reinforces the foregrounding of the gun cycle as signifier. See *On Directing* (31–32).

8. Mamet is quoting from his earlier screenplay, *The Untouchables*. Both films include in early scenes silent rifle stake-outs, and the valise bomb noted by the little girl in *The Untouchables* gets recycled in the valise bomb given to Gold by the Jewish woman guerilla.

9. Vorlicky comments that in Mamet and other contemporary playwrights men "repeatedly resort to violence as a final solution to their immediate professional or private conflicts" (37).

10. Krutnik suggests that the phallus, and through inference the gun, is the male's "membership card." In his psychoanalytic reading of the noir construction of masculinities, Krutnik states that "desire which [is] potentially transgressive of the phallic regime has actively to be held in place, and the 'psychic machinery' which keeps it there will not always succeed in its work of repression" (82).

11. Belsey states that "the phallus is a signifier. No one has it, neither women nor men. It signifies the unnameable object of desire, the desire of the Other, and it re-presents (stands in the place of) the *objet a*, the lost object in the real" (63). Hall presents a clear analysis of the Lacanian "phallus" suggesting that Margaret herself is a phallic prop.

12. Vernet notes how French cinephiles were struck by the "erotic daring" of specific objects in the film noir vocabulary (24). An example would be the glove in *Gilda*. Mamet certainly appropriates this cinematic vocabulary in both of these films.

13. The epilogue of *House of Games* calls attention to another Mametian technique of mystification: insider jokes and self-referentiality. Margaret's flowered dress and Bloody Mary link to important details in Bob Rafaelson's *Black Widow*, a film that also deals with the releasing of female sexuality. Amusingly, in a poker game sequence in *Black Widow*, Mamet is cast as one of the players.

14. Indeed, some of Mamet's shot set-ups resemble scenes from *The Big Gamble* (1931). As in Vidor's *Gilda*, with its central setting of a gambling casino, the phallic signifier reveals its totemic power in the games men play.

15. Copjec suggests that the femme fatale represents a figure of deceit, "a two dimensional figure with no hidden sides . . ." (193). However, one might argue that contrary to this stereotypical femme fatale imaged in classic noir, Mamet reconstructs the parameters of the femme fatale in the characterization of Margaret, whose subjectivity is complex and who is the victim (as well as the perpetrator) of deceit. With regard to high-heel shoes we might recall the famous close-up on Barbara Stanwyck's shoes from *Double Indemnity*.

16. After the bullets have been fired, Mamet moves the camera to a high angle, split screen mise-en-scene, a diagonal bar separating the spaces of the two figures. This shot echoes, in another noir allusion, Hathaway's beautiful scene of the crime in *Niagara* when Loomis (Joseph Cotton) kills Rose (Marilyn Monroe) in the bell tower. Isolation of the figure in an expanded spatial ratio is a characteristic shot of the noir aesthetic, expressive of an equally characteristic psychology: the lonely figure in the urban landscape. The shooting sequence also recalls the conclusion of Welles' *Lady from Shanghai*. Welles, playing a character named Mike, walks away from the shot down femme fatale (Rita Hayworth) as she pleads for her life. In *House of Games*, Mike refuses to plead for his life, while gunned down by the femme fatale. The web of cross-referentiality

operates in other playful ways. That Mamet names his family-man killer Welles, the man who would teach Gold the nature of evil, surely must allude to Orson Welles and *A Touch of Evil*, a pivotal work in the evolution of film noir.

Works Cited

Belsey, Catherine. *Desire: Love Stories in Western Culture*. Oxford: Blackwell, 1994.

Cassirer, Ernst. *The Philosophy of the Enlightenment*. Trans. Fritz A. Koelln and James P. Pettegrove. Boston: Beacon Press, 1955.

Copjec, Joan, ed. *Shades of Noir*. London and New York: Verso, 1993.

Hall, Ann C. "Playing to Win: Sexual Politics in David Mamet's *House of Games* and *Speed-the- Plough*." In *David Mamet: A Casebook*. Ed. Leslie Kane. New York: Garland Publishing, Inc., 1992, 137–60.

Jameson, Fredric. *Postmodernism, or, The Cultural Logic of Late Capitalism*. Durham: Duke UP, 1991.

Kane, Leslie, ed. *David Mamet: A Casebook*. New York: Garland Publishing, Inc., 1992.

———. *The Language of Silence: On the Unspoken and Unspeakable in Modern Drama*. Cranbury, N.J.: Associated UP, 1984.

Kristeva, Julia. *Powers of Abjection*. Trans. Leon S. Roudiez. New York: Columbia UP, 1982.

Krutnik, Frank. *In a Lonely Street: Film noir, Genre, Masculinity*. London and New York: Routledge, 1991.

Lacan, Jacques. *Ecrits*. Trans. Alan Sheridan. New York: Norton, 1977.

MacLeod, Christine. "The Politics of Gender, Language and Hierarchy in Mamet's *Oleanna*." *Journal of American Studies* 29 (1995): 199–213.

Mamet, David. *Oleanna*. London: Methuen, 1993.

———. *On Directing Films*. New York: Viking, 1991.

Otto, Rudolf. *The Idea of the Holy*. Trans. John W. Harvey. New York: Oxford UP, 1958.

Varnet, Marc. "Film noir on the Edge of Doom." In Copjec, 1–31.

Vorlicky, Robert. *Act Like a Man: Challenging Masculinities in American Drama*. Ann Arbor: U of Michigan P, 1995.

Worster, David. "How To Do Things with Salesmen: David Mamet's Speech-Act Play." *Modern Drama* 37 (1994): 375–89.

CONTRIBUTORS

THOMAS P. ADLER has been teaching since 1970 at Purdue University, where he is Professor and Chair of the English Department. He has published extensively on modern British and American drama, with a special emphasis on Tennessee Williams. The latest of his five books, *American Drama, 1940–60: A Critical History*, was reprinted in paperback in 1997. He recently contributed essays on Williams, Miller, and Hellman to three different volumes in the Cambridge Companion Series.

KELLIE BEAN is an Assistant Professor at Marshall University where she teaches drama and film. Her area of expertise is dramatic and feminist theory. She has published on Shakespeare, Stoppard, Beckett, and Pinter, with her most recent essay, "The (Al)lure of Independent Women: Disney's 'Feminist' Seduction in *The Hunchback of Notre Dame*," (forthcoming). Currently Bean is working on a book-length manuscript, *Trauma and Theatre*, which explores the relationship between performance and violence against women in both the specular arts and the popular media.

KAREN C. BLANSFIELD is an Assistant Professor in the Dramatic Art Department at the University of North Carolina, Chapel Hill. She is the author of *Michael Frayn: A Research and Production Sourcebook* and *Cheap Rooms and Restless Hearts*. Her articles and essays have appeared in *South Atlantic Review*, *Journal of American Drama and Theatre*, *Studies in American Humor*, *New England Theatre*, and other journals as well as in *British Playwrights 1956–95: A Research and Production Sourcebook*, *Woody Allen: A Casebook*, *Notable Gays and Lesbians in American Theater History*, and *World Literature Criticism*.

DIANE M. BORDEN is Professor of Literature and Film and Chair of the Film Studies Department at the University of the Pacific. She is co-editor and contributor to the recent *Bertolucci's "The Last Emperor": Multiple Takes*. Borden has published numerous journal articles, including the forthcoming "Manifest Landscape/Latent Ideology: Afterimages of Empire in the Western and Post-Western." She also conducts seminars on film and psychoanalysis for the San Francisco Psychoanalytic Institute and is a Visiting Scholar at the University of Florence in Italy.

RICHARD BRUCHER is Associate Professor of English at the University of Maine where he teaches courses on English and American drama. He has published essays on nostalgia in *Glengarry Glen Ross* (in *Glengarry Glen Ross: Text and Performance,* edited by Leslie Kane) and on parody in Eugene O'Neill and Arthur Miller. He has also published several articles on revenge and violence in early modern drama. He is currently writing on Lillian Hellman's cold war plays.

Prior to her untimely death, LINDA DORFF was an Assistant Professor of Theatre History, Theory, and Criticism in the School of Theatre at the University of Houston. Her previous work on David Mamet appeared in *Glengarry Glen Ross: Text and Performance.* She was completing final revisions of her unpublished manuscript *Disfigured Stages: The Late Plays of Tennessee Williams, 1958–83* at the time of her death and also engaged with the multi-faceted project "Working with Tennessee," which included a documentary for PBS and a collection of interviews.

IMTIAZ HABIB is Associate Professor of English at Old Dominion University where he teaches Shakespeare and English Renaissance literature. He is the author of *Tennessee Williams: A Descriptive Bibliography* and of *Shakespeare and Race: Postcolonial Praxis in the Early Modern Period* (forthcoming) and of essays on English Renaissance and modern literature. Habib earned his B.A. from New College, Oxford, and his Ph.D. from Indiana University, Bloomington.

JANET V. HAEDICKE is Associate Professor of English and Director of Concerts at Northeast Louisiana University. She has published numerous book reviews, bibliographical essays, chapters for edited volumes, and journal articles on contemporary American drama, having won a cash award from *Modern Drama* for her essay on Beth Henley and Sam Shepard. Currently Haedicke is completing a book on family, feminism, and American drama.

CHRISTOPHER C. HUDGINS, former Chair and Associate Professor of English at the University of Nevada, Las Vegas, is the author of numerous essays on Harold Pinter, David Mamet, and other film and theater figures. He is completing a book on Harold Pinter's filmscripts. Co-founder (with Leslie Kane) and Vice President of the David Mamet Society, Hudgins is co-editor of *The David Mamet Review* and also serves as Vice President of the Harold Pinter Society. The former Chair of the Nevada Humanities Committee, Hudgins is a Board Member of Cities of Asylum, Las Vegas, which provides refuge and stipends for politically persecuted writers.

ILKKA JOKI was original staff member of the Academy of Finland's Literary Pragmatics Project, based in the English Department of Åbo Akademi University. A textual reviser at the European Union Translation Services, he has carried out field studies on development theater in Mali and in Tanzania. His publications include essays on theory and *Mamet, Bakhtin, and the Dramatic: The Demotic as a Variable of Addressivity* (1993), the first study of Bakhtin and drama and the demotic in Mamet's work. His current research interests center on the function and effects of intermediate (third) language versions used as stepping stones between the source and the target text, taking poetry as the test genre.

LESLIE KANE is Professor of English at Westfield State College. She is the author of *The Language of Silence: On the Unspoken and the Unspeakable in Modern Drama* and *Weasels and Wisemen: Ethics and Ethnicity in the Work of David Mamet*. She has edited *David Mamet: A Casebook, Israel Horovitz: A Collection of Critical Essays*, and *"Glengarry Glen Ross": Text and Performance*. Her essays, reviews and interviews have appeared in *The Pinter Review, American Drama, American Theatre, Theatre Journal*, and *The Yearbook of English Studies*, and in collections of critical essays. President of the David Mamet Society, which she co-founded with Christopher Hudgins, she is co-editor of *The David Mamet Review*. Kane is also editor of *David Mamet in Conversation*, forthcoming in 2001.

STEVEN PRICE, Lecturer in English at the University of Wales, Bangor, has published widely on British and American drama. He is the author of "Negative Creation: The Detective Story in *Glengarry Glen Ross*," published in *David Mamet's "Glengarry Glen Ross": Text and Performance*, as well as recent essays on Beckett and Pinter, which appeared in *Cyncos*. He is also co-author of *Oscar Wilde: Salome* (1996). A regular contributor on American drama to *The Year's Work in English Studies*, and book reviewer for *Modern Language Review*, Price serves as European editor for *The David Mamet Review*.

ROBERT SKLOOT teaches theater literature and history and is a staff director at the University of Wisconsin-Madison. He has published numerous articles on modern drama and theater, is editor of *The Theatre of the Holocaust* (v. 1, 1982; v.2, 1999) and author of *The Darkness We Carry: The Drama of the Holocaust* (1988). A three-time Fulbright Lecturer to Israel, Austria, and Chile, he has directed three NEH seminars for school teachers on the subject of "The Theatre and the Holocaust." Skloot also directs the UW Center for Jewish Studies and serves as Associate Vice Chancellor for Academic Affairs.

Index